and Center

Christina Xydias

Beyond Left, Right, and Center

The Politics of Gender and Ethnicity in Contemporary Germany

TEMPLE UNIVERSITY PRESS
Philadelphia • Rome • Tokyo

TEMPLE UNIVERSITY PRESS
Philadelphia, Pennsylvania 19122
tupress.temple.edu

Copyright © 2024 by Temple University—Of The Commonwealth System
 of Higher Education
All rights reserved
Published 2024

Library of Congress Cataloging-in-Publication Data

Names: Xydias, Christina, author.
Title: Beyond left, right, and center : the politics of gender and
 ethnicity in contemporary Germany / Christina Xydias.
Description: Philadelphia : Temple University Press, 2024. | Includes
 bibliographical references and index. | Summary: "Challenges prevailing
 expectations about left-right ideological frameworks and advocacy for
 women's rights and interests in democracies"— Provided by publisher.
Identifiers: LCCN 2023044295 (print) | LCCN 2023044296 (ebook) | ISBN
 9781439923764 (cloth) | ISBN 9781439923771 (paperback) | ISBN
 9781439923788 (pdf)
Subjects: LCSH: Women—Political activity—Germany. | Minority
 women—Political activity—Germany. | Women and democracy—Germany. |
 Right and left (Political science)—Germany. | Political
 parties—Germany. | Representative government and
 representation—Germany.
Classification: LCC HQ1236.5.G3 X935 2024 (print) | LCC HQ1236.5.G3
 (ebook) | DDC 320.0082/0943—dc23/eng/20231212
LC record available at https://lccn.loc.gov/2023044295
LC ebook record available at https://lccn.loc.gov/2023044296

∞ The paper used in this publication meets the requirements of the
American National Standard for Information Sciences—Permanence
of Paper for Printed Library Materials, ANSI Z39.48-1992

Printed in the United States of America

9 8 7 6 5 4 3 2 1

To my father, who sought out new worlds

Contents

	List of Figures and Tables	ix
	Acknowledgments	xi
1.	Introduction	1
2.	Theoretical Framework	21
3.	Gender, Ethnicity, and the German Political System	42
4.	German Political Parties: Representing the Problem of Underrepresentation	62
5.	German Political Parties' Actions to Promote Inclusion	81
6.	Rates of Election and Party Leadership	114
7.	The Incomplete Citizen in Germany	130
8.	Political Parties across the OECD	160
9.	Conclusion	186
	Appendices	191
	Notes	211
	References	223
	Index	245

Figures and Tables

Figures

3.1	Women's rates of election to the Bundestag, 2009–2017	43
7.1	German political parties: women in the Bundeswehr	141
7.2	German political parties: ending the Wehrpflicht	149
8.1	Political parties across the OECD	163
9.1	Tweet photo of SPD candidate Scholz with banner, "He can be madam chancellor"	187

Tables

2.1	Summary of theoretical expectations	40
3.1	Summary of ideological axes	44
3.2	German political parties: ideological categories	55
4.1	Parties' acknowledgment of women's political underrepresentation	70
4.2	Parties' acknowledgment of women's underrepresentation × ideological axes	76
5.1	German political parties' adoption of gender quotas	87
5.2	Candidate gender quotas × ideological axes	91
5.3	German political parties' mentorship programming for women	95
5.4	Level of mentorship programming × ideological axes	95
6.1	Members of the Bundestag with a Migrationshintergrund	118

6.2	Women's proportion of candidacies: 17th–19th Bundestag elections	119
6.3	Women's rates of candidacy × ideological axes	121
6.4	OLS regression models of women's candidacies	123
6.5	Elections to the Bundestag: 2009, 2013, and 2017	124
6.6	Women's rates of election to the Bundestag × ideological axes	125
6.7	OLS regression models of women's rates of election to the Bundestag	126
6.8	Fourteen German political parties' chairpersons in 2017	128
8.1	Variation across the OECD	163
8.2	Ideological features of party families in the OECD	167
8.3	Proequality activities in party families across the OECD	170
8.4	All parties' rates of electing women	172
8.5	Party families' rates of electing women	173
8.6	All party leadership's inclusion of women	175
8.7	Party families' leadership's inclusion of women	176
8.8	All parties' support for WLFP policies	178
8.9	Party families' support for WLFP policies	179
8.10	All party leaders' prioritization of minority rights	181
8.11	Party families' leaders' prioritization of minority rights	182
A.1	German political parties' names and abbreviations	191
B.1	Documentation for imputing ideology of German parties	193
C.1	Snapshot of 2016 survey respondents	196
D.1	Interviews conducted in 2007–2008	202
D.2	Interviews conducted in 2014 and 2017	203
E.1	Countries and parties in the cross-national dataset	204
E.2	Descriptive statistics for variables in cross-national analyses	208
E.3	Parties' rates of electing women	209
E.4	Whether party leaders include women	210

Acknowledgments

I write about Germany, because my father was a Greek guest worker in Dortmund in the 1960s. He told many stories about these experiences, such as being offered a sandwich by a nun when he first arrived at a train station in Germany. My father passed away from pancreatic cancer in 2016, and exploring elements of his life through my scholarly work has been very meaningful to me. He and my American mother met in a "German language for foreigners" classroom, and they returned to the United States together in 1973. Because of their international interests and my extended family in Greece, I had early opportunities for travel and language-learning that were central to my development as a political scientist; for these reasons and more, I am profoundly grateful to them both.

I have been privileged to enjoy the camaraderie and smart feedback of numerous political science communities since I completed my Ph.D. at The Ohio State University in 2010. Many thanks to my comparativist besties, including Amy Atchison, Malliga Och, Jenn Piscopo, and Meg Rincker. I belong to a Zoom writing group that transformed my experience of the pandemic, nurturing both friendship and knowledge; I extend particular thanks to regulars Bethany Albertson, Mirya Holman, Shannon McGregor, and Kirsten Rodine-Hardy. I also owe a great deal to a supportive and intellectually vibrant German politics crew, especially Louise Davidson-Schmich, Barbara Donovan, Dan Hough, Melanie Kintz, Erich Langenbacher, Joyce Mushaben, Jonathan Olsen, David Patton, Angelika von Wahl, Sarah Wiliarty, and

Jen Yoder. Until her devastatingly early death in 2016, Danielle Langfield and I were among each other's loudest comparativist cheerleaders.

I received helpful comments on numerous pieces of this project over the years it was in progress, such that there are too many people to name here. However, I am especially grateful to Rosalyn Cooperman, Louise Davidson-Schmich, Michael James, Scott Meinke, Malliga Och, and Shauna Shames for their feedback on earlier versions of Chapters 7 and 8.

For their support of fieldwork in 2007–2008 and 2014, I thank the Coca-Cola Critical Difference for Women Grant at Ohio State, Ohio State's Mershon Center and the Office of International Affairs, the American Hellenic Educational Progressive Association, and the Carrie Chapman Catt Center for Women and Politics at Iowa State University. I am very grateful to the seventy-one German state- and national-level legislators who agreed to be interviewed during these and other fieldwork trips. For exceptional research assistance, especially in connection with this book's cross-national chapter, I thank Ellie Fallon, supported by Bucknell University's Presidential Fellows Program. I also thank two fastidious and thoughtful anonymous reviewers of the book manuscript with Temple University Press as well as my editor Aaron Javsicas, whose insights significantly improved the project.

Last but not least: this book is complete only with the support of my spouse, Brian Hauser, whose patience and humor are seemingly endless. You're the balm.

Any errors that remain in this book are, of course, my own.

Beyond Left, Right, and Center

1

Introduction

Introduction

Prevailing expectations about advocacy for women's rights and interests—known in the political science literature as *women's substantive representation*—generally consist of positive associations with left-leaning parties and negative associations with right-leaning parties. We see evidence of these expectations in many settings. Among scholars, studies tend to describe actors associated with "the left" as better at the representation of women's interests and actors associated with "the right" as worse.[1] In turn, political parties themselves campaign in response to these expectations. The content of their campaign advertisements and candidates' speeches, and their efforts to maintain long-standing supporters or mobilize new ones, tell us who they believe they are already effectively reaching. Civil society organizations often self-identify as left or right. The international women's organization Womankind Worldwide, for example, describes itself as even "more important for combating violence against women than . . . left-wing political parties."[2] Much news coverage of political parties expresses recognition of actors on the left who step up to advocate for women and, conversely, surprise or skepticism when actors on the right do so.[3] A significant feature of these expectations is that, by the late twentieth and early twenty-first centuries, women who support or are active in parties on the right are viewed as a puzzle.[4]

This book proposes revisions to these prevailing expectations of which political parties and policymakers associated with them more fully and effectively advocate for women's rights and interests. It argues that the left-right axis must be disaggregated into finer-grained ideological differences to better explain the variation among political actors in their extent and kinds of advocacy for women as a group. Further, it shows that these left-right axes, even when they are disaggregated, are largely meaningless for explaining variation in advocacy for multiply marginalized women. In developing these arguments, this book adds to the empirical evidence for the persistence of patriarchy both across parties and across the ideological spectrum, and it adds to our understanding of how and when women's rights and interests are promoted.[5]

First, prevailing expectations of associations between women's political representation and "the left" and "the right" risk overstating the extent to which women are a homogeneous group. In order to expect that ideological categories neatly map onto policies that benefit (or do not benefit) women as a social group,[6] we must overlook that even policies designed "for all" women, in practice, benefit only some subgroups of women (e.g., women of majority ethnic status[7]). Through an intersectional lens—a lens that focuses our attention on individual persons' multiple, simultaneous social structural positions—*very few parties* of any ideological profile appear to do particularly well by multiply marginalized women, who comprise the largest subgroups of women. Crenshaw (1989), Davidson-Schmich (2017), Nash (2008), and others define multiple marginalization as "relationships of inequality among social groups and changing configurations of inequality along multiple and conflicting dimensions" (McCall 2005, p. 1773). Proportionally, most women are multiply marginalized: they are not members of the social upper class, and they are the most economically disadvantaged. In most settings, women who are not majority ethnic status experience the most acute exclusion from opportunities for political influence.

Further, women constituents view their own circumstances and needs through different ideological filters. Women do not all share the same preferences, even when they share experiences of gendered household labor or other social expectations (see, e.g., Cassese and Barnes 2018). In this spirit, some scholars use the term "responsiveness" to emphasize that measures of women's political representation should include advocacy from the many varied ideological orientations that women themselves identify with (Severs 2010). A burgeoning research program on right-leaning parties' and policymakers' contributions to women's political representation emphasizes the importance of integrating these actors into our theoretical expectations.[8]

Standard left-right expectations also overstate the extent of uniformity within standard left and right ideological clusters. Huber and Inglehart (1995) assert that "the ideological and programmatic *meaning* of [a left-right axis] varies over time and across cultures" (p. 75, emphasis in original). A single-dimensional left-right axis that differentiates ideologies based on their belief in state intervention in the economy does not hold post–Cold War. The emergence in the latter half of the twentieth century of a left-right cultural axis further fragments ideological categories globally. "The left" and "the right" are not fixed ideological positions cross-nationally when it comes to advocacy for women's rights and interests any more than for other constituents or issue areas. Finally, a noteworthy subset of parties that risks erasure with an emphasis on "left" and "right" is situated at the "center." These parties engender muddier expectations about their advocacy for specific social groups, but conceptually it is vital to include them in a broader framework about the role of ideologies in shaping political representation.

These critiques are especially visible in comparative perspective. Some settings may, indeed, manifest parties commonly viewed as on the left that deserve their positive association with women's advocacy; other settings may subvert conventional expectations by manifesting right-leaning parties that do so.[9] This book contends that these acts of representation do not arise idiosyncratically. Instead, specific ideological and institutional factors help us understand where, when, and why advocacy for women and marginalized subgroups of women occurs. Deconstructing the component parts of "left" and "right" is an essential part of this analysis.

In order to evaluate these assumptions and their implications for what we know about women's political representation, this book focuses on political parties as key actors in the formal political process. Certainly, actors outside the formal process, such as civil society organizations and social movements, also engage in interest creation, aggregation, and promotion. Weldon (2011) and others show that these informal political actors are highly engaged in advocating for women and marginalized subgroups of women, and, therefore, they play an important role in the wider policymaking process (see also Htun and Ossa 2013; and Walsh and Xydias 2014). However, in spite of what we know about the importance of civil society organizations, strong expectations persist among scholars, activists, and the general public regarding women's rights and interests and formal actors. This book addresses the validity of these strong expectations in asking the following question: Which political parties promote the rights and interests of women *or* marginalized subgroups of women? In which ideological and institutional settings are they more likely to do so?

The book takes two complementary empirical approaches. First, it undertakes a within-country analysis of contemporary Germany, an advanced industrial multiparty democratic setting. Second, it presents cross-national analyses of variation among political parties in their divergent settings (data drawn from 2017). These two approaches establish conditions under which parties advocate for women, and they test the expectation that minoritized women will find little advocacy among political parties across ideological categories. The within-Germany analysis holds broader historical-cultural and institutional context largely constant. Cross-national analyses then test a series of hypotheses about the role of social and institutional context in shaping whether and how political parties promote women's rights and interests, with particular attention to the limits of conventional "left," "center," and "right" ideological categories for explaining this variation.

In the case of Germany, a multiparty parliamentary system, the early twenty-first century politics of gender and race-ethnicity have become partially unmoored from standard left-right categories, in particular on matters that are more easily integrated into a wider range of beliefs about gender and social roles, such as women's participation in politics as candidates and officeholders. These findings pose challenges to political science accounts of these phenomena that build on foundations of stable ideological categories. Examining this single case offers the benefit of holding constant a variety of system-wide factors, such as voters' preferences and the electoral system, that shape parties' programmatic commitments and their actions. Additional alternative explanations for parties' varying approaches to these policy areas can be examined in comparative perspective, and findings in Chapter 8 show that the salience of left-center-right distinctions varies cross-nationally.

Contemporary German society widely views the state as bearing some responsibility for communities' well-being. These responsibilities are written into the country's post–World War II constitution, called the Basic Law.[10] The 1949 Basic Law also specifies provisions about the state's obligations to the family as a fundamental social unit: "Marriage and the family shall enjoy the special protection of the state" (art. 6).[11] At the same time, Germany is a multiparty political system where dozens of diverse political parties regularly field candidates. Thus, a basic value regarding the relationship between society and the state is held relatively constant, which makes it possible to observe ideological and strategic differentiation among political actors on other matters. The within-Germany analysis is organized around three issue areas, selected to showcase important sources of variation in advocacy for women and subgroups of women:

1. Informal and formal intraparty practices for diversifying candidate pools
2. Parties' rates of nomination, election, and appointment of women and minoritized women as candidates and party leaders
3. Policies on gender inclusion in the military in the context of evolving citizenship laws

The choice to look at these distinctive issue areas follows Htun and Weldon (2018). These issue areas pose different kinds and extents of challenges to socially traditionalist gender norms and the normative social order. Inclusion in public decision-making poses a lesser challenge to these norms than inclusion in the military. In turn, debates over citizenship laws reveal attitudes toward the intersection of gender and ethnicity. Looking at these issues separately makes it possible to observe how political actors vary in their policy promotion depending on the scale of these challenges: which rights and interests they pay attention to as well as which they promote and how.[12]

Taken together, this empirical approach uncovers the varying extent to which five ideologies distinguish political actors who are likely to ignore or act against the rights and interests of women and marginalized subgroups of women: patriarchy (contrasted with gender egalitarianism), economic liberalism (vs. redistributionism), social traditionalism (vs. progressivism), materialism (vs. postmaterialism), and hegemonic-ethnic supremacy (vs. multiculturalism). Patriarchy manifests across all political parties, while the latter four (economic liberalism, social traditionalism, materialism, and hegemonic-ethnic supremacy) are characteristics of a subset of some but not all parties typically categorized as "on the right." If we arrange existing political parties in a conventional left-right ordering, these characteristics do not increase monotonically from left to right. In other words, a party we consider in conventional terms to be "furthest right" might not be the party that manifests the most extreme version of a given ideological dimension, such as materialism. These nontrivial nuances to "left" and "right" categories contribute to disrupting conventional expectations.

Because patriarchy is universal, much of this discussion focuses on the latter four. Issues that pose *lesser* challenges to these four characteristics are those that are possible or even likely to be integrated into the agendas of a wider range of political parties and policymakers. The promotion of women's presence in office, for instance, is a relatively easy case for a wider range of political actors. At the same time, political parties are likely to implement distinctive strategies; for example, some parties avoid regulatory mechanisms like formal gender quotas. By contrast, norms surrounding gender and the military are consistently very rigid across cultural settings.[13] Allowing women into combat roles is, therefore, a relatively hard case for a wider range of political actors. The juxtaposition of representational activities around these issue areas demonstrates the limits of the expectation that "the left" does particularly well at promoting the rights and interests of women who are marginalized by other dimensions of their social positions, at the same time as it exposes otherwise unexpected advocacy from "the right." Disaggregating the left-right dimension makes our theoretical expectations more nuanced, and it highlights the persistence of patriarchy among political parties and their associated policymakers across the ideological map.

Following van der Haar and Verloo (2013), intersectional analysis includes recording whether and how these formal political actors distinguish among subgroups of women based on their varying access to social, political, and economic power. As later sections and chapters discuss in greater detail, a snapshot measure of attention to subgroups of women cannot discern how multiple marginalization evolves over time.[14] It can, however, offer important insights into which actors play roles in this process by reaffirming or challenging existing power relationships through the policies that they promote.

Ultimately, the purpose of this framework is to challenge a simple left-right distinction in terms of both which parties will be categorized as left or right (i.e., where meaningful "lines" might lie between left and right) and whether left or right will promote women's rights and interests. Although research increasingly seeks to understand the interaction between left-right categorization and other factors for explaining policy attention, conventional expectations persist in favoring parties "on the left" as champions of the rights and interests of historically marginalized groups. However, these expectations are in part an artifact of the construction of these categories of "left" and "right," and the very same political party may be categorized differently as left or right depending on the ideological dimension of focus.

Key Concepts: Intersectionality, Women's Rights and Interests, and Ideology

This section begins with a discussion of concepts central to the book: intersectionality, the rights and interests of women as a political group, and ideology. This discussion presents and justifies the book's operational definitions, in conversation with existing research on women's political representation. It lays the foundation for the book's theoretical expectations, developed in Chapter 2.

Intersectionality and Intersectionality-Plus

Women comprise a political group, at the same time as women are diverse, with varied interests and identities. This view of women as a group is informed by intersectionality, the theoretical lens that focuses our attention on the multiple social structural positions that any individual person occupies simultaneously. A person does not only encounter other people and social and political institutions in terms of sex-gender; they navigate the world in terms of socioeconomic status, race-ethnicity, and potentially many other social structures. Their occupation of multiple structural positions corresponds with simultaneous membership in multiple groups. In this way, intersectionality reveals that a policy designed "for" a wider social group may have different consequences for subsets of group members. For example, a specific policy on the availability of childcare will distribute benefits differently across women, depending on their financial circumstances (e.g., work schedule), marital status, cultural practices that may prescribe maternal responsibilities, and so on.[15]

In her original exposition of intersectionality, Crenshaw (1989) critiques then prevailing social scientific analyses for focusing on one social structural axis at a time. Writing about race-gender in the United States, she notes that studying each social structural axis individually "[treats] race and gender as mutually exclusive categories of experience" (p. 139). She argues that "this focus on the most privileged group members marginalizes those who are multiply-burdened and obscures claims that cannot be understood as resulting from discrete sources of discrimination" (p. 140). In other words, an analysis of women's political representation (women in the aggregate) focuses on "the most privileged group members," and, in doing so, it ignores and likely misinterprets the experiences of multiply burdened women. Models of the policymaking process must instead take these multiple social structures into account, both to understand policy outcomes and to assess which groups those policies advance or hinder. Although this analysis may be complicated, it is necessary. As Smooth (2006) puts it, intersectionality is a "mess worth making," lest we mischaracterize the processes and outcomes we aim to understand. Its complexity is the very reason it is "such a fruitful area of study" (p. 413).

Crenshaw's (1989) critique founded a rich body of research, which has taken intersectionality to places and research questions both narrower and wider than its origins. Scholars "using" intersectionality have been critiqued for applying this lens without further theorizing about the broader context of social identities, their origins, and how they evolve over time and in different settings.[16] Cautioning against intersectional studies that treat social categories as immutable, Dhamoon (2011) advocates for "a shift from studying identities and categories to studying processes and systems" in order to "[foster] ... more rigorous critique of how and why differences are interpreted in privileging and penalizing ways" (p. 240). Other scholars aim to retheorize intersectionality as a discursive analytical tool, in order to avoid essentializing subjects (see Anthias 2012; and Nash 2008).

One answer to these concerns is Weldon's (2008) concept of *intersectionality-plus*. In place of a model that views a person's political or social power as an additive or multiplicative function of a list of social identities or structures, she posits that these structures partially overlap, and their effects vary by context or issue. Weldon writes, "Combinations of gender-race-class (or other axes) produce distinctively different effects, effects of phenomena that other social groups do not even experience" (p. 205); further, she states, "In some times or places, systems of race and class may undermine each other, while in other places they reinforce each other" (p. 206). Weldon thus emphasizes how critical it is to attend to context, including the policy environment (Which issues and policies are we talking about?), the historical-cultural setting (What are the opportunities and constraints associated with specific sociocultural locations?), and the relevance of historical-cultural details for these specific issues and policies.

The empirical application of intersectionality and intersectionality-plus in the social sciences has taken many paths. McCall (2005) draws particular attention to the complexity of lived experiences, promoting qualitative and ethnographic work as better suited to the contextual contingencies of social identities. She writes, "In personal narratives and single-group analyses, then, complexity derives from the analysis of a social location at the intersection of single dimensions of multiple categories, rather than at the intersection of the full range of dimensions of a full range of categories, and that is how complexity is managed" (p. 1781).

In this spirit, many intersectional analyses make use of case studies, and this research points toward the contextual nature of political and social power. For example, Walsh and Xydias (2014) contrast Guatemala and Germany to rule out system-wide factors, such as economic development and level of democracy, which may promote advocacy for multiply marginalized subgroups. Their analysis of these most different cases shows that focused and specific civil society organizations are crucial to intersectional policy success. Davidson-Schmich (2017) assembles case studies of various issue areas within Germany to show that persistent within-country institutional and cultural factors drive policy success or failure for multiply marginalized groups. Collins's (2000) case study of Black women's experiences at the work/family nexus reveals *families* as a site where intersectionality is forged and reinforced, "[framing] particular understandings of property" (p. 48). Hawkesworth (2003) studies the experiences of African American congresswomen, showing that these legislators' subjugation happens through repeated interactions with other congresspeople. African American congresswomen were repeatedly silenced, ignored, or denied credit for policy production, reconstituting their status over time.

Much of this intersectional analysis is qualitative. Dubrow and others, therefore, ask how to apply intersectionality in quantitative work. Dubrow (2008) advises quantitative researchers engaged in cross-national work, in particular, to "[consider] country level processes that generate disadvantaged categories within social groups" and to "[analyze] separate effects for each country" (p. 98). Dubrow's (2008) advice improves upon additive models, but Weldon (2008) has in turn cautioned against "merely" multiplicative modeling of the intersection(s) of social structures, on the grounds that an interactive model cannot in and of itself account for the shifting salience of overlapping social identities and structures in different contexts.

I argue that one answer to these critiques lies in the earlier stages of research design and data collection. A study's conceptualization of variables and of variation is crucial for successfully observing political and social power in the first place. For example, van der Haar and Verloo (2013) apply intersectionality-plus to a quantitative analysis of political texts (laws, policy plans, and civil society documents) by selecting four issue areas for study: equal treatment/equal pay, reconciliation policies, reproductive policies, and domestic violence. They ask, "How are social inequality categories articulated in policy and civil society texts? How do such texts categorize gender and other social and political 'boundaries' at the same time? What is the extent of intra-(gender) categorizing?" (p. 3). Their data collection records observations about each text in categories such as: "(1) are the actors to whom the code is referring only female/male? and (2) do gendered codes refer to any other main inequality axis, more specifically to (a) age, (b) minoritization, (c) class, (d) disability, or (e) sexual orientation?" (p. 4). This operationalization achieves attention to context, and it achieves more than multiplicative intersectionality, in a quantitative intersectional study. It does so in its very research design. This is the model for subsequent empirical chapters.

In sum, a focus on advocacy for the rights and interests of a sex-gender category of women "marginalizes those who are multiply burdened" (Crenshaw 1989, p. 140). An analysis that aims to draw meaningful conclusions about sources of advocacy for *all women* must, therefore, disaggregate the implications of policy for different groups of women. As van der Haar and Verloo (2013) show, "intra-gender categorizing" in policymaking varies across both issue areas and policies. To apply intersectionality-plus, this book examines variation in the engagement of political actors in advocating for women across different policy areas: parties' orientation toward, policies on, and success at promoting more diverse candidates for office; their inclusion of women and ethnic minorities in party leadership; and their arguments about policies on gender in the military, which shifted significantly circa 2000 at the same time as citizenship laws fundamentally evolved. Taken together, analyses of these issues reveal parties' capacity to evolve on fundamental questions of political inclusion. These analyses look for parties' explicit attention to multiple axes of marginalization across these issue areas (i.e., they implement intersectionality-plus).

In the case of Germany, the primary axis of political marginalization that intersects with gender is racial-ethnic-minority status. The importance of this axis is due to the extent of explicit and formal exclusion of "non-Germans" from political equality, an issue that receives extensive attention in

Chapter 7. Women situated within racial-ethnic-minority groups in Germany have very limited political resources for demanding attention to their needs and interests, and (like all women) they simultaneously experience patriarchy within their coethnic communities. More specifically, Muslim communities are, arguably, especially marginalized in Germany, because these are communities that remain, informally, sharply segregated. Turkish-heritage Germans are the largest group in this category, by a wide margin: by 2016, 3 million Turkish ethnics lived in Germany but only 246,000 held German citizenship (McFadden 2019).

Rights and Interests

Throughout this book, sex-gender categories refer to how people are "received" rather than to objective biological facts. To be received as a woman is to be recognized as a woman and expected to conform to social expectations related to women's status. West and Zimmerman (1987) refer to individuals "doing gender," which is conceptually similar to Butler's (1990) theory of gender as performative. Research across the social sciences shows empirically that privileges and disadvantages, and advantages and inequalities, relate to how people are *received* (see, e.g., Schilt 2006).

Social expectations of people *received as women* vary cross-culturally and have changed over time; that is, women are not systematically less empowered than men in the same ways in all settings. Some societies have historically been matrilineal or matriarchal, for example, and in contemporary, industrialized democratic settings, *women* experience relatively few formal inequalities, such as the legal prohibition on voting. However, people who are received as women in high-income countries still earn 72 percent of men's income,[17] and they occupy just 23.6 percent of national legislatures worldwide.[18] The World Health Organization estimates that 30 percent of women experience intimate-partner sexual or other physical violence in their lifetime.[19] These are among the enduring patterns in sex-gendered inequality collectively termed *patriarchy*.[20]

As intersectionally informed research shows, women vary widely in their life experiences and the extent and kinds of resources at their disposal. Multiply marginalized women may experience disadvantage in terms of patriarchy and, depending on the context and issue area, also race-ethnicity and other sociostructural factors. Having said that, a more abstract definition of rights does not itself need to be disaggregated for subgroups of women, because "the category 'women'... relates to something real" (Gunnarsson 2011, p. 24). Even while women vary, the category of people received as women clearly exists. Other sociostructural dimensions differentiate further among them, but people received as women have been systematically excluded from positions of social and political power on the basis of sex-gender.

Although the rights themselves do not vary in definition across subgroups of women, the particular policies needed to achieve these rights do vary. Preferences for those particular policies comprise *interests*. As Gutmann (2003) writes, "In paradigmatic form, identity group politics is bound up with a sense of who people are, while interest group politics is bound up with a sense of what people want" (p. 15). Interests can be conceived of as a pathway to rights, and people vary in their preferred pathways. For example, socially traditionalist versions of women's interests might well involve not choosing to take part in the public sphere, but women's rights involve having the choice. Anti-feminist positions that advocate for sex-gender-differentiated citizenship on the premise that women's political, social, and economic equality to men is not compatible with traditional gender norms do advance a specific flavor of women's interests, but they do not advance women's rights.

This conceptual distinction between rights and interests is important for an analysis of interparty differences in several respects. In this book, women's substantive representation occurs when political actors work to expand women's opportunities in the public sphere. This is a relatively broad definition, which encompasses but distinguishes between a range of pathways to these rights. On the one hand, this definition resonates with feminist conceptions of women's rights. Squires (1999) characterizes feminism as a series of strategies for unmaking traditional gender hierarchies. Ferree (2012) refers to these strategies as "heuristics for empowering women in their political choices" (p. 6). Similarly, Offen (1988) writes, "Feminism makes claims for a rebalancing between women and men of the social, economic, and political power within a given society, on behalf of both sexes in the name of their common humanity" (p. 151). On the other hand, *expanding opportunities in the public sphere* is purposefully inclusive to avoid ex ante defining nonfeminist political actors out of the pool of potential advocates.[21] Xydias (2014) shows that a wide range of political parties actively support expanding women's opportunities in the public sphere; by contrast, parties and ideologies differ starkly in whether they support actively working to change women's outcomes in public life. An inclusive approach that values both *opportunities* and *outcomes* renders advocacy visible that would otherwise be invisible. For instance, it recognizes nonquota strategies for increasing women's rates of election, rather than aiming to explain why some parties do not implement quotas.

Many studies of women and politics have restricted their operational definitions of women's interests in several standard ways. Scholars look to policy areas that they argue disproportionately affect women or women's typical social roles, such as education, social welfare, and reproductive issues.[22]

The greater relevance of these policies for women as a group is sometimes characterized in terms of shared experiences. Sapiro (1981), for instance, points to women's shared experiences as a basis for talking about women's interests. These studies tend to focus on women's household and caregiving labor and their shared exclusion from political and public life.[23] In this line of research, even those experiences that all woman share are nonetheless expected to give rise to women's interests. For example, Phillips (1998) argues, "The variety of women's interests does not refute the claim that interests are gendered. That some women do not bear children does not make pregnancy a gender-neutral event" (p. 68). Phillips makes this claim on the premise that a person received as a woman is affected by expectations of the wider group. In the terms developed earlier: these scholars argue that women share interests in the sense that they walk similar pathways toward achieving equal rights.

A separate wave of studies seeks evidence of women's substantive representation in less standard places, that is, not in terms of shared experiences as women but rather in terms of shared policy preferences (see, e.g., Atchison and Downs 2019; Fredriksson and Wang 2011). These studies measure "women's interests" with public opinion data that show gendered preferences. Proenvironmental policy, in particular, has received attention as a women's interest because women support proenvironmental policy at higher rates than men. In this research, legislators' proenvironmentalism is categorized as women's substantive representation. This and related areas of literature are opening windows on other political consequences of gendered attitudes.

Indeed, gender is everywhere, all the time. Tax and defense policies, for example, also affect women, men, and nonbinary persons, in the aggregate, differently because of gendered patterns in our social, political, and economic lives, but these policies are typically omitted from the category of "women's issues." One consequence of this omission is that we end up observing variation on just a subset of representational activities.

At the same time, even while women share family labor and a history of political exclusion in common, they vary considerably in other salient features of their lives. Gender intersects with other social identities everywhere, all the time. For example, at many points in time, specific forms of labor have been restricted from—or "for"—some subsets of women. In-home eldercare, for instance, is a form of labor increasingly performed by women of marginalized ethnic groups, and often of undocumented citizenship status.[24] Intersectionality-plus highlights how these occupational patterns, and the salience of sex-gender, ethnicity, and other social categories, are highly contingent on context. R. Brown (2016b) shows that migrant caregivers in Israel are predominantly women and deeply disempowered by labor laws that circumscribe their movement and access to rights on the basis of their ethnicity—

at the same time as they are intimately part of elderly Israelis' daily lives and well-being. Women across ethnic groups engage disproportionately in care labor, but these ethnic-minority women caregivers have very different needs from the ethnic-majority women they care for.

Based on the fragmentation and diversity of interests experienced, expressed, and promoted by women as a larger group, this project joins a wave of studies of women's political representation in emphasizing the diversity of claims about "what is best for women" as well as the diversity of sites where those claims are made. Celis and Childs (2012), Celis and Childs (2020), Lovenduski and Guadagnini (2010), Xydias (2013) and others urge studies of women and politics to focus not on whether or under what conditions "women act for women" but rather "how the ... representation of women occurs."[25] It follows that the representation of women may be undertaken, or neglected, by many different political actors.

Each empirical chapter discusses more specific operational choices for measuring the advocacy for women's rights and interests. In abstract terms, this operationalization is disaggregated into three categories:

1. Evidence of a political actor's attention to the rights and interests of women and marginalized subgroups of women
2. Evidence of a political actor's strategies for promoting women's rights and interests in public life
3. Evidence of a political actor's efforts to *remove* barriers to women's full citizenship

Much of this book engages in a single-country case study of contemporary Germany (i.e., the reunited Federal Republic of Germany [FRG], 1990–present). This setting is a multiparty advanced industrial democracy that leads Europe in some social policy areas and lags behind on others. Analyses of Germany ground the operationalization of these three forms of advocacy for women's rights and interests in a systematic collection of German political texts and related materials, including party platforms and statutes, proposed legislation, parliamentary documents, parliamentary speech transcripts, federal ministry website content, political foundations' programming, and transcripts of personal interviews with policymakers. In a final, cross-national chapter, analyses draw from national legislative websites and electoral commissions, and they make use of existing scholarly databases, including the Comparative Political Data Set, the Global Gender Quotas Database (hosted by the IDEA, Inter-parliamentary Union, and Stockholm University), Parline (hosted by the Inter-parliamentary Union), and the Varieties of Democracy Project.

Ideology

Gerring (1997) notes in his review of the concept of *ideology* that the field of political science is littered with different, and even internally contradictory, definitions. Nonetheless, he identifies a core element across definitions, which is that an *ideology*'s content is consistent: it is "a set of idea-elements that are bound together, that belong to one another in a non-random fashion" (p. 980). It is a set of principles that are substantively interconnected by some form of meaning, if not by logic in a scientific sense. In this vein, Putnam (1971) defines ideology as "an explicit, consciously held belief system" (p. 655), which reflects much of the usage in political science. Scholars disagree, however, on whether the strongly held beliefs that constitute ideology are "affective" or "cognitive" (see Gerring 1997, p. 977), conscious or unconscious (Gerring 1997, p. 979), good (in structuring orderly preferences) (see Campbell et al. 1960; and Converse 1964) or bad (in obscuring reality) (see Marx and Engels 1970; and Althusser 1971).

In my usage of the term, *ideology* is visible in political actors' self-presentation and in their differentiation from one another. Ideology consists of words and arguments that political actors produce, which function as "a set of idea-elements that are bound together, that belong to one another in a non-random fashion" (Gerring 1997, p. 980). Theoretically, I discuss expectations about which words and arguments (their stated ideology) are likely to correspond with actions vis à vis women's rights and interests and vis à vis the rights and interests of multiply marginalized women. Empirically, I examine the relationship between the words and arguments (stated ideology) of political actors, such as in the form of party programs, and whether and how they advocate for women.

It is widely recognized that a single dimension is inadequate for capturing ideological variation among political actors. Nonetheless, the typical schema for characterizing ideologies and political parties is at most two-dimensional, composed of two axes that both use the term "left-right." First, a ubiquitous left-right scale is arranged in terms of support for state regulation of the economy.[26] Along this dimension, parties viewed as on the left favor more economic regulation by the state, and parties on the right favor less regulation (Camia and Caramani 2012; O'Brien 2018). A second dimension of variation among ideologies and parties is referred to by Hooghe, Marks, and Wilson (2002) and others as "new politics." New politics consists of postmaterialism and other related sociocultural orientations. Inglehart's (1977) original thesis was that postmaterialism consisted of values that favored individual autonomy and self-fulfillment over more socially rigid and materialist needs. Like its counterpart, new politics uses the spatial terms of left and right: postmaterialism is associated with the left, and its "opposite" (theorized variously as existentialism, survivalism, and social traditionalism) is associated with the right. Much of the literature built on Inglehart's sociological concept of postmaterialism posits that the processes of industrialization and postindustrialization create an environment more conducive to postmaterialist values, because these are settings where individuals and communities are existentially more secure and, therefore, turn to more ephemeral values (Inglehart and Welzel 2005).

These two prevailing dimensions (socioeconomics and new politics) are not the only criteria for differentiating among and spatially categorizing political actors and their ideologies, however. When it comes to explaining variation among these actors' attention to and advocacy for women and marginalized subgroups of women, this book argues that we must take these other dimensions seriously. This section discusses the ubiquity, usefulness, and limits of standard left-right ideological categories.

Despite persistent attention in political science to one- or two-dimensional categories of left and right, there is, indeed, a literature on ideologies and political values that extends these categories in ways that are useful for parsing sources of substantive political representation. Huber and Inglehart (1995) and others citing them (e.g., Budge 2000) identify ten criteria for categorizing parties as left or right, some of which are presented as contrasting pairs of orientations (one orientation being more right and the other more left): economic or class conflict, centralization of power, authoritarianism vs. democracy, isolationism vs. internationalism, traditional vs. new culture, xenophobia, conservatism vs. change, property rights, constitutional reform, and national defense.

These finer-grained dimensions for parsing political actors' ideologies produce inconsistent left-right clusters, and they do so in several ways. First, the boundaries we draw for categorizing a political actor as "on the left" or "on the right" are artifacts of which dimension we are applying (e.g., a party might be left in the socioeconomic sense but right in the new politics sense). Second, the attachment of each dimension to the left or right varies across time and place. Although these criteria differentiate among political parties, they do not hold consistently cross-nationally. Even in the economic and the social values senses, the most commonly applied dimensions, the content of left and right is not globally stable. Instead, the specific policies that are associated with left and right orientations, and the extent to which they differentiate among parties, vary across political systems.[27]

For example, studies of post-Communist Eastern Europe show that leftist parties support free market policies under conditions of simultaneous political and economic transition (Curry and Urban 2003; Hanley 2004). In other settings, policies associated with the left-right axis have simply become less important for party competition. Carmines and Stimson (1993) point to political parties' increased engagement in issue competition (i.e., parties aiming to get their favored—and other parties' disfavored—issues to dominate the electoral competition) rather than competition based on staking out left-right positions (see also Mair, Müller, and Plasser 2004). Relatedly, Green-Pedersen (2007) argues that issue competition has become an increasingly important dynamic in party systems and elections in Western Europe, in particular. Green-Pedersen (2007) shows that attention to standard left-right (economic) issues has declined across most parties in Western Europe since the 1950s, and, indeed, attention to these issues does not differentiate among left-right party families as much as it has historically. By the 1990s, for instance, Green parties had successfully pushed the issue of the environment onto most parties' platforms (Green-Pedersen 2007).

Further, Castles and Mair (1984) show that the way scholars have often studied left-right political scales is fraught with inconsistent decisions regarding which policy preferences qualify as left versus right. They argue that an overreliance on expert surveys exacerbates these measurement issues. One of the results of this data collection strategy, Castles and Mair assert, is that "the empirical foundation for valid cross-national scales rarely exists" (1984, p. 73). Similarly, Keman (2007) argues that analysis of party manifestos is a more objective strategy for characterizing parties' ideological content cross-nationally than expert surveys. However, these very studies using manifestos indicate cross-national heterogeneity in political parties that challenges conventional categories for left and right. Green-Pedersen's (2007) evidence of decreased salience of left-right issues, in fact, comes from Budge's (2001) analysis of Comparative Manifesto Project (CMP) data.

Despite this evidence of ideological heterogeneity, the categories of left and right are ubiquitous in political science, and, in some contexts, they are consistently statistically significant covariates of important political phenomena. As van der Eijk, Schmitt, and Binder write, "Left-right orientations of citizens are customarily found to be one of the most important factors that determine European voters' choices at the ballot box" (2005, p. 167). Work on the media shows that "the right" and "the left" are salient terms to which individual voters respond (Kleinnijenhuis and de Ridder 1998; Thomassen 2005). Extensive research on parliamentary systems posits that the presence in government of left-leaning parties corresponds with policy output that is qualitatively different from the output of right-leaning governments (Kittilson 2006; O'Regan 2000). This is just a sampling of work grounded in a distinction between right and left, showing that scholars and voters alike view this distinction as useful.[28]

Many cross-national studies use the concept of "party families" in lieu of left and right ideological categories.[29] Duverger's (1954) classic work on modern political parties offers one of the earliest uses of this concept. Party family classifications are sometimes based on parties' historical origins. These historical origins consist largely of social context, with particular focus on the social groups who were mobilized at the party's genesis. For instance, labor parties across Europe originated in and through the mobilization of a working class during the industrial revolution. Lipset and Rokkan (1967) refer to these social groups and their political relevance as "social cleavages," arguing that these cleavages produce party families. Much of the subsequent research on comparative parties uses or responds to the concepts of social and political cleavages. In this vein, Marks, Wilson, and Ray (2002) explain parties' attitude toward European integration in terms of their party families.[30] Similarly, Celis, Schouteden, and Wauters (2015) explain variation in political parties' interactions with their constituencies in terms of these family categories, which they define in historical terms.[31]

Other scholars define party families in terms of their shared principles rather than their historical origins. Adams et al. (2004), O'Brien (2018), and others follow the CMP in categorizing political parties into families based on their election platform documents. These scholars do not always use the same family categories, though there is consensus in a broad sense. Caramani and Hug's (1998) meta-analysis of post–World War II scholarly literature on political parties discerns thirteen groups that receive scholarly attention: socialist (including labor and social democratic), Christian democratic, conservative, communist, liberal and radical, right wing and authoritarian, regional/ethnic, agrarian, ecological, left, right, center, and other. Camia and Caramani (2012) observe seven party families that largely capture the thirteen covered by Caramani and Hug (1998): far left, socialist, green, liberal, religious, conservative, and far right. O'Brien (2018) observes eight, locating Christian Democrats, conservatives, and "nationalists" on the right; green and socialist/communist parties on the left; and social democratic, liberal, and agrarian parties in the center (p. 33).

Not all scholars agree that the concept of the party family is more useful than left-right categories. Mair and Mudde (1998) argue that both approaches suffer from similar setbacks, because they are variously developed based on historical origin, manifesto content, and expert surveys. Inconsistent theoretical bases for these categories produce different conclusions. In their study of the European Parliament, Hix, Noury, and Roland (2005) appear to use "party family" and "party group" synonymously. These critiques fit in the broader category of concerns about "concept stretching," which Sartori (1970, 1991) and others have long cautioned comparatists against.

This book is not the first piece of scholarship to observe that heterogeneity within ostensible ideological categories has consequences for our theoretical expectations about political behavior and outcomes. Caul (2001), for instance, differentiates between long-standing social democratic parties and more recently developed parties on the left in her study of gender quota diffusion, arguing that the "new left" is more likely to implement gender quotas than the "old left" (p. 1217). Golder (2003) shows that disaggregating the far right into populist and neo-Fascist categories is important for discerning how differently extremist parties fare electorally: neo-Fascist parties and voters express their political preferences regardless of the state of the economy or concerns about specific migration patterns, while populist patterns rise and fall with broader sociopolitical conditions. Erzeel and Celis (2016) apply a similar logic to their study of women's political representation across fourteen countries in Europe and argue that we must "adopt an understanding of 'ideology' that allows for more variation and is conceptually different from 'party'" (p. 576). However, these disaggregated approaches do not prevail in political science, in spite of their promise.

For the purposes of this book, heterogeneity within ideological categories has significant implications for what we think we know about women's political representation. Chapter 2 develops a series of finer-grained theoretical expectations about numerous varied ideological dimensions and their correspondence with women's substantive representation. In turn, empirical chapters of the book document this heterogeneity, observing it in political actors' activities on and their contestation over selected issue areas.

Road Map for the Book

Chapter 2 draws from existing research in gender and intersectionality, power, political ideologies, and comparative political institutions to generate a series of testable hypotheses about the ideological and institutional underpinnings of women's political representation. These hypotheses express expectations of variation between parties both within Germany and cross-nationally.

Chapter 3 introduces the case of Germany. This introduction provides background on continuity and change in the politics of gender and ethnicity in Germany, contextualizing parties' debates on these matters. It then presents the fourteen parties included in the book's analyses, justifying these parties' left-right placements in terms of the four ideological axes developed in Chapter 2. These ideological categories are the basis for much of the analyses in the empirical chapters on Germany that follow. The chapter concludes with a profile of the former chancellor Angela Merkel as a figure who represents many different faces of Germany.

Together, Chapters 4–6 apply the book's theoretical framework to explaining variation in parties' words and actions regarding women's political underrepresentation. This includes whether and how parties acknowledge the issue of women and especially minoritized women's underrepresentation

(Chapter 4), formal and informal intraparty strategies for addressing underrepresentation (Chapter 5), and their success at nominating and electing women and ethnic minorities into office and appointing them into parties' top leadership positions (Chapter 6). Increasing underrepresented groups' rates of officeholding is a relatively "easy case" for a wider range of political actors. Chapter 4 concludes with a profile of Ina Lenke, a politician with the Free Democratic Party (Freie Demokratische Partei; FDP) and former member of the Bundestag, whose policy priorities exemplify the complexities of explaining who will speak up for women's rights and interests. Chapter 5 concludes with a profile of Die Partei Mensch Umwelt Tierschutz: the Wellbeing of Humankind, the Environment, and Animals (TIER), a small German political party that illustrates what we can learn by inspecting rather than ignoring parties that do not fit into standard left-right ideological categories. Chapter 6 concludes with a profile of Annalena Baerbock, the Alliance 90/Greens (Bündnis 90/Die Grünen; B90/Gr) chancellor candidate in the 2021 federal election—at once an illustration of the Greens' successful institutionalization of gender equity and its limitations.

Next, Chapter 7 examines the policy changes that expanded women's inclusion in the German military against the backdrop of expanding pathways to citizenship for women and for ethnic-minority groups. Whether citizens can be banned from military service on the basis of sex-gender is a relatively "hard case" for a wide range of political actors both in Germany and around the world. This issue is embedded in traditional gender hierarchies, and difficult to find advocates for, across distinctive ideological dimensions.[32] In the case of Germany, the issue simultaneously challenges deep-seated beliefs about "Germanness," at the intersection of gender and ethnicity. The origins of Germany's categorical exclusion of women's participation in combat are intertwined with categorical exclusions of ethnic minorities' access to citizenship, and the evolution of both policy areas is also intertwined. Whether and how parties' orientations evolved on these intertwined issue areas presents a case study in the salience of finer-grained ideologies for understanding variation. The chapter concludes with a profile of the *Innere Führung*, the "leadership principle" of the FRG's military since its inception in 1955.

Taken together, the contrasting issue areas covered by Chapters 4–7 highlight the persistence of both patriarchy and limited advocacy for multiply marginalized women among and across political actors. Chapter 7's attention to intertwined military and citizenship policies contributes closer attention to whether, when, and how political parties have the capacity to evolve in their orientation toward ethnic-minority "others," in particular in gendered ways.

The final empirical chapter presents statistical tests of party-level data across the Organization for Economic Co-operation and Development

(OECD) for 2017. This cross-national analysis makes it possible to address system-level hypotheses, such as whether multiparty systems are more likely to include parties that promote women's rights and interests. It also provides empirical support for the claim that conventional "left" and "right" ideological categories are not stable across divergent political settings, concluding with a profile of the Chilean party system.

2
Theoretical Framework

Introduction

Even when a broad definition of women's rights and interests is applied, ultimately very few political parties and policymakers are active in promoting them. Some of the parties on the right perform as poorly as conventionally expected, advancing policies that are explicitly designed to constrain women's political opportunities within narrow social roles. In turn, advocacy for marginalized subgroups of women, foreclosed from full citizenship rights by sex-gender, class, race-ethnicity, and other social structures, is not a priority even for those political ideologies and parties from which we might conventionally expect it (the left).

In spite of this grim assessment of political actors' priorities, the rights of women and subgroups of women have advanced over the past century. These successes consist of both the removal of barriers, which we talk about as formal equality (e.g., the removal of constitutional strictures on women's right to work for pay without a husband or father's approval), and the creation of policies that actively promote social and political equality. They arise from the efforts of both civil society and formal political actors, working together, changing paradigms, and forging new legal landscapes. This book contends that political actors who seek to advance the rights and interests of historically marginalized social groups do not do so idiosyncratically. Instead, some parties (and individual policymakers associated with those parties) are more likely to engage in this advocacy than others, and their broader ideological and institutional context plays a powerful role in mitigating this potential. These patterns in advocacy are multidimensional, and they conform inconsistently to left-right categories.

This book argues that variation within conventional left and right categories should disrupt our expectations regarding whether and how political parties will advocate for the rights and interests of women and historically marginalized subgroups of women. In the face of the complicated picture of women's advocacy, this book proposes a comparative framework for situating political actors in their social and political context. Following Celis et al. (2008), Escobar-Lemmon and Taylor-Robinson (2016), and others, this chapter develops a series of testable hypotheses of women's political representation. Disaggregating ideological categories that are often conflated together, it posits factors that play a role in whether parties and policymakers will pay attention to women and to marginalized subgroups of women, direct that attention into meaningful and substantive policies that promote those groups' rights and interests, and engage in efforts to remove barriers to women's full citizenship. In turn, it theorizes that a broader context provides both constraints and opportunities that function differently for some parties compared to others.

This theoretical framework explains variation in advocacy for women and subgroups of women between political parties *within* a political system as well as *across* systems, with an emphasis on the shared importance of ideological commitments and institutional arrangements. Toward this aim, subsequent sections present and contextualize these expectations about political parties and their corresponding party-level observable implications.

Who Promotes the Rights and Interests of the Multiply Marginalized?

A growing body of research has arrived at the conclusion that multiply marginalized groups find advocates only in political actors who have specifically pledged to do so. By contrast, political actors who represent more expansive (less specific) groups of constituents overwhelmingly focus on the most advantaged members of these constituencies. These findings hold across a wide range of settings. For instance, in Guatemala *Indigenous women's* advocacy groups advocate for Indigenous women, while women's *or* Indigenous groups do not.[1] In the United States, Black women's advocacy organizations work to advance the rights and interests of Black women, while women's organizations' "wider" mandate conversely addresses the most advantaged (white, middle- and upper-class) women's issues and does not prioritize women of color.[2] This is further reflected in the policy agendas and bill sponsorship of legislators. Reingold, Haynie, and Widner (2020), for example, show that U.S. state legislators who are women of color are considerably more active than white women in advocating both for women more broadly and for multiply marginalized women. Importantly, policies that advance the interests of the most advantaged women may never benefit those who are the least advantaged.

This research points to the depressing expectation that parties and policymakers on neither the left nor the right as conventionally defined are likely to advocate for multiply marginalized subgroups of women, unless they are explicitly dedicated to doing so. "Explicitly dedicated" means that the party's stated core mission, identity, founding, principles, and priorities revolve around promoting the rights and interests of these subgroups. A political party that forms to advocate for a specific subgroup of women (e.g., Indigenous women) would constitute such an actor for that specific subgroup. This expectation applies across the ideological map. Political actors on the left and right (by any definition) who are not explicitly dedicated to advocating for multiply marginalized women are unlikely to do so.

As later chapters' empirical attention to multiple marginalization in Germany discusses, ethnic minorities comprise many diverse groups. Many members of these groups share the experience of formal exclusion from the political rights enjoyed by citizens. Women within these communities are especially unlikely to find advocates within formal politics.

Theoretical Expectation #1: *Unless a political party explicitly acknowledges the political rights and interests of multiply marginalized women, it is highly unlikely to undertake efforts to advance them.*

Patriarchy

Theories of gender, power, and feminism describe a social hierarchy that benefits the group of people received as men. The structure of this hierarchy, the values that underpin it, and the institutions producing and following from it are collectively termed *patriarchy*. For example, a long history of women's formal exclusion from politics has produced gendered stereotypes about what constitutes good leadership.[3] This formal exclusion and the persistent beliefs that result from it are all constitutive of patriarchy.

Patriarchy is by definition pervasive, embedded in formal institutions and in social practices alike. Walby (1989) defines patriarchy as "a system of social structures, and practices in which men dominate, oppress, and exploit women" (p. 214). Similarly, Rifkin (1980) writes, "By patriarchy, I mean any kind of group organization in which males hold dominant power and determine what part women shall and shall not play" (p. 83). Patriarchy is, therefore, ubiquitous. However, it is at the same time "just" about sex-gender, which is not the only salient social structure for people's lives. Intersectionality highlights variation among subgroups of women in their various social positions, which introduces questions about whether, when, and how patriarchy overlaps with other systems of domination, oppression, and exploitation. These systems of domination organize around race-ethnicity, socioeconomic class, and other social identity markers. They operate alongside patriarchy, and they have the potential to enhance or mitigate patriarchy's effects.

Research shows that interactions between patriarchy and other social systems depend, in part, on the setting, but arguments and findings about how they do so are inconsistent. For example, some theorists argue that "the family is not oppressive to women of the most subordinate groups" on the premise that "it is part of an alliance of the oppressed group against the superordinate group" (discussed in Walby 1989, p. 221). By contrast, Walby argues that women's oppression as women within the family is not necessarily far less than (less morally urgent than) their oppression as members of marginalized class and ethnic groups (p. 222). The family might be a site where other kinds of marginalization are produced and reinforced.

This debate over whether families within multiply marginalized settings will "overcome" patriarchy exemplifies shortcomings of some versions of intersectional theory in presupposing that an individual's multiple structural positions are all equally salient in all situations. By contrast, *intersectionality-plus*, discussed in Chapter 1, argues that women who are members of otherwise marginalized socioeconomic or ethnic groups do not need to "pick" which axis of marginalization matters more. Instead, intersections of multiple social structures have different salience and urgency depending on the issue area and, more broadly, on the context. Sometimes, the family setting may be empowering for women, including those women who are also marginalized by other social structures. At the same time, Walby (1989) and others remind us that the family's interests must not be conflated with women's interests. According to intersectionality-plus, there may be some family settings that enhance rather than detract from women's rights and interests. However, the persistence of patriarchy across diverse settings suggests that systematic private-sphere benefits are unlikely to occur in the absence of wider-ranging public-sphere advances in women's rights and interests.

If patriarchy is pervasive, then political actors are unlikely to act freely of it. A political actor who is *explicitly dedicated* to resisting it is expected to be categorically different from other political actors. For a political party, "to be explicitly dedicated to resisting" means that its core mission, identity, founding, principles, and priorities revolve around resisting patriarchy. In other words, only a feminist political party is likely to be free of patriarchy in its principles and aims:

> ***Theoretical Expectation #2****: Unless a political party explicitly states that it is antipatriarchy, it is propatriarchy.*

Ideologies

Patriarchy is an ideology: a set of values and beliefs that structure how individuals and groups think their broader societies and political institutions should be organized.[4] However, political parties across systems and across countries consistently embody patriarchy, making this ideology unhelpful for differentiating among them and, thus, also unhelpful for generating expectations about variation among political actors' advocacy for women.

This section, therefore, returns to Chapter 1's discussion of left and right ideologies, those clusters of values and beliefs that differentiate across political systems and among parties. It starts with the premise that political actors do not operate in a vacuum. Instead, they are situated within a broader ideological context, which sets the stage for parties' emergence and their competition with one another over both issue ownership and voters.[5] This ideological "stage" set for political actors has several names in the literature. One of these is "cultural systems," which include wider sets of political and social values; another is "broader ideology."[6] Scholars characterize these cultural systems in terms of (variously) the principles or values either that underpin its society or that structure its political institutions. Sometimes scholars base these characterizations on a holistic and qualitative assessment of the society in question (e.g., in describing an East Asian society as Confucian). Other scholars examine survey data for aggregate attitudes that can be characterized as, for example, individualistic (Inglehart and Carballo 1997). Regardless of the specific operationalization for it, a cultural system provides sets of parameters for how political actors appeal to and communicate with wider audiences. In short: a political actor is constrained by the wider political culture in which they are situated.

A society that largely shares communitarian values—something that can be measured with the World Values Survey or similar attitudinal data—for example, is likely to give rise to a different array of political parties compared to a society where individualism predominates. In a broadly communitarian society, a party that espouses individualistic values will struggle to get elected at all. Analogously, a communitarian party in an individualistic society is unlikely to emerge or survive. The upshot is that some societies are unlikely places for finding political parties or policymakers working to advance the rights and interests of women and subgroups of women.

A society that is deeply socially traditionalist, valuing traditional gender hierarchies in daily life as well as in patterns of political and economic behavior, is a hostile setting for political actors who aim to "smash the patriarchy." Especially in a majoritarian electoral system that structurally hinders the emergence of more than two political parties, a feminist political party, for example, is unlikely to emerge or survive. In a system where all viable political parties are socially traditionalist, individual feminist would-be policymakers are not likely to find a party that aligns with their values, nor to find a party willing to nominate them to run for office.

Once this stage is set, political actors vary in their promotion of the rights and interests of women. This section focuses on the connections between political actors' apparent ideological commitments and their advocacy for women, with an emphasis on the limitations of aggregated left-right categories.

Ideologies are constructs. They are not direct measures of, say, brain waves. Thus, *ideology* as an independent variable for explaining variation in political actors' advocacy for women is like many independent variables in political science: methodologically, the measure of ideology can be difficult to differentiate from the measure of the very same political activities (e.g., acts of representation) that we are interested in understanding. As Gerring (1997) notes, "Ideologies direct, or at least influence, political behavior. It is impossible, therefore, to study ideological phenomena as purely ideational" (p. 967). We risk tautologizing "ideology" with "observed political actions." At the same time, the ideological content of a party (its expressed principles and values) is often well known to constituents, and it is self-consciously part of the image that a party presents to the public. In other words, ideology matters for voters, and it matters for parties. These critiques underscore the importance of careful and well-justified operationalization. Measurement choices that follow (here and in subsequent empirical chapters) aim to avoid such a tautology.

This section discusses a series of ideologies, which subsequent empirical chapters test, as correlates of attention to and advocacy for women's rights and interests. This list is not intended to include all possible ideologies that a party might espouse or that might structure a party's priorities and proposed policies. Instead, the ideologies discussed are sets of values and beliefs that meet the following criteria:

1. Associated with political actors
2. Well established in the existing literature and can be inferred from relevant political texts (such as party platforms)
3. Widely accepted dimensions of differentiation between "left" and "right"
4. Theoretically expected to have a relationship with those actors' advocacy for women

5. Not one and the same as advocacy for women (i.e., this section does not include a discussion of the contrasting orientations of "pro-women versus anti-women")

Criterion 3 is because the book overall focuses on ideologies that scholars view as relevant for differentiating left from right in order to test the limits of these categories. The goal throughout is to challenge prevailing and aggregated expectations about the origins of advocacy for women and subgroups of women. Criterion 5 is to avoid a tautology between principles and policies.

The ideologies and value orientations in the discussion that follows are largely drawn from Huber and Inglehart (1995) and Budge (2000). These scholars identify ten criteria for categorizing parties as left or right, some of which are presented as contrasting pair of orientations (where one of those pairs is more left and one more right): *economic or class conflict* (i.e., economic redistributionism vs. liberalism), centralization of power, democracy vs. authoritarianism, internationalism vs. isolationism, xenophobia (which this book refers to as *multiculturalism vs. hegemonic-ethnic supremacy*), *change vs. conservatism* (i.e., social progressivism vs. traditionalism), *new vs. traditional culture* (i.e., postmaterialism vs. materialism), property rights, constitutional reform, and national defense. The four pairs from Huber and Inglehart (1995) are included in italic here.[7]

This book selects these four ideological dimensions for several reasons. First, these dimensions differentiate between the left and the right, but they are not one and the same with values or priorities directly speaking to gender roles. Second, as subsequent sections discuss, these dimensions generate divergent expectations about gender values and priorities; that is, they facilitate an exploration of the stability of the labels "left" and "right" for making sense of political actors' engagement in advancing women's and multiply marginalized women's rights and interests. The specific operationalizations of these ideologies (how they are observed and measured) are discussed in subsequent empirical chapters. These ideological dimensions are expected to correspond with different kinds of variation depending on the wider ideological and institutional context, expectations that are developed in the following sections and testable in comparative perspective.

Economic Redistributionism vs. Liberalism

Economic redistribution is consistently associated with "the left," and economic liberalism with "the right."[8] These sets of values regarding the role of the state in the economy are usually understood as opposites. I argue that existing literature supports the expectation that political actors who espouse *either* orientation have the potential to pay attention to and advocate for women's rights and interests. However, this attention is unlikely to be identical: these actors may express similar general goals, but they are expected to propose different policies to achieve them. Although many feminists argue that economic systems are tightly connected with whether and how societies value feminized labor, orientations toward state intervention in the economy are not in and of themselves about gender.

Political actors associated with economic liberalism are sometimes dismissed as unlikely advocates for women, because this negative expectation is often bundled together with a more general expectation about parties on the right (see O'Brien 2018), and it mirrors the expectation that policymakers who support economic redistribution will be likelier advocates for women. However, some research shows that actors "on the right" in terms of their economic orientations are not necessarily opposed to the broader goal of, and other means for, promoting women. For example, Xydias (2013) shows that members of Germany's FDP, which is primarily a free market party, actively talk about and endorse issues and concerns specific to women. Piscopo (2011) shows that women on the right in Argentina's Chamber of Deputies actively engage in debates on women's interests (specifically regarding sexual health, in 2001 and 2006), but they do so through different ideological lenses from those of their left-leaning counterparts. In Argentina, right-leaning women from parties including Acción por la República, Demócrata Progresista, Peronista Federal, Propuesta Republicana, and Unión Cívica Radical all energetically contributed their own perspectives *as women* on women's sexual health. All of these parties are economically liberal.

Conversely, political actors associated with economic redistributionism are not in fact consistently supportive of women's rights and interests. Political actors advocating for economic redistributionism exhibit a long history of ignoring gendered inequalities, due to both an emphasis on socioeconomic class over other structural positions and the embeddedness of Marxism in patriarchal institutions. For example, although official policies of the Soviet Union at its origin nominally promoted the equality of women and men, historians and sociologists have shown that these policies were ineffective at altering the power dynamics of the workplace, home, and political life.[9]

> ***Theoretical Expectation #3****: Political parties that espouse economically liberal values have the potential to advance women's rights and interests, doing so through policies that emphasize individual choice over achieving equal outcomes [all other things being equal]. Correspondingly, political parties that espouse redistributionist values have the potential to advance women's rights and interests, doing so through*

policies that emphasize achieving equal outcomes [all other things being equal].

Social Progressivism vs. Traditionalism

Social progressivism is consistently associated with "the left," and social traditionalism with "the right." As in the previous section, these sets of values are typically understood as opposites. Social traditionalism consists of placing high value on long-standing cultural practices, with corresponding resistance to new practices. Cultural practices include how respect and authority coalesce around individual people and individual roles, how respect and authority are expressed and maintained, etc. Beliefs about gender are, therefore, deeply embedded in cultural practices (Phillips 2010).

A large body of sociological work observes social attitudes and values through surveys and demonstrates a clear relationship between individual people's extent of social traditionalism and their beliefs about gender and equality. For example, Inglehart (2008) shows through simultaneous cohort and cross-national analyses that socially traditionalist values have declined in prevalence across Western societies in the 1970–2006 period. This decline corresponds both at the individual level and in the aggregate with support for gender equality—for example, in the form of disagreement with the statement, "A university education is more important for a boy than for a girl" (World Values Survey).[10]

Although these shifts in values may seem straightforward, they are not. "Social traditionalism" is instead multipart. One widely recognized component of social traditionalism is not just gender-differentiated social roles but hierarchical positions defined by gender, that is, men's position in authoritative roles and women's position in subservient roles. This hierarchical arrangement is fundamentally at odds with women's equality to men in political, social, and economic terms. If social traditionalism consisted only of hierarchically gendered values, then we could not observe variation in socially traditionalist political actors' promotion of women's rights and interests. But recent research has disaggregated the various components of social traditionalism in order to resolve otherwise puzzling observations. For instance, Cassese and Holman (2017) investigate explanations for the persistent finding that women are more religious—an orientation associated with social traditionalism—yet more progressive than men in the United States. They argue that "gendered beliefs about authority embedded in the religious experience" (p. 5) play an important mediating role in the relationship between religiosity and political values. Specifically, religious women who view God as a masculine authority are less likely to identify as socially progressive than their equally religious counterparts who do not view God as a masculine authority. In other words, this research indicates that religiosity itself is not a staple of political conservatism once religiosity is disaggregated.

Taken together, this existing literature supports the expectation that social traditionalism does not *preclude* advocacy for women, but it is likely to be associated with both less in overall quantity and a narrower range of issues. Further disaggregation of the components of social traditionalism is also likely to produce yet more nuanced findings.

> ***Theoretical Expectation #4***: *Political parties that espouse socially traditionalist values will have the potential to advance women's rights and interests, but they will do so to a lesser degree: less frequently and extensively, and on a narrower range of issues than their progressive counterparts [all other things being equal].*

Postmaterialism vs. Materialism

Postmaterialism is consistently associated with "the left," and its opposite, materialism (alternately termed "existentialism"), is consistently associated with the "the right." Inglehart (1971, 1977) defines materialism as a value orientation that emphasizes existential security over more ephemeral goals such as a feeling of accomplishment. Inglehart's (1971) premise is that "individuals pursue various goals in hierarchical order," with an emphasis on assuring sustenance before proceeding to satisfy other more symbolic goals (p. 991). Postmaterialism bears some resemblance to social progressivism. Postmaterialism as an orientation consists of an emphasis on such values as "a freedom of expression and participation in governmental decisions" (Inglehart 1977, p. 440). Inglehart and Welzel (2005) argue that postmaterialism emerges after materialism, as people's surroundings change and their existential security increases. They argue analogously that a step back (or down) in existential security, in turn, corresponds with a return to materialism/existentialism.

Postmaterialism and materialism are, therefore, closely related to, but not one and the same as, the orientations of social progressivism and traditionalism (see previous section). The issue of the environment and environmentalism neatly illustrates important distinctions between the axes of social progressivism/traditionalism and postmaterialism/materialism. Social traditionalism might correspond ideologically with environmental sustainability, while materialism is unlikely to do so. At the level of the political party, for instance, Christian Democrats show considerable interest in environmental sustainability, in Germany and elsewhere.[11] Sociologically, greater religiosity among social conservatives is associated with environmentalism, while conservatism on its own is not (Woodrum and Wolkomir 1997). Postmaterialism and progressivism are also not synonymous sets of beliefs. Cotgrove and Duff (1981), for example, show that environmentalists are particularly postmaterial and subject to other sociological forces. Mostafa (2013) shows that environmentalism has grown cross-nationally, even and also among poor countries (i.e., it is not contingent upon affluence).

In terms of the rights and interests of women and multiply marginalized women: materialism intersects with ubiquitous patriarchy, making it unlikely that an individual or society focused on survival will view women's rights and interests as a priority, however essential they are to women's own lives and existential security. This previous research, therefore, supports the expectation that, compared to postmaterialism, materialism will be associated with far less attention to women's rights and interests, and any attention that is paid will be on a narrow range of issues. Postmaterialism and materialism are close cousins to social progressivism and traditionalism, but they yield different theoretical expectations about political actors' likelihood of actively promoting women's rights and interests.

Theoretical Expectation #5: Political parties that espouse materialist values are much less likely to advocate for women compared to their postmaterialist counterparts, and any advocacy will be to a lesser degree: less frequent and extensive, and on a much narrower range of issues [all other things being equal].

Multiculturalism vs. Hegemonic-Ethnic Supremacy

Like the other sets of values previously discussed, hegemonic-ethnic supremacy is not a commonality across all political actors on "the right." However, it is historically and theoretically located on the right. Many scholars locate hegemonic-ethnic supremacy more specifically on the far right. Indeed, Mudde (2007) argues that "right-wing parties outside the mainstream" share nativism as a lowest common denominator. Nativism is "an ideology, which holds that states should be inhabited exclusively by members of the native group ('the nation') and that non-native elements (persons and ideas) are fundamentally threatening to the homogenous nation-state" (p. 19). This is conceptually very close to the ideology that Huber and Inglehart (1995) term *xenophobia*. In turn, the set of values often referred to as multiculturalism is strongly associated with "the left." Multiculturalism is the recognition, acceptance, and inclusion of varied cultural practices (Taylor 1994).

It is important to parse the extent and ways that hegemonic-ethnic supremacy corresponds with and departs from the conventional categories of left and right. Not all political actors associated with the right evince hegemonic-ethnic supremacist values; however, hegemonic-ethnic supremacy is largely located on the right. That said, some scholars identify an essential characteristic of hegemonic-ethnic supremacy that they argue is shared across the right and manifests most forcefully on the far right. With Bobbio (1994) and Seidel (1988), Mudde (2007) asserts that "the right" is defined by its orientation toward inequalities. In all right-leaning ideologies, they argue, inequalities are viewed as natural, and the state should not intervene to unmake them. This belief in the moral value of the status quo underlies economic liberalism's opposition to state intervention in the economy, materialism's prioritization of [men and humankind's] survival over political rights and civil liberties, and social traditionalism's opposition to external forces that apply pressure for change in social practices that they perceive as long-standing.

Political actors who evince hegemonic-ethnic supremacy apply this core belief in natural inequalities to specific ethnic groups other than their own: they view "other" ethnic groups as naturally unequal and lesser. This attitude toward natural ethnic inequalities is a short jump from a belief in natural inequalities between genders (see also Seidel 1988). Sociologist Kimmel (2019), for example, argues that hegemonic masculinity is intrinsically part of the political right.

In terms of women and gender, Mudde (2007) observes that "solid studies of the role of women in the organizations and ideologies of populist radical right parties are practically nonexistent" (p. 91). A gender analysis of the far right tends to emphasize hegemonic masculinity (Blee 2007; Kimmel 2019). However, as rightist populism rises in Europe in the twenty-first century, we are seeing increasing research on the dimension of gender and the role of women in parties organized around these values. For instance, Erzeel and Rashkova edited a special issue of the journal *West European Politics* (2017) expressly in order to address this long-standing gap in our knowledge about parties on the right. In this journal issue, Rashkova and Zankina's (2017) data on women's presence in radical right parties in Bulgaria show that these parties do elect fewer women than other parties in the Bulgarian system, but that by their measures "both radical right women and men have been more active in women's issues than their gender counterparts from other political parties" (p. 848). On the basis of these findings, they argue that "the classification of radical right parties as *Männerparteien* [men's parties] based on descriptive representation only, is too simplistic and to an extent, misleading" (p. 848).

This research on the radical right in Bulgaria notwithstanding, decades of sociological studies of nativism and ideologies of the right show evidence of a strong connection between hegemonic-ethnic supremacy and belief in traditional gender roles pointing in particular to the salience of motherhood as the primary vehicle for nurturing (hegemonic-ethnic supremacist) values.[12]

At the same time as hegemonic-ethnic supremacy clearly corresponds with low valuation of women's equal rights, research shows that multiculturalism is not always aligned with the promotion of women, either. This is because many persistent cultural practices are at odds with gender equity. The commitment to multiculturalism is a relativist position from which it may be difficult to assert any specific value, including the value of gender equity. Political theorists have discussed extensively how a group's right to practice its values potentially conflicts with individual group members' rights (Kymlicka 1995; M. Williams 1998). For example, Okin (1999) lists cultural practices that have defenders in spite of their clear injury to women members of the cultural group, including polygamy, forced marriage, female genital mutilation, punishing women for being raped, differential access for men and women to health care and education, unequal rights of ownership, assembly, and political participation, unequal vulnerability to violence (p. 8). These practices sometimes persist even in spite of wider legal systems. Rimonte's (1991) legal case study of the use of "the cultural defense" by Hmong communities in California against domestic violence and sexual assault charges, for example, shows how a cultural group can and does successfully assert its cultural practices against individuals' rights, even when those rights are enshrined in California state and U.S. federal laws.

In light of these persistent issues, Okin (1998) argues that women's "rights cannot be recognized as human rights without some significant challenges to that concept itself and to institutions basic to the various human cultures, certainly families and religion" (p. 32). Truly *feminist* multiculturalists "confine their defense of group rights largely to groups that are internally liberal" (Okin 1999, p. 11).

In sum, while hegemonic-ethnic supremacist values are clearly expected to correspond with opposition to gender egalitarianism, multiculturalist values sometimes correspond with allowing gender inegalitarian practices to persist.

Theoretical Expectation #6: *Political parties that espouse hegemonic-ethnic supremacist values are much less likely to advocate for women compared to their multiculturalist counterparts, and any advocacy will be to a lesser degree: less frequent and extensive, and on a much narrower range of issues [all other things being equal].*

Institutions

Beliefs alone do not produce action. Instead, political actors operate in specific institutional contexts: sets of formal and informal rules that produce opportunities and constraints. Some of these rules may function as institutional tools for political actors to shift the status quo.

In light of what we know about the persistence of agendas and privilege, this book starts with the expectation that a political actor who advocates for women, *and especially for multiply marginalized women*, does so against the currents of history. They must have some institutional tools at their disposal for resisting these forces. Political actors must have structural opportunities to place women's rights and interests on their party and legislative agenda, and they must have opportunities to bring important legislation up for a vote. This section, therefore, turns to key institutions that vary between political systems and produce different environments for parties and for policymakers as agenda setters. Even details such as how nominations for candidacy are produced—openly or anonymously, consensus-driven or by majority vote, at the national or subnational level, and so on—matter for political representation. However, this book does not discuss or test the salience of every possible institutional variant for women's advancement. Instead, it focuses on institutions that make space both for parties to add issues to the conversations taking place in their wider ideological context and, in turn, for policymakers to expand the agenda. This emphasis on *expansion* is because the concerns of women, and, especially multiply marginalized women, are still relatively new on the political agenda.

In 1960, Schattschneider observed in his oft quoted line that "the flaw in the pluralist heaven is that the heavenly chorus sings with a strong upper-class accent" (p. 35). This observation predicted decades of further research that agrees that pluralism and interest group representation are significantly biased against the marginalized.[13] Some of this bias is due to resources of varying kinds, such as education, money, and social networking (Verba, Schlozman, and Brady 1995). Research has also discerned institutional mechanisms for enabling or constraining dissenting or marginal voices. Across different political systems, even ideologically highly similar political actors are not all equally likely to stake out new issues (i.e., to expand the attention paid to groups previously ignored), because they operate within different institutional arrangements. Political actors pursue their agendas within rules that stipulate how drafts of laws are proposed and by whom, whether these laws must first run the gauntlet of multiple legislative committees and their respective veto points, whether parties and policymakers must anticipate the need for a majority or supermajority vote to pass legislation when it finally comes up for consideration in the plenary session, and so on.

This discussion generates theoretical expectations from two clusters of political institutions, multipartism and the institutions that directly precede and follow from it, and the legislative rules that make political parties more or less flexible to policy change. These represent important institutional tools for shifting the status quo.

Multipartism

Research in political science supports several interconnected explanations for the origins of multipartism, which is when a party system includes more than two political parties that regularly win seats. Here, I argue that the fact of multipartism, regardless of its origins, has powerful system-wide consequences for whether political actors will advocate for women and how they will do so. In brief: the coexistence of multiple parties in a political system results in these parties differentiating themselves in order to compete over voters. Structurally, in these systems there is a greater likelihood that at least one individual party will expressly promote gender equality (contingent upon public opinion). Thus, multipartism is an institutional feature that is applicable to cross-national comparisons.

As Lijphart (1999) notes, multiparty systems tend to include a greater number of issue dimensions for both clear spatial reasons and historical reasons. There are more parties to differentiate themselves from one another, and the system is likely multiparty, in the first place, because of the existence of multiple social and political cleavages. Issue dimensions consist of issues on which political parties offer distinct alternative perspectives and policy solutions. The ideological range and variety of political parties in a given political system has a direct relationship with the number of available issue dimensions.

One of the many ways that political parties may differentiate themselves is on issues related to women's rights and interests. If all political parties in a system shared a position on women's rights and interests (i.e., these parties were not distinguishable from one another in those domains), then women's rights and interests would not constitute an issue dimension in that party system. Parties would also not be distinguishable from one another on these matters, either in left-right terms or by any other criteria.

Multipartism itself derives from several origins and is, of course, no guarantee that parties will be meaningfully differentiated on any given issue, including issues central to women's right and interests. Taagepera (1999), for example, draws a triangle whose points consist of the number of parties in an assembly, institutions (electoral system permissiveness), and historically and socially relevant issues and cleavages (sociopolitical heterogeneity). This triangle shows that the number of issue dimensions is interrelated with the number both of parties and of electoral institutions, but in a recursive and nonlinear way. While multipartism is not a guarantee of the presence of multiple political parties that differentiate themselves on issues related to women's rights and interests, it is likely to be a prerequisite.

Political parties typically categorized on the right have a greater potential to play a role in advancing women's rights and interests in a system that can and does include multiple distinct right-leaning platforms. When parties on the right have space to differentiate themselves further, some platforms will express ideological commitments that are more likely to correspond with advocacy for women. For instance, in a multiparty system there is space for a political party that occupies a "right" position in socioeconomic terms (more likely to advocate for women) but not in postmaterialist or cultural-ethnic terms (which would make it less likely to advocate for women) (see Lijphart 1999, pp. 78–79). The fact of multipartism on its own makes it more likely that a wider diversity of these ideologies on the right will be present, including greater potential for ideologies that can and do support gender equity.

This expectation applies to "left" parties as well. Even while parties typically categorized on the left enjoy a positive reputation for advancing women's rights, these parties are also heterogeneous. Not all ideologies that can be associated with "the left" prioritize women's rights and interests. Further, the pervasiveness of patriarchy across societies suggests that, in a mainly two-party system, a single major party on the left *or* the right will advocate less for gender equity than they (strictly theoretically) have the potential to do. They may view it as an unworthy issue dimension or not to their competitive advantage, or they may not think of it at all. A multiparty system, by contrast, allows space for a wider diversity of political parties to actively promote gender equity.

The potential for multiparty systems to create structural space for women's advocacy by parties and individual policymakers is also mirrored in the dynamics of two-party systems. For example, Thomsen (2015, 2017) shows that the U.S. Republican Party's shift to the right and its ideological narrowing has squeezed moderate Republicans, including many women, both out of the party and also out of politics entirely. These are not individuals who will run on a Democratic ticket, meaning that they have no ticket to run on at all.

Another way to think about the consequences of party system attributes for women's rights is in terms of parties' strategic incentives. Much research in political science aims to explain policy change. On the matter of women's rights and interests, many of these studies specifically examine when, why, and how political actors empowered in the status quo might nonetheless support significantly changing that status quo through an expansion of the electorate. In this vein, research shows that political parties' competitive environment helps explain their support for enfranchising new social groups and, subsequently, their advocacy for these groups' rights and interests. Teele (2018), for example, demonstrates across the divergent cases of the United States, France, and Great Britain that women's suffrage is more likely in settings where parties perceive an advantage in an expanded electorate and women's organizations are strong. In turn, Boix's (1999) longitudinal 1875–1990 study of electoral institutional changes across twenty-three countries shows that these changes hinge on the weakness of longtime parties and the potential for new parties to mobilize voters. McConnaughy (2013) investigates parties' strategic choices within U.S. state legislatures, and Wolbrecht (2009) theorizes that strategic actors *within* parties lead the charge on policy shifts when they believe this will mobilize voters.

Taken together, research on multipartism, issue dimensions, and explanations for expanding suffrage to new social groups suggests that multiparty systems have the potential to incentivize greater attention to shifting the status quo.

Theoretical Expectation #7: Political parties that actively engage in promoting gender equity are more likely to be found in multiparty systems compared to two-party systems [all other things being equal].

Legislative Rules

Legislative rules directly shape the extent to which political parties can and do "discipline" their members, thereby shaping opportunities for individual policymakers to expand the agenda to include more or different policy items (Kam 2009). These rules are held constant across all parties in the same legislature, subject to the same legislative rules. This factor is, therefore, applicable to cross-national comparisons, with the general expectation that interparty variation will be different depending on context.

Much of this research models legislative behavior from a rational-choice perspective, and it distinguishes between exogenous and endogenous rules. Exogenous rules are those that legislators and parties effectively cannot change during the time frame of the legislative process they are active in, while endogenous rules are not fixed, can be changed, and can, therefore, reflect rather than shape political actors' incentives.[14] In this vein, Cox (2000) argues that a legislature's rules of procedure affect which bills pass by shaping the agenda (which bills are considered, in the first place), which amendments are allowed, and how legislators vote. In some systems, these rules work to bolster the power held by the majority party or government, such as by restricting the actors who can put legislation on the agenda. In other systems, these rules empower opposition parties against the majority or government, such as by allowing a wider range of actors to add to the agenda. For instance, legislative rules that restrict amendments once draft legislation is beyond its committee of origin and being considered by the legislature at large, called "closed rules," empower the members of the committee (Krehbiel 1992).

Further, these rules vary considerably across countries. Döring (2001), for example, shows variation in "agenda setting devices" even among the parliamentary systems of Western Europe (p. 148). This variation in government control of the agenda "contributes to a reduction of 'legislative inflation,' the proliferation of many small and incoherent pieces of legislation" (p. 147).

Some studies, of course, focus on more issue-specific rules, such as rules surrounding the budget (see, e.g., Döring 2001; Hagen 1992). But research shows that even a more general distinction between the government's control over the agenda helps explain both quantity and quality of legislation. Following this research, I focus on the flexibility of the legislative body in question for (1) political parties to affect the legislative agenda and (2) individual policymakers to introduce items on the agenda (see earlier discussion regarding policymakers' opportunities to expand their parties' agendas beyond the historical status quo). I extend findings regarding budgetary legislation to argue that political actors will be more likely to advocate for women when they are structurally allowed to add items to the agenda. As discussed in earlier sections, my premise is that the rights and interests of women, and, especially of multiply marginalized women, are still relatively new on the political agenda. A political actor must be institutionally empowered to promote women's rights and interests in spite of the status quo. Thus, analogous to the mechanism proposed earlier in theoretical expectation #7, a setting with more rigid rules for agenda setting limits tools for officeholders to expand their parties' agendas to include the rights and interests of women and marginalized subgroups of women. A setting with less rigid agenda-setting rules may accomplish the reverse effect. To test this expectation, Chapter 8 uses Döring's (1995) index for measuring "the degree of agenda-setting control exercised by the government" (quoted in Döring 2001, p. 157).

Theoretical Expectation #8: Political parties in a legislature whose rules empower the government in agenda setting will be less likely to promote the rights and interests of women and multiply marginalized women [all other things being equal].

Wider Sociocultural Context

The previous section introduced theoretical expectations for women's advocacy that follow from research on institutional differences between political systems, which are expected to produce constraints and opportunities for political parties. Parties also face constraints and opportunities shaped by their sociocultural setting. As Inglehart and Norris (2003) and other studies show, societies' social values matter for many political processes and outcomes, including political equality across social groups. Widely held social attitudes toward traditional gender roles, in particular, correspond powerfully with whether and how women enjoy full and equal citizenship with men counterparts. In turn, widely held attitudes toward minority rights set the stage for marginalized groups' political rights. In terms of political parties, the wider sociocultural context provides a crucial backdrop for parties' emergence, their agendas, and their strategic choices. Following Kunovich and Paxton (2005) and Paxton and Kunovich (2003), this book views political parties in their national contexts. In analyses focused on Germany, this context is shared across parties. Subsequently, cross-national analyses illuminate how "political parties mediate and interact with the effects of country-level variables in producing political outcomes for women" (Kunovich and Paxton 2005, p. 507). In particular, differences between *otherwise similar* political parties illuminate the role of wider context.

> ***Theoretical Expectation #9****: The extent of proequality attitudes in society will moderate political parties' likelihood of promoting the rights and interests of women and multiply marginalized women: more egalitarian settings will correspond with more advocacy [all other things being equal].*

Alternative Explanations

This theoretical framework (for a summary of the theoretical expectations discussed in this chapter, see Table 2.1) has presented both ideological and institutional explanations for variation in parties' advocacy for women and multiply marginalized women, explanations that deprioritize the bottom-up efforts of social movements and, more generally, civil society actors. This book's proximal explanations for interparty variation nonetheless contribute to a broader argument about the origins of advocacy. In other words, although civil society actors' voices and action are not explicit in this book's account, they may be operative behind policy changes.

Analyses in this book that focus on contemporary Germany largely hold this competitive environment constant. Chapter 7 adds insights to this question by examining parties' capacity to evolve on fundamental questions of citizenship rights. In turn, cross-national analyses in Chapter 8 show whether and how parties' wider political context, including social values, shapes interparty variation.

Conclusion

Chapter 1 introduced four ideological characteristics, arguing that three of them—social traditionalism, materialism, and hegemonic-ethnic supremacy—especially distinguish political actors who are likely to ignore or act against the rights and interests of women and marginalized subgroups of women.

TABLE 2.1 SUMMARY OF THEORETICAL EXPECTATIONS	
Theoretical Expectation #1: Multiple Marginalization	Unless a political party explicitly acknowledges the political rights and interests of multiply marginalized women, it is highly unlikely to undertake efforts to advance them.
Theoretical Expectation #2: Patriarchy	Unless a political party explicitly states that it is antipatriarchy, it is propatriarchy.
Theoretical Expectation #3: Economic Redistributionism/ Liberalism	Political parties that espouse economically liberal values have the potential to advance women's rights and interests, doing so through policies that emphasize individual choice over achieving equal outcomes [all other things being equal]. Correspondingly, political parties that espouse redistributionist values have the potential to advance women's rights and interests, doing so through policies that emphasize achieving equal outcomes [all other things being equal].
Theoretical Expectation #4: Social Progressivism/ Traditionalism	Political parties that espouse socially traditionalist values will have the potential to advance women's rights and interests, but they will do so to a lesser degree: less frequently and extensively, and on a narrower range of issues than their progressive counterparts [all other things being equal].
Theoretical Expectation #5: Postmaterialism/ Materialism	Political parties that espouse materialist values are much less likely to advocate for women compared to their postmaterialist counterparts, and any advocacy will be to a lesser degree: less frequent and extensive, and on a much narrower range of issues [all other things being equal].
Theoretical Expectation #6: Multiculturalism/ Hegemonic-Ethnic Supremacy	Political parties that espouse hegemonic-ethnic supremacist values are much less likely to advocate for women compared to their multiculturalist counterparts, and any advocacy will be to a lesser degree: less frequent and extensive, and on a much narrower range of issues [all other things being equal].
Theoretical Expectation #7: Multipartism	Political parties that actively engage in promoting gender equity are more likely to be found in multiparty systems compared to two-party systems [all other things being equal].
Theoretical Expectation #8: Parliamentary Control of the Agenda	Political parties in a legislature whose rules empower the government in agenda setting will be less likely to promote the rights and interests of women and multiply marginalized women [all other things being equal].
Theoretical Expectation #9: Cultural Context	The extent of proequality attitudes in society will moderate political parties' likelihood of promoting the rights and interests of women and multiply marginalized women: more egalitarian settings will correspond with more advocacy [all other things being equal].

- #1–9 all pertain to political parties.
- #1–6 are examined both in the case of contemporary Germany and cross-nationally.
- #7–9 are examined cross-nationally.

As discussed, these ideologies also map onto some (but not all) criteria for defining the left and the right. The research design of subsequent empirical chapters, therefore, selects issue areas that represent varying challenges for differentiating between left and right. Issues that are *less* at odds with social traditionalism, materialism, and hegemonic-ethnic supremacy are *more* likely to find advocates across a more diverse range of political actors. Each empirical chapter presents and justifies specific operationalization and measurement for the theoretical expectations articulated here.

3

Gender, Ethnicity, and the German Political System

Introduction

This chapter introduces the case of Germany, joining other scholars in characterizing the country as, simultaneously, "a reluctant newcomer to combating discrimination against women" and "an exemplary case of feminist political leadership" (Ferree 2012, p. 2). Indeed, across diverse issues and policy domains, Germany presents many faces. Contemporary Germany is a conservative social welfare state where significant social and economic infrastructure assumes a man breadwinner,[1] and where the political and social integration of immigrant ethnic minorities is globally poor. As *Der Spiegel* reported in 2009, "Foreigners who come to live in Germany tend to remain strangers, even after 50 years and three generations in some cases" (Elger, Kneip, and Theile 2009). Yet, at the same time, German women's presence in elected legislative office outpaces many of the country's European and global counterparts (see Figure 3.1), and, by 2021, Germany was home to the highest number of migrants in crisis in Europe: 1.24 million refugees (half of these from Syria), 233,000 asylum seekers, and 27,000 stateless persons.[2]

Germany's second-longest-serving chancellor is a woman, and the 2021 federal elections produced a supermajority of women in the Bundestag's *Präsidium*: Bärbel Bas serves as the Bundestag's president, and four of five vice presidents are women.[3] Former Chancellor Angela Merkel's service (2005–2021), successes, and legacy point to important ways in which *specifically wom-*

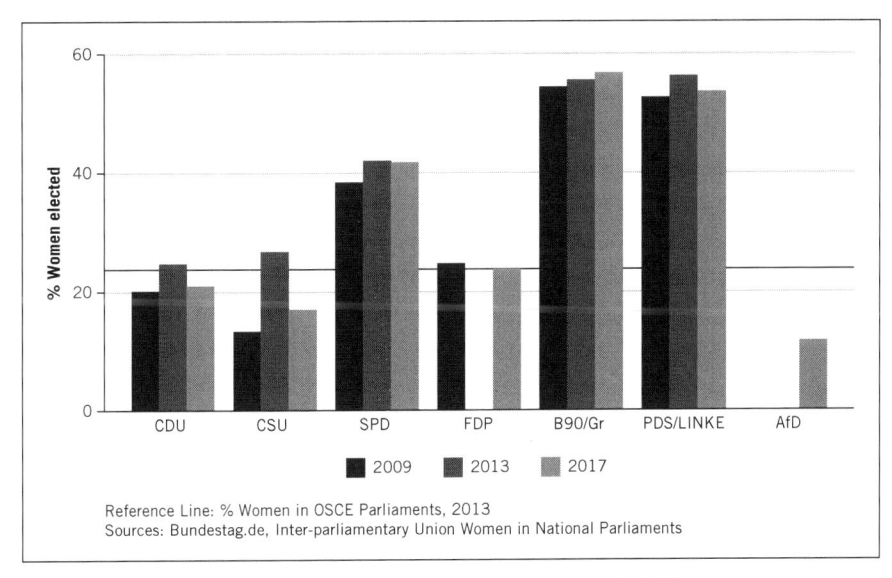

Figure 3.1 Women's rates of election to the Bundestag, 2009–2017.

en leaders have forged Germany since the country's reunification in 1990. By contrast, racial-ethnic-minority women have remained outside much of the formal policymaking process, because pathways to citizenship have been highly limited; later chapters explore profound changes to German nationality laws, in 2000, that are leading to greater political opportunities for racial-ethnic-minority group members.

In many countries, social movements have produced advances in the rights of historically marginalized groups. Such movements coalesce around the shared experience of unequal political rights, and they mobilize grievances with the goal of changing the status quo. They are more likely to both cohere and mobilize and succeed in their goals under conditions that are conducive to change. As Tarrow (2011) writes, "Changing political opportunities and constraints create incentives to take action for actors who lack resources of their own" (p. 9). German women's movements in the twentieth century illustrate the contributions of these efforts to achieving suffrage and opening greater educational opportunities to women (Gerhard 1990). However, in the case of post–World War II Germany, social movements on behalf of women have largely rejected formal politics. Unlike in the United States, postwar German feminists have not focused on achieving formal equality within existing institutions. German feminist movements have generally been hostile to the state, focusing instead on developing women's autonomy and self-fulfillment in spheres outside formal politics (Ferree 2012; Wiliarty

2010). This orientation is shared across West and East Germany in spite of these regions' otherwise distinctive social legacies. In the case of ethnic-minority populations, political mobilization has been significantly curtailed by their exclusion from the electoral process.

Methodologically, the case of Germany presents an opportunity to examine political parties' ideological variation in a wider context where many other salient factors for explaining advocacy for women are held constant. Taken together, this is a setting where the potential for social change is arguably high and, yet, stagnation is persistent. As Davidson-Schmich (2016) writes, "Germany's decentralized political institutions . . . offer multiple points of access where intersectional groups and their allies can influence state and national policymakers" (pp. 9–10), yet successes remain noteworthy and have unfolded gradually.

Three goals guide this chapter's presentation of the German case. First, the chapter briefly introduces significant axes of debates in the politics of gender and ethnicity in contemporary Germany. Second, it describes key German institutions, with a focus on electoral and party rules, in order to develop a case for the validity of inferences based on interparty comparisons. Finally, it introduces the fourteen parties included in the book's analyses of Germany, substantiating these parties' left-right placement in terms of the four ideological axes, which were introduced in Chapter 1. This placement builds from existing scholarly datasets, which generally include only nationally successful or longer-lived parties; therefore, it categorizes smaller parties based on evidence drawn from their current statutes and their 2017 election platforms.[4] Political parties' ideological placements are the basis for analyses in subsequent empirical Chapters 4–6, which explore whether and how the "usual suspects" in Germany work to promote the rights and interests of both women and minoritized women. As throughout the book, parties' left-right positions are defined not in terms of their attitudes toward and policies regarding sex-gender but rather in terms of other issue areas that inform typologies of ideology in the existing literature. The same party might be categorized as left or right depending on the axis. Table 3.1 summarizes the ideological axes included in these analyses. The chapter concludes with a pro-

TABLE 3.1 SUMMARY OF IDEOLOGICAL AXES	
Ideological Axes	
Left	*Right*
Economic redistributionism	Economic liberalism
Postmaterialism	Materialism
Social progressivism	Social traditionalism
Multiculturalism	Hegemonic-ethnic supremacy

file of former Chancellor Angela Merkel, whose biography and career illustrate numerous contradictory features of the German gender and political systems.

Politics of Gender in the FRG

Debates around gender in Germany have long focused on women's traditional roles within their families as wives and mothers. In 1949, the new FRG (West Germany) readopted the 1900 Civil Code. It then took decades to remove explicitly gendered provisions from this legal framework, provisions that especially targeted the rights and roles of married women.[5] The 1900 Civil Code restricted wives' property ownership, automatically awarded custody to fathers in case of divorce, and explicitly held women responsible for domestic labor. A limited Equal Rights Act in 1957–1958 allowed joint ownership of property by spouses, ended the legal requirement for women to have husbands' permission to seek paid employment outside the home, and (as discussed at greater length in Chapter 7) addressed married women's differential citizenship rights. However, even after 1958, section 1356 of the Civil Code stated that the woman "is entitled to take on paid employment" but only "as far as this can be combined with her duties in marriage and family" (Kolinsky 1993, p. 49). The subsequent Marriage and Family Law Reform Act (1976–1977) amended the Civil Code so that family law was no longer sex- or gender-specific; that is, both spouses were legally equals in areas that now included equal child custody (Gerhard 1990; Meyer 2003).

Although the country's legal frameworks no longer specify domestic labor, German society and political parties continue to express concern about "reconciling work and family" (*die Vereinbarkeit von Beruf und Familie*), and this shared attention exemplifies several simultaneous truths about contemporary Germany: the persistent commitment to having a primary, at-home caregiver for young children, who is still much more likely to be a woman/mother figure; the fact that working outside the home, particularly full-time, is incompatible with the expectation of within-home childcare; and, finally, the social and economic pressures to address demographic change, namely, an overall below-replacement birthrate (Goldenberg 2020).

Over the past thirty years, parental leave policies have become more generous and expanded to include men and fathers. Indeed, policies that are associated with "the left" were picked up and promoted by a long-serving federal officeholder with the Christian Democratic Union (Christlich-Demokratische Union; CDU): Rita Süssmuth, who served as federal minister for Youth, Family, Women, and Health (1985–1988) and as Bundestag president (1988–1998). At the same time, however, childcare infrastructure remains too limited to meet need and demand. As of 2020, parents of one in seven young children cannot secure a childcare spot.

Politics of Ethnicity in the FRG

As Chapter 7 addresses at much greater length, Germany's citizenship laws are globally restrictive and have long emphasized German ethnicity as the basis for access to political rights. This citizenship principle is known as jus sanguinis (citizenship by blood or inheritance), as distinguished from jus soli (citizenship by place of birth) (Brubaker 1992). One reaction to the Nazi era was the FRG's commitment to welcoming and repatriating people of German ancestry who had been expelled and wished to return, in addition to the descendants of Germans who had been persecuted, expelled, or murdered by the regime. Article 116 of the Basic Law assures renaturalization for victims of Nazi persecution who lost their German citizenship between January 30, 1933, and May 8, 1945, and it assures citizenship for these victims' descendants. A Federal Constitutional Court decision in 2020 (2 BvR 2628/18) further expanded the definition of "descendants" to include individuals who were born to unmarried parents in the following categories: those born prior to April 1, 1953, whose mothers' German citizenship had been unjustly revoked, and those born prior to July 1, 1993, whose fathers' German citizenship had been unjustly revoked. Other legal provisions for (re)naturalization have facilitated the immigration of ethnic Germans from Eastern Europe after the end of the Cold War.[6]

However, even these expanded provisions specifically address *Germans* who were persecuted or expelled. These restrictive citizenship laws coexisted with foreign-worker policies developed in the immediate postwar period (starting in 1955), which brought millions of southern Europeans to Germany to address the country's labor shortage in its period of rapid economic redevelopment. Bilateral agreements between the FRG and workers' home countries facilitated short-term work contracts, without the expectation of longer-term stays. Thus, by the time of the country's reunification in 1990, approximately 8 percent of the population comprised a category that Germans refer to in terms of their Migrationshintergrund (having a migrant background).[7]

Integration of "non-Germans" into German society has been poor, for numerous structural reasons. Broadly, ethnic-minority communities reside in "parallel societies," with relatively little interaction with other communities (Müller 2006). This isolation is especially stark for Muslim communities, whose religious practice is both institutionally and culturally separate from wider society. For example, the civil society association that organizes mosques in Germany is actually run by the Turkish government: the Türkisch-Islamische Union der Anstalt für Religion (Turkish-Islamic Union for Religious Affairs). Further, Muslim religious instruction is not integrated into public school systems, meaning that many young Muslims in Germany receive religious instruction within segregated settings. As Bale (2017) shows in an analysis of a movement for educational policy change in the northern German city of Hamburg, structural efforts to improve the educational performance and attainment of ethnic minorities meet with significant resistance from other groups in society. Indeed, in October 2010, then Chancellor Merkel famously asserted that the country's *multikulti* (multicultural) policy had failed. Writing more specifically about the political opportunities for ethnic-minority women, Donovan (2017) argues that conversations have largely shut out voices that do not focus on women as victims of "headscarves, honor killings, and forced marriages, to the detriment of other issues or perspectives" (p. 111).

The 1999–2000 citizenship law is the first significant increase in access for members of most racial-ethnic-minority groups in Germany seeking political status as citizens. At the same time, dual citizenship for naturalized German citizens is allowable for only a narrow set of circumstances, which has discouraged some potential applicants. By 2016, just 8 percent of the largest ethnic-minority group—first- and multigeneration Turkish-migrant background residents—enjoyed the political rights associated with citizenship status.[8] Legally, non-German-ethnics have systematically lacked levers for producing social and political change.[9]

The German Party and Electoral Systems

According to classic treatments of political party systems, the party "is a miniature political system. It has an authority structure. . . . It has a representative process, an electoral system, and sub-processes for recruiting leaders, defining goals, and resolving internal system conflicts" (Eldersveld 1964, quoted in Sartori 1976, p. 71). This is the case in Germany, as elsewhere, at the same time as German political parties are highly regulated from the top down, written into the country's constitution (called the Basic Law; Grundgesetz) and into the national policymaking process. Specifically, article 21 of Germany's Basic Law states that parties' "internal organization must conform to democratic principles" (clause 1) and parties that "seek to undermine or abolish the free democratic basic order or to endanger the existence of the Federal Republic of Germany shall be unconstitutional" (clause 2). The Parteiengesetz (Party Act) of 1967 further specifies details ranging from the composition of executive committees and the process for nominating candidates to the transparency of each party's financial accounts.

Germany's sixty-five-member constitutional committee, called the Parliamentary Council (Parlamentarischer Rat), in 1948–1949, designed this level of national regulation in a conscious effort to limit structurally the potential for extremist actors' reentry into politics, reflecting on causes of the Weimar Republic's dissolution into the Nazi regime. Karl Arnold, cofounder of the CDU in Nord-Rhein-Westfalen and the first Bundesrat president in 1949, famously stated in 1948, "We must be sure that what we construct will someday be a good house for all Germans" (Quoted in "International: Berlin to Bonn" 1948). Arnold was referring specifically to regional interests that members of the Parliamentary Council were balancing, but barring antidemocratic forces from politics was also a widely held goal.

Scholars and commentators refer to postwar Germany as a *Parteienstaat* (party state) for the centrality of political parties to the function of German democracy. In this vein, Katzenstein's (1987) concept of the semisovereign state interprets German politics as having three essential elements, starting with (1) the party system and also including (2) a form of federalism that he terms "cooperative" and (3) "parapublic institutions" (i.e., corporatist arrangements that integrate social groups into the policymaking process). This political design simultaneously diffuses authority and concentrates processes along specific pathways, including within political parties.

In terms of its electoral institutions, more specifically, at the national level Germany is a mixed-member proportional system. Roberts (1988) uses the phrase "the two-lane route to Bonn" to describe the two-vote legislative ballot for Bundestag elections.[10] Each voter casts a first vote to select an individual candidate to represent their constituency, and then a second vote in support of a political party. This first vote elects 299 individual constituency representatives, and the second vote elects the remainder of the Bundestag's membership, drawing officeholders from a party list. As of 2002, the total number of Bundestag constituencies in Germany is 299, (i.e., 598 seats is the body's base size). Overall seat distribution in the Bundestag is proportional to parties' share of second votes. Each party starts with seats it has won with first votes (i.e., direct mandates in constituencies), and then its remaining proportional seat share for each Land (state) is filled with candidates from party lists.

The CDU and the Social Democratic Party (Sozialdemokratische Partei Deutschlands; SPD) have historically won more first-vote constituencies than they "deserve" proportionally; therefore, the total number of seats in the Bundestag may expand beyond its base size so that parties' seat allocations remain proportional with the second votes they have received. Small parties less frequently win first-vote constituency mandates; that is, their route to Berlin is more likely to be from the second vote (party list). A party must clear a 5 percent electoral threshold to take its proportional share of seats; however, it may keep its first-vote seats regardless of its overall proportion of second votes. For example, the Party of Democratic Socialism (PDS) held two seats in the 2002–2005 Bundestag, which were direct mandates won in Berlin, even though their overall second-vote share was below 5 percent.[11]

A 2008 Federal Constitutional Court ruling declared overhang seats unconstitutional, because they so disproportionately advantaged larger parties. Thus, as of the 2013 federal election, small parties also gain seats to bring the overall allocation of seats into proportionality with the distribution of second votes. The expansion of smaller parties and contraction of larger parties have contributed to significantly more seats in the Bundestag in recent election cycles, prompting the prospect of lowering the number of constituencies to 280 and the chamber's base size to 560 seats (Schumacher 2021).

Germany's federal design requires further attention both to contextualize the alliance between the CDU and the Christian Social Union (Christlich-Soziale Union; CSU) and to justify the parties and the elections that receive closer analytical attention in later chapters. Germany's local and state elections are organized at the subnational level, meaning that (for the purposes of systematic comparison) state legislatures are not included in subsequent empirical chapters. In addition, Gunlicks (2003) notes that German state parliaments ultimately undertake more administration and constituency service than legislative work, which further distinguishes them as sites of political representation from the Bundestag (pp. 221–229).

Local and state elections in Germany operate within federal regulations for transparency and internally (within-party) democratic processes, but there is considerable variation in the rules. Many of the sixteen state legislatures' seats are filled through mixed-member proportional rules by which voters cast two votes (a first vote for an individual constituency representative, and a second in support of a political party), but five states use modified rules. The duration of a legislative term ranges from four to five years, and, as of February 2021, the size of state legislatures ranged from 51 seats (Saarland's Landtag) to 205 seats (Bavaria's Landtag; Gunlicks 2003, pp. 274–276). Bavaria had an upper house until it was abolished by referendum in 1998; today, all state legislatures in Germany are unicameral.[12] As noted elsewhere, the CDU operates in fifteen states and the CSU just in the state of Bavaria. These two closely allied parties form a party group in the Bundestag, but they are treated as separate parties in most analyses in this book, because they articulate distinctive priorities that are visible in party programs, in statutes, in public statements by party leaders, and in some limited issue domains in officeholders' voting records. Further, their political recruitment models diverge because their electoral environments are different.

Dozens of parties have regularly fielded candidates for elected office at all levels in the postwar period. Nonetheless, for decades just four parties were successful at winning national seats: the CDU, CSU, SPD, and FDP. These parties have been ideologically spaced around the center in an arrangement that scholars refer to as "a 2.5 party system" (CDU/CSU, SPD, FDP). Edinger and Nacos (1998) characterize this postwar party system in the following words: "The CDU/CSU and the SPD were either the strongest government or opposition parties, with the small Free Democratic Party holding the balance of power most of the time" (p. 72). This constellation preserved a fairly conservative and stable approach to everything from macroeconomics to social policies. For gender politics, a stable and conservative orientation largely worked to preserve traditional social roles.

Germany's party system, including the constellation of parties within it, offers several methodological advantages for testing this book's theoretical framework. First, inspection of these "miniature political systems" has the potential to offer particular insights into the role of ideology in the discretionary structural choices that are possible within German legal regulations. Second, and more specifically for the purpose of studying efforts to dislodge the status quo on the matter of gender and intersectional inequalities: divergence from this status quo and from the significant inertia of this stable party system is quite visible.

Political Parties in Contemporary Germany

As of 2017, the contemporary German system includes three more nationally successful parties in addition to the original postwar roster (CDU, CSU, SPD, FDP): the Green Party (first entering the Bundestag in 1983; called the Alliance 90/Greens, abbreviated here as B90/Gr, as of 1990), PDS/LINKE (as the PDS, 1990; LINKE emerged in 2007), and the Alternative for Germany (Alternative für Deutschland, AfD) (2017).[13] This means that fewer than ten political parties hold or have recently held seats in the Bundestag. This represents a level of stability that is especially noteworthy in comparison to other European countries also wracked by repeated turmoil for the first half of the twentieth century, many of which are now significantly more fragmented, such as Italy. Contemporary German political parties are generally viewed as differentiable along both socioeconomic and "new politics" axes, though Green-Pedersen (2007) shows evidence of convergence on several specific issue areas, most notably environmental sustainability.

The two largest parties in the German political system, the SPD and the CDU, are at the center-left and center-right, respectively, and are longtime political actors. Both of these political parties are rooted in historically fundamental social groups that are found across Europe, at the same time as they emerged in the specific competitive environment of a newly formed German state in the late nineteenth century.[14] In Lipset and Rokkan's (1967) terms, these are parties that responded to and mobilized constituencies in terms of politicized social cleavages. Neither parties' origins lie with the mobilization of communities who are or have been marginalized in terms of their ethnic or immigrant status.

On the center-left, the SPD has been part of national German politics for more than a century. The SPD emerged out of the trade unions central to the labor movement at the turn of the past century (Vössing 2017). On the center-right, the CDU has similarly been active for more than one century. The CDU is simultaneously known as a "confessional party" and a secular party, a right-leaning proponent of both social order and social well-being. In Kalyvas's (1996) terms, Christian Democracy in Europe "was the unplanned... byproduct of the strategic steps taken by the Catholic church in response to Liberal anticlerical attacks" (p. 6). In the case of Germany, Christian Democracy mobilized religious communities for political strategic ends at a time of regional power brokering. Writing about the late nineteenth century, a period during which the German confederate states were coalescing into the federated empire, H. Schulze (1998) refers to the "great variety of intersecting, often antagonistic social and economic interests"... which "solidified into political parties" (p. 159). One of these was the Center Party, which became Germany's CDU.

The CDU's sister party, the CSU, fields candidates only in the state of Bavaria, where the CDU does not participate in elections. The CDU and CSU form a single party group in the Bundestag, though this relationship is not without tension. CSU is markedly more socially conservative than the CDU, reflecting the conservatism of Bavaria. Recent scholarship argues that the CSU is increasingly right-wing populist (Arzheimer 2015; Falkenhagen 2013).

Numerous small liberal[15] parties developed immediately at the end of World War II, rooted in communities regionally, and they coalesced midcentury into the present-day FDP. Leuschner (2005) argues that precursors to the national FDP shared in common an emphasis on private enterprise and secularism, combined with a rejection of socialism (p. 2). The FDP, consistently small, has frequently served as a coalition member in the postwar period.[16]

The fourth party to emerge nationally in Germany grew out of pacifist, anti–nuclear energy movements and the new women's movement of the 1970s: the Greens.[17] Located on the left, with a particular focus on the environment, Germany's Green Party entered the Bundestag with twenty-eight seats in 1983. After Germany's reunification, the existing West German Green Party merged with an East German coalition called Alliance 90 (Bündnis 90), yielding the contemporary party name: Bündnis 90/Die Grünen (B90/Gr). Over the past forty years, the B90/Gr have served as a coalition partner in the fourteenth (1998–2002), fifteenth (2002–2005), and twentieth (2021–present) legislative terms.

West and East Germany reunited in 1990 at the close of the Cold War. Upon reunification, the former German Democratic Republic's (GDR) Socialist Unity Party took form as the PDS. The PDS gave way to the Die Linke in 2007, following a merger between the PDS and former members of the SPD (LINKE).[18] The LINKE are currently the leftmost mainstream contemporary party. The party has won between two and seventy-six seats in the Bundestag since 1990, never serving as a coalition partner.

Finally, the newest entrant into Germany's national party system is the AfD, established in 2013. It originally coalesced around opposition to economic bailouts for Southern Europe in the Great Recession, although its development has also drawn from the anti-Islamic movement in Germany as exemplified by PEGIDA, or the Patriotic Europeans against the Islamicization of the Occident (Patriotische Europäer gegen die Islamisierung des Abendlandes).[19] This party is unambiguously right-leaning, though it is variously described as Euroskeptic, populist, and radical right wing.[20] Based on an analysis of 2014 European Parliament election manifestos, Arzheimer (2015) argues that the AfD is programmatically closest to the CSU. In Arzheimer's (2015) assessment, the AfD is far right compared to other contemporary German political parties on the basis of its "nationalism, its stance against state support for sexual diversity and gender mainstreaming, and its market liberalism" (p. 551). However, the party actively mutes nativist and racist elements in its manifesto, party website texts, and social media presence. Hansen and Olsen (2019) argue that the party and its followers are primarily motivated by "attitudes towards immigrants/refugees and antiestablishment sentiment/satisfaction with democracy in Germany" (p. 1), orientations that have mobilized erstwhile supporters of parties across the German system. Writing about the AfD and gender, Xydias (2020) discusses causes and consequences of women's low presence in the AfD, both as members and as officeholders, in terms of the party's masculinism and nativism. The AfD is the materialist, hegemonic-ethnic supremacist party par excellence at the national level in Germany.

Like many other countries in Northern Europe, Germany has seen the emergence of a political party called the Pirate Party (Die Piratenpartei Deutschland; PIR), a niche party whose platform focuses on transparency of data, open access, and more participatory democracy through internet technology. As in other countries, the German Pirates first fielded candidates in the early 2000s. After winning seats in the European Parliament (2014) and in four state legislatures (2011–2012), this relative newcomer has had significantly less success than the AfD. They have largely disappeared from office, though they have one Member of the European Parliament (elected 2019), and the party continues to field candidates in elections. Schlegel (2016) describes the PIR as benefiting from and portraying themselves as part of the digital revolution. He writes that this digital revolution "has played a central role in the party's organization, programmatic goals, and internal development" (p. 18).

In turn, several dozen small parties regularly field candidates in elections at all levels of German government. These small parties play an important role in the country's party system. They are consistent participants in electoral politics even when they do not regularly win seats at any level. Over time, some of these parties have integrated into larger organizations, and individual candidates have in some cases become active in etablierten Parteien (parties that do win seats). However, much less scholarly attention has been paid to small parties in Germany, focusing instead on seat holders at the national level. As A. Schulze (2004) writes, "Small parties and factions are a terra incognita in the social sciences" (nicht etablierte Klein- oder Splitterparteien stellen . . . eine terra incognita der Sozialwissenschaft dar, pp. 8–9). Schulze goes on to note that small extremist parties are those that have garnered closer attention, in particular, because of their role in Germany's political history (p. 10), but ignoring other small parties misses valuable opportunities to theorize more broadly about the incentives that the party system produces. We must instead examine all small parties, including those nonextremist organizations with greater potential to build coalitions with others.

On the far right in Germany lie numerous small parties with limited longevity, such as the Deutsche Volksunion (1987–2011). More persistent, though not nationally successful, parties include the National Democratic Party (NPD; Nationaldemokratische Partei Deutschlands), with which the Deutsche Volksunion merged in 2011, and the Republikaner (REP). These smaller parties tend to organize around narrower, and sometimes eccentric, sets of issues. As a result, many of them fit less cleanly within existing cross-national frameworks for categorizing political parties. Existing comparative parties' datasets place many of these parties—when they include them, in the first place—in a miscellaneous category, indicating that they lack "a clear left/right position."[21] In particular, smaller parties that are not easily categorizable as far right or far left are typically omitted from much cross-national analysis.

Omitting smaller parties that fit less cleanly into a unidimensional ideological framework is a mistake for a variety of reasons. First, their omission mischaracterizes the party system, in terms of both parties' strategic environment and voters' choices. Parties that win few or no seats are not irrelevant to either processes or outcomes. For example, these smaller parties may draw voters away from other parties, or their presence and platform may incentivize other parties to change their tune. Second, including smaller parties increases the sample size and thereby empowers statistical analyses. Finally, these parties present the opportunity to examine theoretical expectations about unusual combinations of ideological dimensions.

For these reasons, this book's analyses include seven small German parties in addition to the seven nationally successful parties. These parties were selected because they are consistent participants (but not seat winners) in Bundestag elections, they represent ideological diversity (i.e., they offer an opportunity to test the theoretical implications developed in previous chapters), and, finally, they represent both extremists and nonextremists. They include the following: the Free Voters (FW/FWD), the Marxist-Leninist Party of Germany (MLPD), the NPD, the Ecological Party of Germany (ÖDP), the PIR, the REP, and the TIER.

German Political Parties in Four Ideological Dimensions

Chapter 2 introduced four pairs of ideological dimensions that it argued correspond with expectations of advocacy for the rights and interests of historically marginalized groups in Germany: economic redistribution vs. economic liberalism, social progressivism vs. traditionalism, postmaterialism vs. materialism, and multiculturalism vs. hegemonic-ethnic supremacy. This section discusses and justifies German parties' placement into each of these categories. Data on parties' ideological placement draw from both existing comparative datasets and the application of these datasets' coding rules to party statutes and platforms. As discussed earlier, parties' explicit orientation toward gender issues is not considered as a basis for categorization. Table 3.2 summarizes parties' categorization. (Abbreviations for party names are summarized in Appendix A.)

Party Families and Left-Right Categories in Comparative Politics

Table 3.2 juxtaposes several standard aggregated left-right measures with four additional ideological dimensions for distinguishing left from right. These are the ideological categories used for analyses in subsequent chapters.

The first column in Table 3.2 displays German parties' party family categorization, following existing research. Specifically, it draws from the Comparative Political Data Set, which in turn cites Lane, McKay, and Newton (1997), like many existing comparative datasets. These party families have been used in other studies of parties and political representation, such as Mudde (2007) and O'Brien (2018). Political parties are grouped together in a family on the basis of their broad policy orientations as well as their history and the social groups in which they are rooted (Mair and Mudde 1998).

The second column in Table 3.2 shows "aggregated party positions in four major dimensions" (Döring and Manow 2020), ranging from 0 to 10, where higher values are further to the right. In the ParlGov dataset, these dimensions

TABLE 3.2 GERMAN POLITICAL PARTIES: IDEOLOGICAL CATEGORIES

Party	Lane, McKay, and Newton (1997) and CPDS Party Family Categorization	L-R (ParlGov: Döring and Manow 2020)*	Economic Redistributionism (L) or Liberalism (R)?**	Social Progressivism (L) or Traditionalism (R)?***	Postmaterialism (L) or Materialism (R)?[†]	Multiculturalism (L) or Hegemonic-Ethnic Supremacy (R)?[‡]
AfD	Right	8.8	L	R	R	R
CDU	Religious	6.3	R	R	R	R
CSU	Religious	7.3	R	R	R	R
FDP	Liberal	5.9	R	L	L	L
B90/Gr	Environmental/Green	2.9	L	L	L	L
PDS/LINKE	Communist	1.2	L	L	L	L
SPD	Social Democratic	3.6	L	L	L	L
FW/FWD	Right	7.4	L	R	R	R
MLPD	Communist	[no L-R value in ParlGov]	L	L	L	L
NPD	Right	9.8	L	R	R	R
ÖDP	Environmental/Green	2.5	L	L	L	L
PIR	Liberal	[no L-R value in ParlGov]	L	L	L	L
REP	Right	9.3	R	R	R	R
TIER	Environmental/Green	[no L-R value in ParlGov]	L	L	L	R

Note: A party is categorized as L (a) if its V-Party value is at or lower than the median value for that variable, or (b), for parties not included in V-Party, based on the application of existing datasets' coding rules to the party's 2017 or most recent Bundestag election program. See more extensive discussion in the text.

* Source: This column presents Döring and Manow / ParlGov (2020) for an aggregated "left-right" variable; each party gets a 0–10 value, where zero denotes left-most and ten denotes right-most.

** Source: V-Party (2020) includes an Economic Left-Right scale variable.

*** Source: V-Party (2020) includes a Social Liberalism-Conservatism variable.

[†] Source: V-Party (2020) includes a variable for "position on democratic freedoms and rights" (GALTAN).

[‡] Source: V-Party (2020) includes a Cultural Superiority variable.

are time-invariant and impute missing party positions with "mean values for the respective party family."[22] ParlGov aggregates several prominent expert surveys in the discipline of comparative politics, and its dataset includes eleven of the fourteen parties here.[23] This is a continuous and unidimensional measure, in which the LINKE is the overall left-most German party in the ParlGov dataset and the NPD is the right-most German party in the dataset.

This book's central claim is that ideological heterogeneity within standard left and right categories has implications for whether and how parties will work to promote the rights and interests of all women and of minoritized women. More generally, critiques of aggregated party groupings take several forms in the literature. Considerable methodological scholarship has weighed the merits of competing approaches to categorizing political parties into party families and other similar typologies. As Mair and Mudde (1998) write, "Family groupings are often treated in practice as self-evident categories, requiring neither justification nor specification," making them "various and problematic" (p. 214).

The criteria for grouping parties together, therefore, are central to concerns about the substantive meaning and implications of these categories. The cross-national study of political parties relies on several standard empirical approaches to categorizing political parties, with corresponding trade-offs. First, questionnaires to political scientists who are experts in a given party system, called "expert surveys," have the advantage of providing global coverage within the same dataset.[24] Conversely, expert surveys risk relying too heavily on individually biased evaluations of these parties; some expert survey approaches average experts' responses in an effort to address this latter issue (Mair and Castles 1997). However, Budge (2000) and Huber and Inglehart (1995) argue that these aggregated left-right expert measures risk overstating the cross-cultural comparability of these family categories. As Benoit and Laver (2007) write, although "overall in western Europe, party placements on the four core policy dimensions explain a large part (75–90 percent) of the variation in their placements on the left right dimension," this is not as consistently the case in all regions of the world (p. 92). In turn, any party family measures that are static over periods of political and social change risk mischaracterizing these parties as they and their electoral environments evolve (Budge 2000, p. 104). Further, what an aggregate expert survey is showing may lack both reliability and validity. This manifests in two ways: variation in whether any given expert's evaluation reflects the ideological positions of party leaders (as distinct from officeholders or rank-and-file members), and inconsistency in whether the evaluation reflects a party's behavior and actions versus the orientations that theoretically underlie them (Budge 2000, pp. 103–104).

As an alternative to country experts, the impressive and widely used CMP employs content analyses of parties' election programs to characterize their policy positions and hence their ideological orientations. However, efforts like the CMP's to assign left-right positions are stymied by several issues, including the aforementioned cross-national variation in the meaning of ideological categories[25] as well as questions about the external validity of the left-right index (RILE) constructed from CMP data (see Mölder 2016). Further, Gemenis's (2012) meta-analyses show a systematic centrist bias in parties' categorization.

Finally, the above-mentioned ParlGov Project (Döring and Manow 2020) identifies what they call a "special" category of political parties, which they do not categorize as left or right. These are "parties that cannot be classified into the eight categories" in Döring and Manow's (2020) typology, because they are "special issue parties without a clear left/right position."[26] However, the heterogeneity of these special political parties is, I argue, direct evidence of the inadequacy of standard left-right categories. This point receives more attention in Chapter 5.

Economically Redistributionist (L) or Economically Liberal (R)?

This ideological dimension differentiates among parties on the basis of their orientation toward the state's intervention in the economy. CHES (2019), an expert survey, covers nine of the fourteen parties in this book's dataset, and the ParlGov (2020) dataset covers seven. The CHES "redistribution" variable indicates each party's "position on redistribution of wealth from the rich to the poor," on a ten-point scale (where 0 = Strongly favors redistribution, and 10 = Strongly opposes redistribution). The ParlGov "state-market" variable indicates each party's rejection of state regulation of the economy (also 0–10). Parties were categorized as "left" if they were at or lower than the median value for these variables.

Five parties' values for this variable were imputed based on inspection of their 2017 or otherwise current party programs. Documentation and quotations that substantiate this imputation are in Appendix B.

Table 3.2 shows that more political parties in this book's analyses of Germany are redistributionist (left-leaning) in their orientation toward the state's role in the economy. However, three key parties in the postwar period are liberal (right-leaning) in this regard: the CDU, CSU, and FDP.

Socially Progressive (L) or Socially Traditionalist (R)?

This ideological dimension differentiates among parties on the basis of their valuation of sociocultural traditionalism. Lührmann et al.'s V-Party dataset (2020) includes data for seven German political parties for a variable called, "Social Liberalism-Conservatism" (V-Party 4.2.3, ep_v6_lib_cons).[27] Seven parties' values for this variable were imputed based on inspection of their party programs for 2017. Documentation and quotations that substantiate these imputations are in Appendix B.

As shown in Table 3.2, several German political parties that are left-leaning in their economic orientations are coded as socially traditionalist (right-leaning), and one party—the FDP—is liberal but coded as socially progressive. These are not "switches" but rather an indication of parties' multidimensional ideological complexity.

Postmaterialist (L) or Materialist (R)?

This ideological dimension differentiates among parties on the basis of their orientation toward individual persons' options for fulfillment (i.e., steps beyond merely survival-based concerns). As discussed in Chapter 1, Inglehart (1977) proposes a distinctive ideological orientation that prioritizes environmental sustainability and individual autonomy regarding life choices over socially rigid and survival-focused matters. Lührmann et al.'s V-Party dataset (2020) includes a variable called, "Liberal-Traditional Scaling" (V-Party 4.2, ep_galtan). As noted in the previous section, V-Party includes data for seven German political parties. The V-Party codebook defines this variable as follows:

> "Libertarian" or "postmaterialist" parties favor expanded personal freedoms, for example, access to abortion, active euthanasia, same-sex marriage, or greater democratic participation. "Traditional" or "authoritarian" parties . . . value order, tradition, and stability, and believe that the government should be a firm moral authority on social and cultural issues.

Seven parties' values for this variable were imputed based on inspection of their 2017 or otherwise current party programs. Documentation and quotations that substantiate these imputations are in Appendix B. In the twenty-first century, numerous political parties are simultaneously economically right-leaning yet postmaterialist in their orientations, especially regarding the environment. Although social traditionalism and materialism remain conceptually distinct, parties' left-right placements along these two axes largely overlap in Germany today.

Multiculturalist (L) or Hegemonic-Ethnic Supremacist (R)?

This ideological dimension differentiates among parties on the basis of their xenophobia, which captures nationalism and natalism, as contrasted with their openness and valuation of cultural diversity. Lührmann et al.'s V-Party dataset (2020) includes a variable called "Cultural Superiority" (V-Party 3.2.9, v2paculsup). This variable has values for seven parties in the German system. The V-Party codebook defines the variable as whether

> the party leadership promote[s] the cultural superiority of a specific social group or the nation as a whole . . . [referring] to key non-economic cleavages in society, which could, for example, be based on caste, ethnicity, language, race, region, religion, or some combination thereof. This question further refers to cultural issues related to the national history and identity of a country. This question does not pertain to social groups based on gender or sexual orientation.

In the V-Party dataset, this variable can take five values ranging from zero ("strongly promotes the cultural superiority of a specific social group or the nation as a whole") to four ("strongly opposes"). As noted earlier, political parties were dichotomously categorized as "left" if they were at or lower than the median value for these variables. Values were imputed for the seven small parties included in this book's analyses based on inspection of their 2017 or otherwise current party programs. Substantiating documentation is in Appendix B.

Table 3.2 shows that three nationally successful parties in the Bundestag since Germany's reunification, in 1990, are simultaneously "left" along all four ideological axes, including multiculturalism: B90/Gr, LINKE, and SPD.

The German Party System in Four Dimensions

Previous sections have justified the placement of fourteen German political parties along four ideological dimensions. Later empirical chapters test whether these parties' words and actions in support of women's rights and interests covary with each ideological dimension, respectively.

Angela Merkel and the CDU

A 2005–2007 social marketing campaign called *Du Bist Deutschland* aimed to unite Germans in their diversity. Supported by a coalition of companies, it consisted of posters and advertisements showcasing many varied Germans with the caption: "You Are Germany." Posters featured Germans such as nineteenth-century aviator Otto Lilienthal, twentieth-century feminist journalist Alice Schwarzer, and twenty-first-century chef Tim Mälzer. Reactions to this campaign were mixed and included the criticism that it resembled National Socialist posters (Erenz 2005). Other commentary observed that the campaign expressed unity without solidarity (Holly 2009).

Who are the Germans? Angela Merkel, second-longest-serving postwar chancellor, led both Germany and the CDU across a series of debates on this and related questions. Merkel herself represents many dimensions of Germany all at once. Born in 1954, she is the guise of the contemporary FRG and yet was raised and educated in the former GDR—*da drüben* (over there)—in the words of Böhme's (1983) influential essay collection on East German society and identity. Merkel grew up in a Lutheran household "over there" yet later served as the leader of a political party with Catholic roots in Southern Germany.

She is the first and, thus far, only woman chancellor, paradoxically elected under the banner of a socially traditionalist party. Merkel completed graduate degrees in physical chemistry, she is twice married, once divorced, and she is the stepmother to her husband's two sons from his previous marriage. She is famously reserved yet powerful. In Mushaben's (2017) words, Merkel "provides a one-woman laboratory" for addressing many important questions about both contemporary German politics and gender in this context (pp. 2–3). As Wiliarty (2008) describes her, Merkel is either "a sign of hope, or the exception that proves the rule."

Merkel's leadership also offers insights into the evolution of Germany's party system. In December 2018, nearly thirty years after German reunification, Merkel stepped down from her role as CDU party leader, expressing the desire for a smooth transition within the CDU to her successor. When she retired in 2021 at the conclusion of the nineteenth Bundestag term, she had served as chancellor for sixteen years and sixteen days, just ten days fewer than the longest-serving post–World War II German leader, Helmut Kohl (Lane 2021).

The CDU is in some ways a different party now. Commentators and critics attribute a "leftward" shift in the CDU over the past twenty years to Merkel, especially on the issue of welcoming refugees into Germany when the civil war in Syria escalated in 2015. Over this same time frame, the CDU also moved "leftward" on the environment. However, painting with four brushes—the four ideological dimensions highlighted in this book—produces a more complicated picture. The CDU remains a center-right party, in the German context. During Merkel's tenure, the CDU remained largely consistent in its economic liberalism and social traditionalism but arguably became less materialist and more multicultural. These are the directions in which Germany, more broadly, is moving. At the same time, the CDU faces the loss of right-leaning voters to the AfD. In other words, variation among parties "on the right" is highly consequential for voters and for policymaking, alike.

Coalition negotiations after the September 2021 elections took nearly three months to conclude. The coalition partners, SPD, B90/Gr, and FDP, signed their governing contract on December 7, 2021. Michaela Kuefner, chief political editor of the German news source *Deutsche Welle*, observed in a social media post on Twitter (now X), "This is the moment the post-Merkel Era begins for real."

Conclusion

Germany is a multiparty political system, and this system has evolved with political and social change over the post–World War II period. At the national level, the FRG's "2.5 party system" expanded in the early 1980s to include the Green Party (later B90/Gr). Germany's reunification in 1990 introduced the PDS (later LINKE). In the 2010s, financial crises and rising xenophobia introduced the AfD. All of these parties have also evolved over this time frame. Although subsequent empirical chapters focus on parties' contemporary guises, these discussions also aim to place parties in their historical context and to consider where the parties have been before now.

The CDU under the leadership of Angela Merkel (2000–2018; chancellor 2005–2021) offers an example of simultaneous continuity and change. Table 3.2 shows that the contemporary CDU is right-leaning, right of the median for all four disaggregated ideological dimensions. That was true at the party's ascendance after World War II, and it remains true. Yet, by the twenty-first century, this party "on the right" has enacted bylaws to increase women's presence in elected office, endorsed quotas for corporate boards, and presided over the arrival of more than one million refugees from Syria's civil war. The meaning of "the right" has changed even within the relatively stable setting of Germany.

4

German Political Parties

Representing the Problem of Underrepresentation

Introduction

This chapter lays the foundation for an exploration of variation among German political parties in whether and how they (1) acknowledge the disproportionate absence of women and marginalized women from politics in their statutes and election platforms and (2) take action to redress this absence through recruitment, training, and candidate nomination processes. Here, women's rights and interests take the form of their inclusion at a stage prior to political recruitment: at the parties' description of the problem, that is, whether and how parties acknowledge political underrepresentation. This approach to examining variation in political actors' advocacy for women and marginalized women follows Bacchi (2009) and Bjarnegård and Murray (2018) in seeking evidence of parties' acknowledgment and framing of disproportionately low rates of political officeholding as a problem, in the first place.

In Bacchi's (2009) terms: What is the problem represented to be? This chapter's analyses yield two key findings. First, German political parties manifest extensive variation in whether and how they view increasing women's presence in office as a goal that should be pursued. Parties' ideological differences are multidimensional, and these dimensions inspire a range of framing choices and electoral provisions in their statutes and election programs. Both otherwise-left and otherwise-right parties neglect the problem of women's underrepresentation in politics. Second, German political parties manifest little to no variation in their attention to the exclusion of women from marginalized social groups. The relative absence from political office of women with a migrant background in Germany, for instance, receives no attention in the statutes and programs of both otherwise-left and otherwise-right parties. This finding is null but important: it establishes a basis for comparison in the future, and it reaffirms the persistent impact of parties' roots in social groups on much of their subsequent development.

Earlier chapters have discussed three more abstract indicators of *advocacy for women and multiply marginalized women*: (1) paying attention to women and to marginalized subgroups of women, (2) directing that attention into meaningful and substantive policies that promote those groups' rights and interests, and (3) working to remove barriers to those rights and interests. In this chapter, *advocacy* consists of political parties' acknowledgment of unequal representation in elected office. This includes whether they name unequal representation as a problem, in the first place, as well as whether they articulate the needfulness of acting on it. In Chapter 5, advocacy consists of parties' formal and informal activities to encourage and recruit aspirants from underrepresented groups and, ultimately, their level of success at nominating more diverse candidates and electing them to legislative office. Because formal restrictions on the basis of sex-gender were dismantled over the course of Germany's twentieth century,[1] *removing existing barriers* to women's candidacy, election, and officeholding is conceptually integrated into measures of the formal and informal tools (quotas and mentoring programs) that may work to overcome the status quo of women's exclusion (covered in Chapter 5).

Subsequent sections of this chapter proceed as follows. First, a discussion of the literature on the political representation of historically marginalized groups establishes political officeholding as a right and interest; that is, this domain is justified as an area for seeking to understand variation between political parties in their advocacy for these groups. Second, a discussion of factors shaping men's *overrepresentation* justifies the empirical focus of these chapters on political parties and gatekeepers. Parties and their gatekeepers are political actors in the position to nominate and otherwise encourage candidates from historically marginalized groups, and they are the actors who may act to accomplish this in opposition to long-standing practices that advantage ethnic-majority men.[2]

Analyses of fourteen ideologically varying political parties' election platforms and statutes for 2017 focus on whether and how parties acknowledge the disproportionate absence of women and marginalized women from elected office. These are all parties that fielded candidates in the Bundestag elections of 2009, 2013, and 2017.

Finally, the chapter considers the ideological and institutional context of a "renegade" policymaker: Ina Lenke, an FDP Member of the Bundestag (MdB) who has advocated for gender quotas in spite of her party's repeated rejection of positive discrimination as a tool for diversifying candidate pools. This short concluding profile showcases Lenke's *problem representation* regarding women's absence from political officeholding.

Political Officeholding as a Right and an Interest

Direct participation in the political process through officeholding is, unambiguously, both a political right and a political interest. In their essay on the significance and the shortcomings of one-hundred-year anniversaries of women's suffrage, Piscopo and Shames (2020) call this "the right to be elected." Political parties' varying levels of commitment to redressing exclusion provide meaningful insights into their commitments to other democratic principles as well as to fundamental questions of equity both across gender and across race-ethnicity.

First, being able to participate in public decision-making is a right from the perspective of the individual. Since the mid-twentieth century, suffrage, including the legal rights to both cast votes and run for office, has been a universally accepted component of full citizenship (see Marshall 1950 and Walby 1994). As Chapter 1's discussion of intersectionality shows, people received as women share the experience of exclusion from full citizenship on the basis of their sex-gender. However, *inclusion* is accomplished differently for different women. Multiply marginalized women struggle for inclusion in the face of different challenges, which are historically contingent. In the U.S. South, for example, Jim Crow laws curtailed the voting rights of people of color, but the effects of Jim Crow were also inflected by gender. Writing about the one-hundred-year anniversary of the Nineteenth Amendment of the Constitution of the United States, Wolbrecht and Corder (2020) emphasize that it "left in place . . . legal and extra-legal practices which denied voting rights on other bases, most notably on the basis of race in the American South" (p. 5). Focusing on the politics of the state of North Carolina in the late 1800s and early 1900s, Gilmore (2019) argues more specifically that "racial repression at the turn of the [last] century did not simply institutionalize the prevailing trend in race relations; rather, it profoundly reordered society," including the disenfranchisement of Black men (p. xxi). Black middle-class women in this setting navigated gendered-raced pathways toward political justice. Gilmore's findings are globally applicable: worldwide, marginalized subgroups' pathways toward political justice are inflected by both political institutions and cultural practices.

Globally, women who are racial-ethnic minorities are consistently disenfranchised and absent from formal politics at higher rates than majority-status women (Barker and Coffé 2018; Hughes 2011). Writing about Germany,

Schönwälder (2012) describes how German political institutions, including historically restrictive naturalization laws (the subject of this book's Chapter 7), have inhibited the political engagement and influence of ethnic minorities. Assessing the political presence of Germans with a migrant background in 2012, Schönwälder observes that "parties contribute very unevenly to the growth of immigrant representation" in office (2012, p. 76). Davidson-Schmich (2017), Donovan (2007), and Walsh and Xydias (2014) similarly show that opportunities for ethnic minorities within Germany to organize effectively for political change are limited. These institutional barriers are even greater for women within these minority communities in Germany, because intersectional civil society advocacy groups—those for and by marginalized *women*—are absent at the national level (Donovan 2017; Walsh and Xydias 2014).

Women's disproportionate absence from public office is unjust and signals clear symbolic deficiencies (Mansbridge 1999). A wealth of empirical research shows that this absence is also likely to be associated with less attention to issues that may be of greater urgency for women as a group. Political scientists have paid extensive attention to connections between women's presence in office (often termed *descriptive representation*) and advocacy for women's rights and interests (*substantive representation*). This literature has studied a variety of mechanisms for this connection, including the role of, alternately, a "critical mass" and "critical actors" acting on behalf of women and the possible importance of officeholders' personal experiences in motivating their attention to women's interests. It consistently finds that women officeholders advocate for women at greater rates than their men counterparts. These differences are often small, but they are both statistically and substantively significant, and they persist cross-nationally.[3] That said, while women holding office may produce benefits for women as a larger group to some extent, research also shows that the presence in office of multiply marginalized women in decision-making roles may be crucial for the explicit and effective promotion of multiply marginalized women's preferences.[4] This is the case for at least two reasons. First, "women are not a voting bloc," either as policymakers or as constituents (Wolbrecht and Corder 2020, p. 5). Women's interests are varied and inflected by many other intersecting factors. Second, the interests and perspectives of marginalized women are less likely to align with the interests of nonmarginalized men, who remain in the distinct majority in most policymaking settings.[5]

The mother of this strand of contemporary research on political representation, Hanna Pitkin, defines descriptive representation as "[standing] for" others, "by virtue of a correspondence or connection between them, a resemblance or reflection" (Pitkin [1967] 1972, p. 61). The presence of women—or of members of a specific racial-ethnic minority—matters for "being present, being heard" (Pitkin [1967] 1972, p. 63). In this way, presence is important for the actions that it makes possible.

As Diamond and Hartsock (1981) argue, "Only women can 'act for' women in identifying 'invisible' problems" relevant to women; that is, only women can give accurate information about the problems that they experience directly (p. 720). But how accurate is this information for the circumstances of multiply marginalized women? All of these problems, in their various forms, can find policy solutions only when they are recognized and articulated by policymakers. Phillips (1998, p. 25) similarly emphasizes that ideas (i.e., interests) cannot be fully separated from presence (i.e., people who share those interests being there to vocalize them). The necessity of *presence of ideas* further underscores how important it is for women from many different sociostructural positions to hold public office.

The benefits of inclusion arguably include better decision-making and better policy for everyone. In this vein, Young (1997) makes the case for "public discussion and decision making" that "includes and affirms all particular social group perspectives," including women and multiply marginalized women, "in the society and draws upon their situated knowledge as a resource for enlarging the understanding of everyone and moving them beyond their own parochial interests" (p. 399). Writing about the varied benefits of more diverse officeholders, Mansbridge (1999) also argues that having a group member in office may be particularly substantively important when interests are "uncrystallized" (i.e., on issues that are emergent or lesser known). Deliberation over these nascent issues especially needs the input of varied perspectives. Mansbridge's argument about uncrystallized interests resembles Phillips's contention that ideas (interests) and presence may be difficult to fully separate.

In addition to arguing for ways in which descriptive representation is likely to improve the qualities of substantive representation, Mansbridge (1999) makes the case for other symbolic benefits. These benefits include the existence of role models for groups who have historically been formally excluded or otherwise absent from public life and the legitimacy that their visible presence in office confers on the political system. M. Williams (1998) similarly argues that self-representation by historically marginalized groups is vital for democratic legitimacy. These social groups who have experienced injustices perpetrated by the state are especially in need of purposeful inclusion. In turn, empirical studies such as Lombardo and Meier (2014) argue that women in previously men-dominated spaces, such as defense ministries, discursively alter public life by shifting assumptions about how roles are gendered. These symbolic and role model effects may, therefore, also profoundly reshape "social [meanings] of 'ability to rule'" (Mansbridge 1999, p. 628).

In sum, the abilities to stand both for political candidacy and for election are a right and an interest. Although other political and social factors play significant roles in the policymaking process, advocacy for the political preferences of all women and of marginalized subgroups of women is less likely when members of these groups are fully absent from office. Advocacy for women's rights and interests, therefore, includes actions to promote their presence in policymaking roles.

Factors Shaping Men's Overrepresentation and Women's Underrepresentation

Globally, by the late twentieth century, very few political systems still imposed restrictions on suffrage on the basis of sex-gender. Aside from nondemocratic regimes, where citizens received both as women and as men lack the formal or effective right to participate directly in political decision-making, just two otherwise democratic settings formally excluded women from the electorate until the 1990s–2000s: Western Samoa (1990) and the Swiss canton of Appenzell Innerrhoden (1991).[6]

Although barriers to women's officeholding no longer consist of legal or constitutional exclusion on the basis of sex-gender, extensive research shows that other forces reduce their likelihood of being nominated for political office.[7] Informal social practices that discriminate against women, and opaque intraparty nominating rules, contribute to persistently lower rates of women's nomination.[8] Some scholars argue that this issue should be considered in terms of men's persistent *over*representation in legislatures around the world. For example, Bjarnegård (2013) shows evidence of social practices that comprise what she terms "homosocial capital," by which "men select men, and male dominance in the networks is maintained and reproduced" (p. 22).[9] In the same spirit, Bjarnegård and Murray (2018) refer to flipping attention from women's underrepresentation to men's overrepresentation as a matter of "problem description," and they argue that distinctive and important insights can be drawn from inspecting "factors that enable and reproduce men's presence" among candidates and among officeholders (pp. 265–266). Informal social practices such as these are more difficult to find evidence of, but their relative invisibility does not make them unimportant.

Additionally, research clearly shows that a multitude of social and economic forces reduces women's likelihood of seeking candidacy in the first place. Globally, women in the aggregate are less likely than their men counterparts to have professional and educational backgrounds common for political office, and they consistently participate in the labor market at lower rates.[10] Sociocultural forces also shape political activity. Women are still disproportionately responsible for both childcare and eldercare and for household tasks, which reduces their time and other resources for political engagement.[11] Indeed, Federici (2020) refers to the household as "point zero" for gendered inequities that extend to engagement in public life.

Some research finds that people received as women also view pursuing political candidacy and officeholding more negatively than their men counterparts, both in terms of their own suitability and qualifications and in terms of whether these political activities seem desirable. In this vein, the literature on gendered political ambition shows aggregate differences in self-perceptions of winnability even between women and men who share similar elite occupational backgrounds (e.g., working as an attorney or in civil bureaucracy), levels of educational attainment (e.g., holding an advanced professional degree), and community engagement (e.g., serving on philanthropic boards in their community) (Fox and Lawless 2010; Davidson-Schmich 2016). This research demonstrates that gendered socialization affecting both women's psychology and their material resources makes it less likely that they will consider running for political office than their men counterparts. It does so through several mechanisms. Broadly, gendered socialization shapes respondents' perceptions of what is both required of and experienced by political officeholders. Experimental studies such as Schneider et al. (2016) and Pate and Fox (2018) suggest that gendered frames for seeking political candidacy, including underlying motivations to do so, explain men's greater expressed interest in running. Further, survey data of "ordinary" as opposed to elite women and men—those who are not active in the prestigious, higher-paying occupations that Fox and Lawless's (2010) data focus on—also show differences between women and men in their levels of political ambition. Crowder-Meyer (2020) argues that, among "mass public" women in the contemporary United States, the deterrents to their candidacy (and, correspondingly, factors that might encourage it) are strongly related. This is especially the case for women's access to support resources that are necessary for overcoming the gendered distribution of household and family labor.

The finding that gendered socialization constrains women's resources, their interest in political office, and whether they are viewed as serious candidates extends beyond the United States and across culturally diverse societies. Bjarnegård's (2013) empirical analysis of the role of homosocial capital in maintaining men's overrepresentation among parliamentarians is on the case of contemporary Thailand. Bjarnegård and Kenny (2016) offer a comparative analysis of informal candidate selection practices in Thailand and Scotland to demonstrate how widely this theoretical framework can travel. In a similar vein, Davidson-Schmich's (2016) study of political recruitment in Germany shows that these sociocultural effects are strongest at early stages of the process, where gendered opportunities to play in the community soccer club or chitchat at the local watering hole make it more difficult for women to be viewed as party loyalists. Also writing about Germany, Kintz's (2011, 2014) studies of demographic patterns among officeholders clearly show the disproportionate absence both of mothers and of former Eastern Germans (i.e., the absence of those eligibles with lower resources of time, money, and incumbency).

These findings further apply to multiply marginalized women, though more comparative scholarly attention has been paid separately to *either* women *or* marginalized groups. Donovan (2017) shows that women with a migrant background in Germany face significant challenges against political organizing (i.e., against seeking pathways for influencing the policymaking process). These challenges include the vertical corporatist structure of policymaking in Germany, which becomes doubly challenging for women within marginalized communities. Davidson-Schmich (2017) provides a rare examination of intersectional policymaking outside the United States, focusing on policy successes for multiply marginalized women in Germany, although it does not address political officeholding.

Discussion of Evidence: German Political Parties' Acknowledgment of Inequalities

Earlier chapters introduced Germany's party system, with particular attention to its high level of regulation at the national level. Roberts (1988) writes that, as a result of Germany's history with nondemocracy and the desire to avoid repeating it, "candidate selection occurs within a more rigorously defined regulative context than is the case in many other democratic states" (p. 97). Germany's multiparty system includes dozens of ideologically varied parties, all of which must by federal law make extensive documentation about their internal organization publicly available. These parties also publish manifestos (party programs) at regular intervals, at the time of elections. Candidacy and election data reported by the *Bundeswahlleiter* (federal returning officer) are then central to the empirical analysis in Chapter 5. Taken together, these materials are the basis for characterizing political parties' advocacy for the inclusion of women and multiply marginalized women. These analyses are then further examined in light of material from personal interviews with officeholding members in the Bundestag and in state legislatures.

Significant inertia hinders the advancement of the rights and interests of historically disadvantaged groups. Political parties that promote more diverse candidates for office and within-party leadership positions are acting against this inertia. On the more specific matter of women's relative absence from political office, one signal to this kind of action lies with whether these parties acknowledge gendered inequalities and express a commitment to redressing them. Even while this is "just talk," it is arguably an important starting point (see Xydias 2013). The party that has nothing to say about gender and ethnic marginalization in its membership and in its pool of candidates is an unlikely site for activities in targeted support of these groups. For those parties that have not adopted specific measures, such as a gender or ethnic quota, mention of these issues could portend future action.

This discussion of fourteen contemporary German political parties draws from their platforms for the 2017 Bundestag elections[12] to justify coding each as *acknowledging* or *not acknowledging* women's political underrepresentation. It contextualizes attention to political underrepresentation within each party's acknowledgment of gendered inequalities, more broadly. It does so in order to highlight that, by the early twenty-first century, variation in parties' attention to various dimensions of inequalities is complex. The "usual suspects" are not the only parties that express concern about gendered inequalities and the need for political inclusion. Further, variations in how parties parse these issues is significant. In 2017, the election programs of various parties widely viewed as left-leaning do not pay much attention to women's political underrepresentation. However, this makes a certain amount of sense; women are not, in fact, underrepresented in their ranks! At the same time, inattention from some parties on the right may be integrally part of these parties' failure to act. A small subset of parties expressly rejects framing gendered disproportionate absence from office as a problem.

Table 4.1 summarizes the findings discussed in the following section. Following van der Haar and Verloo (2013), this analysis looks for evidence of political actors (here, parties) paying attention to gender and, in turn, to the intersection of gender with other social categories. The following discussion of each party identifies multiple marginalization as the intersection of two or more social categories that are associated with socioeconomic or political disadvantage. Not one of these fourteen programs mentions the underrepresentation in political office of Germans with a Migrationshintergrund (migrant background) or other source of marginalization, and they also do not call for greater representation of marginalized women. Several platforms dis-

TABLE 4.1 PARTIES' ACKNOWLEDGMENT OF WOMEN'S POLITICAL UNDERREPRESENTATION

Acknowledgment of Women's Political Underrepresentation	Party
Does *Not* Acknowledge	AfD, CDU, CSU, FW, MLPD, NPD, PIR, REP, TIER
Acknowledges	B90/Gr, FDP, LINKE, SPD, ÖDP

cuss various dimensions of marginalization, such as physical difference, without considering them intersectionally, that is, not as a social category that intersects with gender.

AfD

The AfD is a political party that currently has few women officeholders and whose supporters also include relatively few women (see Hansen and Olsen 2019; Xydias 2020). The party's 2017 election program does not frame this as a problem. Section 1.15 of the 2017 program discusses article 3 of the Basic Law in the following manner: "the AfD supports equality before the law, *therefore the party rejects quotas* [emphasis added]" (Die Alternative für Deutschland tritt für die Gleichheit vor dem Gesetz ein. *Deshalb lehnen wir sogennante 'Quotenregelungen' ab*, p. 12). More broadly, this program does not discuss gendered patterns in inequality in any sphere of life, nor does it address multiple marginalization across any combination of axes.

B90/Gr

As discussed elsewhere, this is a political party with a long history of public attention to both gendered inequalities and women's rights, including in its 2017 federal elections program. However, this program pays little attention specifically to women's underrepresentation *in politics*. This inattention becomes less surprising in light of the party's significant success at electing women at high rates. Women's underrepresentation is factually not a problem for the B90/Gr. As later sections address, regarding quotas and rates of candidacy and election, the B90/Gr do not disproportionately undernominate or underelect women. Indeed, for several consecutive national election cycles, the party has nominated and elected women at higher rates than men.

The party's attention to gendered inequalities specifically in the formal political sphere is brief. Section 4, subsection 1, of the 2017 program asserts that "women are massively underrepresented in legislatures" (Derzeit sind Frauen in den Parlamenten massive unterrepräsentiert, p. 149). Later sections of the program reassert the party's commitment to regulations for women's inclusion in many domains, including the workplace (pp. 131, 193). Quotas are presented as a desirable tool for addressing gendered inequalities in the workplace and other domains, and this accords with the party's more general orientation in favor of equal outcomes rather than more narrowly equal opportunities (Xydias 2013). Based on this material, the B90/Gr 2017 program is coded as acknowledging women's political underrepresentation. This attention is clearly expressed, even while it focuses on women's underrepresentation with other political parties and in spheres beyond politics where women are disadvantaged and underrepresented.

In turn, B90/Gr's attention to multiple marginalization is limited and does not include concern about the political invisibility of marginalized women. The 2017 program addresses a range of sources of marginalization, but it does so largely without noting intersectional effects. For example, the program discusses the rights of workers who are differently abled, calling for: "Good jobs for everyone—including for people with disabilities" (Gute Arbeit für alle—auch für Menschen mit Behinderung). This call includes support for a quota for disabled persons' inclusion in educational programs and employment (pp. 220–221), but the discussion is not intersectional. An exception to this omission lies with the party's discussion of asylum seekers, which notes specific gendered challenges and issues among refugees.

CDU and CSU

As sister parties at the national level, the CDU and CSU shared a 2017 program. This program acknowledges women's underrepresentation in the workplace, writing: "We want more women in leadership positions in business and management. With the introduction of women's quotas for corporate boards we have achieved our initial success, but we know that further efforts are necessary" (Wir wollen mehr Frauen in Führungspositionen in Wirtschaft und Verwaltung. Mit der Einführung der Frauenquote in Aufsichtsräten haben wir erste Erfolge erzielt, wissen aber auch, dass weitere Anstrengungen notwendig sind, p. 14). Other sections of the program then express support for regulations to aid these efforts. This shared program does not explicitly support quotas for political office, which makes sense for a shared program between one party with a nonbinding target (the CDU's "Quorum"; see discussion in Chapter 5) and another with no quota target of any kind (CSU). Because this program limits its attention to gender and the workplace, it is coded as not acknowledging women's underrepresentation.

Multiple marginalization gets some attention in the section of the CDU/CSU program on "Safe and Stable Retirement" (Sichere und stabile Renten), which expresses support for additional pension aid for mothers whose children were born before 1992. This policy aims to help women approaching or in retirement whose lifetime income is likely to be lower due to caregiving work (p. 42). However, discussions of women's underrepresentation in politics are not intersectional.

Because the CSU's voters are all regionally in the state of Bavaria, the CSU also had a separate, shorter 2017 *Bayernplan* (Bavaria-specific program). The 2017 *Bayernplan* does not mention gendered patterns in inequality in any sphere of life, and there is, correspondingly, no mention of strategies for inclusion. The CSU program is coded, therefore, as not acknowledging women's underrepresentation. This illustrates the correspondence between low rates of women's election (women's presence in the CSU is lower than in many other German parties) with the party's representation of the problem. It is not framed as a problem, which portends little action.

FDP

The FDP's 2017 program's attention to unequal political representation between women and men positively frames the goal of electing more women while simultaneously avoiding framing current rates of representation negatively: "We Free Democrats want more women in leadership positions, in both the workplace and in public service. Women are very successful leaders, and gender-mixed workplaces are more productive and successful" (Wir Freie Demokraten wollen mehr Frauen in Führungsverantwortung, sowohl in der Wirtschaft als auch im öffentlichen Dienst. Frauen sind in der Leitung von Unternehmen und anderen Führungspositionen sehr erfolgreich, und gemischte Teams arbeiten produktiver und erfolgreicher, p. 72).

This framing is coded as an acknowledgment of women's underrepresentation in the FDP, but additional details are important for appreciating whether and how the party might address it. This program emphasizes equality of opportunity, explicitly rejecting formal rules: "We Free Democrats stand for women's and men's equal chances" (Wir Freie Demokraten setzen uns für Chancengleichheit von Frauen und Männern ein, pp. 71–72) ... "and we reject a legal quota, because this would degrade women's achievements" (Eine gesetzliche Quote lehnen wir jedoch ab: So werden Frauen zu Platzhaltern degradiert und nicht entsprechend ihrer Leistungen gewürdigt, p. 72).

The FDP's 2017 program does not address the intersection of gender with any other axes of marginalization. Though attention to women's higher risk for poverty in old age is low-hanging fruit for other parties, such as the CDU and CSU, it is not mentioned in the FDP's program.

LINKE

The LINKE program for 2017 discusses women and gender at great length, in many sections, about many issues, but its attention to the matter of women in political office is limited. The program asserts, more generally: "We want the equality of women and men" (Wir wollen die Gleichstellung von Frauen und Männern, p. 67). This assertion is backed by commitments to quotas across spheres, with a focus on the workplace: "We want a 50-percent women's quota for every career level" (Wir wollen eine 50-prozentige Frauenquote auf jeder Karrierstufe durchsetzen, p. 56). Like the B90/Gr, the LINKE successfully elects women at parity with men, and beyond. The party does not have a problem with the underrepresentation of women in political office. However, also like the B90/Gr, the LINKE has fewer women in leadership positions. This platform's attention is coded as acknowledgment of women's political underrepresentation, because of the extent of attention to gender equality, more generally, even while its emphasis is really on the workplace.

Intersectional issues receive less attention and, correspondingly, few proposed solutions. For example, the program acknowledges (on p. 72) that "poverty among the elderly is experienced disproportionately by women" (Altersarmut ist weiblich) and that women single parents are also at disproportionately higher risk. However, these forms of multiple marginalization are not expressed in terms of political representation.

SPD

Like the LINKE platform, the SPD's 2017 program expresses support for equality across many spheres of life, without particular emphasis on political officeholding. Most generally, the program asserts: "For more than 150 years, the equality of women and men has been a central goal of our politics" (Seit mehr als 150 Jahren ist die Gleichstellung von Frauen und Männern ein zentrales Ziel unserer Politik, p. 81). In a section on "Emancipation and Equality" (Gleichberechtigung und Gleichstellung, from p. 81), the SPD applauds the success that quotas have had where they have been implemented and expresses support for implementing them across more spheres. For example, they write: "We stand for having a minimum of 40 percent women in leadership positions in science" (Wir setzen uns für einen Frauenanteil von mindestens 40 Prozent in Führungspositionen in der Wissenschaft ein, p. 19). Based on this material, the SPD's 2017 platform is coded as acknowledgment of women's political underrepresentation; it mentions politics, even while its emphasis is on other spheres.

Although other sections of the program mention social inequalities in other terms (ability, sexual orientation, migrant status), there is little attention to multiple marginalization. For example, the gender-neutral group of "single parents" (Alleinerziehende) receives attention rather than women heads of household who disproportionately experience poverty. None of these other forms of marginalization is expressed as an issue of political representation.

Smaller Parties

As later sections show, smaller German political parties nominate women at highly variable rates. These are parties that are unlikely to elect anyone of any gender into the Bundestag, though some of them win small numbers of seats at local and state levels. What do their programs say?

Small parties that are broadly considered "on the left" include the MLPD and the ÖDP. These two parties are inconsistent in their attention to women's political underrepresentation. The MLPD's 2017 program addresses gendered inequalities in many spheres but not politics; for example, one section of the program is titled: "For Women's Emancipation!" (Für die Befreiung der Frau! p. 16). Some of this attention is intersectional, acknowledging the particular challenges faced by elderly women (p. 19) and by women who are situated in war zones (p. 12). However, none of this discussion is about political office. This is coded as not acknowledging women's underrepresentation in politics. By contrast, the ÖDP's 2017 program mentions political office in a list of spheres where women are underrepresented. In a section titled "Equality and Solidarity" (Gleichberechtigung und Solidarität, sec. 2.9, p. 50), the program reads: "the number of women in leadership positions and in politics . . . must be increased" (Der Anteil von Frauen in Führungspositionen und Politik muss . . . gesteigert werden, p. 52). Because the ÖDP's platform asserts unambiguously that women's absence from these positions is a problem, this is coded as acknowledgment.

Three small parties that are broadly considered "on the right" include the FW, the NPD, and the REP. These parties overwhelmingly ignore the issue of underrepresentation, though there is some attention to intersectional interests. First, the FW's 2017 program does not mention women's presence in elected office at all; therefore, the party is coded as not acknowledging the political underrepresentation of women. Its attention to intersectional issues consists of a section on higher poverty rates among elderly women (pp. 17, 61). Second, the NPD's program broadly rejects "Gender Politics" (Genderpolitik), without mentioning specific issue areas: "the NPD recognizes the differences between and equal worth of men and women, and it rejects gender-mainstreaming ideologies as unnatural" (Die NPD bekennt sich zur Unterschiedlichkeit und Gleichwertigkeit von Mann und Frau und lehnt die naturwidrige Gender-Mainstreaming-Ideologie ab, p. 12). This NPD program identifies the poverty of older women as especially acute (p. 27) in its national pension policy. Thus, the program is coded as not acknowledging.

Third, the REP program does not discuss women's presence in political office. References to ways in which the state might support women in the workplace are exclusively in terms of women's traditional caregiving roles. For instance, section 4.3 of the current platform includes the following line: "We support better use of women's labor force potential through the increase in childcare availability" (bessere Ausschöpfung des Fachkräftepotentials von Frauen durch mehr Kindertagesstätten, p. 38). This platform is, therefore, also coded as not acknowledging women's underrepresentation in politics.

Finally, two parties included in this book's analyses are often categorized by scholars as ideologically miscellaneous. As discussed in Chapter 3, Döring and Manow (2020) label these parties "special," including the PIR and the TIER in this category. These two parties are quite different from one another in numerous respects, but neither of them acknowledges women's political underrepresentation. The PIR 2017 program discusses intersectional interests in several sections, including the rights of sexual minorities (p. 15) and of women who are migrants (pp. 16–17). Further, the section on domestic and interpersonal violence advocates for policies that do not focus on women as victims, in order to make resources available for all genders (p. 70), with particular concern for the needs of trans victims. This intersectional attention is not, however, about representation in political office. The TIER 2017 program mentions women once, in a sentence about opportunities for equal pay (p. 8). There is no mention of women's political underrepresentation, and there is no discussion of intersectional issues.

Discussion of Results

Table 4.2 shows the direction and statistical significance of the relationship between a party's program acknowledgment of the need to diversify their

TABLE 4.2 PARTIES' ACKNOWLEDGMENT OF WOMEN'S UNDERREPRESENTATION × IDEOLOGICAL AXES

Ideological Axis	(Direction of Relationship) Statistical Significance of Fisher's Exact Test	Affirms Theoretical Expectations? (Y/N)
Economic Redistributionism/ Liberalism (dichotomous 0/1)	(n/a; not significant) 0.597	Y
Social Progressivism/Traditionalism (dichotomous 0/1)	(−) 0.031	Y
Postmaterialism/Materialism (dichotomous 0/1)	(−) 0.031	Y
Multiculturalism/Hegemonic-Ethnic Supremacy (dichotomous 0/1)	(−) 0.021	Y
	(Direction of Relationship) Statistical Significance of T-test	
ParlGov L-R Measure (continuous 0-1)	(−) 0.026*	

Note: $N = 14$ parties
* This is a one-tailed t-test for whether parties' ideological placement differs between parties that do acknowledge women's underrepresentation and those parties that do not acknowledge women's underrepresentation.

ranks and a series of left-right ideological measures: (1) economic redistributionism/liberalism, (2) social progressivism/traditionalism, (3) postmaterialism/materialism, (4) multiculturalism/hegemonic-ethnic supremacy, and (5) Döring and Manow/ParlGov's (2020) aggregate left-right continuous measure. Statistical tests between categorical variables (the relationship between dichotomous left-right position and acknowledgment of underrepresentation) are Fisher's exact tests, because the sample sizes are small (Agresti 2002, p. 91; Larntz 1978). Does a party's *placement on the right* correspond with its acknowledgment of women's underrepresentation? The final column in this table indicates whether the presence or absence of a statistically significant relationship between these variables affirms the book's theoretical expectations.

The statistical test presented in the final row (i.e., for the aggregate continuous measure of a party's left-right position) is a *t*-test, indicating whether parties that do acknowledge women's underrepresentation are statistically significantly further to the left of those that do not acknowledge women's underrepresentation. This final row therefore shows whether the prevailing account within the existing literature holds for this measure of women's advocacy.

The book's theoretical expectations about the four dichotomous ideological categories were that a party's economic redistributionism/liberalism would not relate to its problem formation, and that a party's social traditionalism, materialism, and hegemonic-ethnic supremacy, would be negatively correlated with their acknowledgment of women's underrepresentation. Table 4.2 affirms these four expectations, even while the final row indicates that acknowledgment is also statistically significant related to ParlGov's aggregated, continuous left-right measure.

Thus, this table affirms statistically the preceding sections' discussion of how German political parties' attention to women's underrepresentation in politics varies in complex ways. Whether a party is left or right in terms of its economic liberalism is not related to its acknowledgment of women's absence of political office, while social traditionalism, materialism, and hegemonic-ethnic supremacy do correspond with less inclination to acknowledge women's absence. Döring and Manow's (2020) aggregate left-right measure shows what the literature largely expects: a negative statistically significant correspondence between rightist ideologies and problem formation. However, this aggregate measure simplifies parties' variation. Further, inattention to multiply marginalized women is universal. No party portrays their absence from political office as a problem.

At this point in the development of Germany's party system, more than seventy years after World War II and thirty years after the country's reunification, acknowledgment of women's relative absence from political office is squarely mainstream. Indeed, the more interesting finding is arguably that parties who have found success (within the German system and in global comparison) have turned their attention elsewhere. Many political parties believe that they have "solved" the problem of diversifying political officeholding. As Davidson-Schmich (2016) shows, however, this solution has not consistently extended to earlier phases in the political recruitment process, nor arguably to society more broadly.

Ina Lenke: Advocating for Women's Presence

Born in 1948, Ina Lenke is a member of the "1968 Generation" in Germany. The 1968ers are the first postwar cohort of Germans, born 1936–1956 and socialized in a period of cultural and social agitation. Historians and cultural critics characterize this group as activist and antiestablishment. Legal and cultural changes regarding sexuality and family roles in the 1960s and 1970s profoundly marked Germans' political sensibilities (Ferree 2012; Gerhard 1999). For example, the Marriage and Family Law Reform Act of 1976–1977 signaled the end to legally different rights for wives and husbands in case of divorce, and it formally removed gendered differentiation of household labor from the German Civil Code (Gerhard 1990; Xydias 2014). This is the context in which Lenke entered politics.

Lenke is a longtime member of and officeholder with the FDP. Active with the party since 1974, she entered local politics in 1981 as a member of the town council of Oyten, Niedersachsen, serving in this capacity until 1999. She then served in the Niedersachsen state parliament 1990–1994, and in the Bundestag 1998–2009. Her other party leadership roles have included the position of chairwoman with the Liberale Frauen. While in office, she was a speaker for her party on issues relating to numerous issue areas, most prominently women's rights and family policy.

As discussed in Chapter 3, Germany's FDP is a European liberal party that emphasizes individual freedoms against the state; that is, it opposes significant state intervention in the economy and in social processes. This has historically included opposition to formal strategies for increasing women's presence in the party as members and officeholders, and this presence has been and remains consistently low. The FDP is widely viewed as right-leaning because of its orientation toward the role of the state, but the party's disaggregated ideological dimensions paint a more complex picture. In terms of the ideological axes central to this book's analyses, the FDP is economically liberal (rather than redistributionist), socially progressive (rather than traditionalist), postmaterial (rather than existentialist), and multicultural (rather than hegemonic-ethnic supremacist).

The FDP's progressivism, postmaterialism, and multiculturalism correspond with supporting gender equity, but we would not expect formal tools for advancing these goals. Lenke, therefore, is noteworthy for her contributions to developing more extensive state infrastructure for supporting women as mothers, job holders, and political candidates and officeholders. News coverage of her time in the Bundestag shows Lenke's commitment to women's rights, sometimes at odds with other members of her political party. For example, in 2005, *Focus Magazin* characterized Lenke as "warning" the FDP's general secretary Guido Westerwelle. The article quotes her: "If the proportion of women among the members does not rise to 30 percent, we will campaign for a women's quorum at the federal party congress."

As an FDP member of the Bundestag's standing legislative committee on Families, Seniors, Women, and Children (Familie, Senioren, Frauen und Jugend), Lenke departed from her party on numerous occasions, most notably on quotas for political and other positions. Her distinctive position on this and related issues was widely acknowledged. In a November 24, 2004, debate on structural changes to Germany's military, Lenke's fellow FDP-legislator Günther Nolting rejected quotas for women's inclusion: "the Liberal position is to reject quota regulations" (Liberale Linie ist die Ablehnung von Quotenregelungen).[13] Later in the same debate, Irmingard Schewe-Gerigk (B90/Gr) quipped that Nolting's "colleague Lenke clearly had more persuading to do" (Ihre Kollegin Lenke muss offensichtlich in Ihrer Fraktion noch viel Überzeugungsarbeit leisten).[14]

Lenke took a similar approach to childcare infrastructure. In a September 29, 2006, Bundestag debate on supports for new parents, Lenke spoke emphatically in favor of better infrastructure as a necessary counterpart to "direct payments to parents" (*Elterngeld*), asking: "What use is one year of direct payments to caregivers if there are not any day care spots or babysitters available"? (Was nutzt Eltern oder Alleinerziehenden ein Jahr Elterngeld, wenn anschießend Krippenplätze oder Tages-mütter und -väter fehlen?)[15] While other members of the FDP emphasized parental choice on the matter of childcare options, which direct payments could support, Lenke argued that in the absence of day care centers this was not a choice, at all.

Lenke was also a longtime champion in favor of more equitable taxation policies, which included opposition to a German tax policy dating to 1958 called *Ehegattensplitting*, translated into English as "income splitting." This policy allows a household to choose to pay lower taxes on the higher-earning spouse's income and higher taxes on the lower-earning spouse's income. This policy is more likely to result in higher taxation of women's incomes due to women's lower income in the aggregate. Lenke has referred to her efforts to address gendered impacts of this policy as her hobbyhorse ("Lieblingsthema").[16]

Lenke's commitment to institutionalizing rules for increasing women's presence in leadership roles is not a matter of merely prioritizing women's presence over the party's principles. Lenke represents the problem of women's low numbers as central to her party's priorities on liberty, democracy, and good governance: "More women *must be* represented in the next federal executive" (*Focus* 2005, emphasis added).

This closer look at Ina Lenke shows that she simultaneously acts with and against the party-level preferences of the FDP. Germany is a multiparty system. Lenke could have been active in another political party that does support quotas for women, among other tools for gender equity. However, for Lenke, supporting a quota is not part of a wider preference for more extensive state infrastructure. It is a prerequisite for a society in which the state interferes minimally. In order to realize libertarian principles for women, Lenke argues that women must be included in political decision-making. In other words, Lenke represents the problem of women's rates of participation in public life as a necessary precursor to a world in which libertarianism can function properly.

5

German Political Parties' Actions to Promote Inclusion

Introduction

This chapter builds on the preceding chapter, which discussed existing literature on the political representation of historically marginalized groups and evaluated how German parties frame matters of *political presence*. Chapter 5 turns to an analysis of whether and how parties translate acknowledgment of unequal representation into action to redress the status quo: whether they implement candidate gender quotas (formal mechanisms) or mentoring programs for encouraging and training candidates from underrepresented groups (informal mechanisms). A formal gender quota generally specifies that a minimum proportion of candidates be women, though in some cases it specifies parity between women and men (such as constitutional *parité* in France), or a minimum of either women or men (such as Germany's SPD). Electoral gender quotas have been adopted worldwide, taking various forms. Where constitutional or legislated quotas have been adopted, they apply to all political parties within the political system. In other countries, a subset of political parties have voluntarily adopted quotas. In some settings, such as India, the quota takes the form of a specific proportion of seats reserved for women or for another subgroup of constituents. Enforcement mechanisms may include, for example, nullification of a party list that does not meet requirements or the removal of public funding, but in some systems these mechanisms are limited or merely nominal.

Political parties vary in the actions they take to increase women's presence among candidates and in elected office. What underlies this variation?

Do the "usual suspects" step up to promote members of underrepresented groups as candidates, or can we better appreciate the variation between parties by distinguishing between them in other ways? This chapter operationalizes *advocacy for women and multiply marginalized women* as the extent to which parties engage in formal and informal activities to encourage and recruit aspirants from underrepresented groups. It finds significant variation among parties in the strategies they develop (if any), and this variation does not conform neatly to a single left-right axis. This chapter starts by discussing the literature on informal and formal mechanisms by which political parties act to increase women's presence in office. Subsequent empirical sections address formal and informal strategies for promoting candidates on the basis of gender.

In a concluding section, this chapter discusses a party that does not fit wider patterns in the German political system, both in its ideological composition and in its actions in support of increasing women's presence in office: the animal protection party, TIER. Many standard party typologies in comparative politics place the TIER in a "special" (miscellaneous) category. Here, closer inspection shows the value of including it in the analysis. It is a party that evinces largely postmaterialist values and nominates women as political candidates at relatively high rates, but it does so without fully embracing strategies for inclusion that are widely touted as part and parcel of women's advocacy. This analysis supports arguments against both aggregating parties into more general ideological categories and omitting informative outlier cases.

Informal and Formal Practices for Redressing Unequal Representation

This discussion of the literature contextualizes and justifies the chapter's attention to mentoring programs in addition to parties' formal gender quotas. As elsewhere in the world, German political parties take varying kinds and extents of actions to diversify candidates and, more specifically, to increase the presence of women and ethnic-minority women. These efforts vary in how institutionalized they are, and research on gender and political recruitment shows clearly that we must look beyond formal gender quotas to explain rates of women's both nomination and, ultimately, officeholding. Formal quotas are no guarantee of women's presence in office. At the same time, informal strategies have varying levels of success, and parties that rely on them are widely viewed as making a lesser commitment to diversifying their ranks.

Taken together, existing research shows that scholars must take these varying social and institutional patterns into account to understand women's rates of candidacy and election. Mackay, Kenny, and Chappell (2010) propose *feminist institutionalism* as a form of new institutionalism that directly acknowledges how significantly patriarchal norms infuse the function of both formal and informal rules. They argue that this approach offers important insights into "real world questions about power inequalities in public and political life as well as institutional mechanisms of continuity and change" (p. 574). The feminist institutional approach has subsequently grown to dominate the comparative study of gendered political recruitment and women's rates of election into political office, and it has been applied to countries in many regions of the world.[1] For example, Kenny (2013) studies the case of women's candidacies and election in Scotland, showing the persistence of longtime political recruitment processes even in a newly devolved system, and Hinojosa (2012) shows the consequences of divergent recruitment procedures in her cross-national study of women's rates of election in the region of Latin America. These and other studies establish the necessity of inspecting political parties, their processes, and the actions (and inaction) of their gatekeepers for understanding women's persistent disproportionately low presence in political office.

Ultimately, empirical studies in feminist institutionalism show that the informal and formal elements of candidate selection may be difficult to disentangle, but this difficulty should not dissuade researchers. Bjarnegård and Kenny (2016) contend that while formal institutions may be more visible than informal practices, ignoring the latter likely mischaracterizes the process of candidate recruitment. Their framework views formal rules as interacting with informal practices: "Understanding formal rules therefore necessitates comparing their content to actual practices" (p. 374). Empirically, case studies lend themselves especially well to the task of tracing these intertwined practices.

At the most formal end of the spectrum in the case of Germany, some political parties have written more inclusive electoral rules into their statutes. Less formally, some political parties support programs that are meant to train or otherwise support members of underrepresented groups in seeking elected office. These latter efforts are not institutionalized tools. Political parties that reject gender quotas sometimes argue that they have mentoring programs in place of quotas, but scholars have argued that these informal efforts are less effective than quotas, and their effectiveness is highly dependent on both context and the preferences of local party actors.[2] Although Roberts (1988) does not offer a specifically feminist analysis of candidate nomination, the following observation further supports a closer look at the full spectrum of parties' recruitment and nomination activities in the case of Germany: "The *formal* process of selection in a constituency is . . . not surprisingly often merely the benediction bestowed by the party on the outcome of *informal* discussions" (p. 105).

An additional reason to examine both formal and informal recruitment and nomination strategies is simply that quotas do not always work. The presence of a formal gender quota guarantees parity in neither candidacies nor electoral outcomes. Although political parties' formalization of processes for diversifying candidates for office and intraparty leadership positions is an important step in support of women and multiply marginalized women, these formalized processes are not the same as successfully electing a more diverse set of officeholders or party leaders. In political systems that have legislated or constitutionally mandated candidate quotas, low compliance rates are associated with weak enforcement mechanisms.[3]

Specifically in Germany, parties with quotas have voluntarily adopted them. Their voluntary nature might suggest a higher level of success at meeting their stated targets. However, as Caul (2001), Matland and Studlar (1996), and others argue, political systems without top-down implementation of a quota nonetheless may manifest the diffusion of quotas across the party system. The potential mechanisms for this diffusion are varied, but scholars have principally favored the idea that competition between parties pressures them to adopt gender quotas to appear more gender-egalitarian in order to avoid losing postmaterialist voters (Kolinsky 1993). This "peer pressure" may induce parties to adopt quotas that they are unlikely to apply strictly.[4]

Finally, whether and to what extent quotas that are adopted succeed in their stated goals is interconnected with nonquota strategies that parties may implement. In a study that demonstrates the importance of considering both formal and informal approaches, Ruf (2021) analyzes the role of nonquota strategies in local elections in the German state of Baden-Württemberg and shows that "parties' capacities . . . for gendered recruitment" significantly affect their nomination of women (p. 74). This finding is especially important in a case like contemporary Germany, where quotas are inconsistent across parties: both formal and informal approaches to recruitment contribute to explaining nomination patterns.

In short, previous research in Germany and beyond supports viewing mentoring programs as conceptually and practically distinct from quotas—even those quotas that are incompletely realized—as tools for redressing women's disproportionate rates of election. Bjarnegård and Kenny (2016) discuss this complex phenomenon in terms of an interplay between formal and informal processes for candidate recruitment and nomination.

The case of Germany offers several advantages for differentiating between peer pressure diffusion and other mechanisms behind women's rates of election and for examining this "interplay between formal and informal processes." As Davidson-Schmich (2016) argues in her analysis of gender quotas within Germany, "The process of quota contagion helps alleviate concerns that feminist party ideology, rather than quotas, drives . . . findings" (p. 13). Further, the voluntary nature of gender quotas in Germany leaves space for significant variation between parties in how they are designed and, in turn, whether and how they are enforced. Germany's between-party variation in quotas makes it possible to evaluate the extent to which the "usual suspects" adopt quotas, to discern sources of variation in the form that these quotas take, and to evaluate whether the quotas are effectively applied, while controlling for the same wider electoral and cultural environment (see discussion in Davidson-Schmich, 2016, pp. 11–13).

An exploration of parties within the case of Germany, and, moreover, an analysis that includes strategies along a spectrum of formality, can reveal the extent to which variation in parties' choices (formal vs. informal tools; nothing at all) conforms to left-right expectations. Comparative analyses that juxtapose informal recruitment tools alongside formal quotas within the same parties, in the same system, make it possible to study parties' choices: Neither tool? Both? If one, which?

Discussion of Evidence: Quotas and Mentoring Programs for Underrepresented Eligibles and Aspirants

This section proceeds in two parts. First, it evaluates the existence and form of quotas across fourteen contemporary German political parties, inspecting the extent to which quota adoption correlates with parties' ideological dimensions. As discussed in earlier sections of this chapter, a gender quota is an explicit commitment either to including a specified proportion of women among candidates for political office or to gender balance. Although the party statute's specification of a quota does not assure the successful nomination and election of any historically marginalized group members, it is a formal mechanism for shifting the status quo, in the sense that it is explicit and written into party rules. In Germany, gender quotas are voluntarily adopted. No party has adopted a quota for the inclusion of ethnic-minority group members (Hughes 2011).

Second, this analysis evaluates the available evidence of mentorship programs for promoting diversity among its officeholders and leaders. Mentorship programs are informal mechanisms for shifting the status quo, in the sense that they are not written into party rules, and they are not regulatory. Therefore, it is also the case that they take a wider range of forms. Because mentoring programs are less institutionalized than formal quotas, it is more challenging to identify systematic and comparable evidence of their existence across political parties. Further, systematically showing the absence of such programming poses evidentiary difficulties. Parties that are described as having developed more extensive infrastructure for supporting women aspirants and candidates generally receive less discussion here that those parties that are described as not having done so.

Relatively little research has been done on mentoring or candidate training programs outside the United States, a system without institutionalized quotas.[5] This has limited our knowledge about how formal and informal tools intersect. By contrast, inspecting a system such as Germany with party-voluntary quotas makes it possible to study parties' choices of which combination of tools to adopt, if any. Piscopo's (2021) discussion of candidate training programs worldwide proposes differentiating among these programs based on two key criteria: "Who funds them, and who runs them" (p. 224). Piscopo describes examples of programs funded and run by NGOs—"internationally supported but locally run"—and, in turn, programs run by political parties themselves (p. 224). This book's analysis of German political parties does not examine autonomous (nonpartisan) civil society organizations that promote the candidacies of women and multiply marginalized women. Nonetheless, Piscopo's distinction between the funding sources and the organizers is useful for identifying the extent to which a commitment to increasing women's rates of candidacy is shared across members and subgroups within the same political party. This discussion, therefore, specifies, to the extent that evidence is available, the organizers of mentoring or training programs, with particular attention to whether it comprises a niche effort as opposed to a project that seems to have broad support across the party.

Quotas

Table 5.1 shows that six parties included in this analysis specify a candidate or party leadership gender quota in their statutes. Most of these quota rules formally express targets for inclusion of women as a percentage of candidates; several express a minimum of either women or men. For example, the TIER party statute refers to the goal of "balance" between women and men in candidacies and leadership positions. Because commitments to balance are expressed in the parties' statutes (i.e., they are part of parties' formal rules and procedures), these are grouped together here with formal quotas, though the language in these statutes varies in important ways. This language offers insight into the level of commitment that party members could agree on to assuring women's greater presence in decision-making roles. Secondary literature cited here further supports the interpretation that this language reflects the process by which parties adopted or debated quotas. This snapshot of contemporary Germany cannot show the extent to which diffusion favors the adoption of quotas across wider ideological ranges of parties than we might otherwise expect. However, as Table 5.1 shows, diffusion has not ex-

TABLE 5.1 GERMAN POLITICAL PARTIES' ADOPTION OF GENDER QUOTAS

Party	Quota for Women's Inclusion as Candidates?*	Provision in Party Statute for Women's Inclusion in Leadership?**
AfD	None	None
CDU	1/3 "quorum" (1996)	1/3
CSU	None	40%
FDP	None	None
B90/Gr	50% minimum (since party's inception)	50% minimum
LINKE	50% (party established in 2007)	50%
SPD	40% (initially set at 25% in 1988; quota is minimum for *either* men or women)	40%
FW**	20% minimum of *either* men or women	20% minimum of either men or women
MLPD*	None	None
NPD	None	None
ÖDP	None	None
PIR	None	None
REP	None	None
TIER	"Balance" between women and men candidates	"Balance" between women and men on executive board(s)

* See Davidson-Schmich (2006) as well as parties' statutes available at https://www.politicalpartydb.org/statutes/.
** See parties' statutes.

tended even to parties where we might expect it (i.e., this variation requires further explanation).

Germany's B90/Gr, for example, have had a 50 percent gender quota for decades. The party's statute further specifies a "zipper" policy, by which the candidate gender alternates on the party list for proportional representation (PR) elections: party lists alternate women and men ("Wahllisten sind grundsätzlich alternierend mit Frauen und Männern zu besetzen"; *Grüne Regeln*, 2017, sec. 11, p. 5). It also specifies that the first candidate in any party list is a woman (the *Spitzenkandidatin*). This is not aspirational language; it is a statement of fact in the present tense, and Davidson-Schmich's (2016) analysis shows that the B90/Gr have been consistently widely successful at electing women into office. These specific positive discrimination policies are not grudging additions to the party's statute; they are original to the party. In a personal interview with me in November 2007, a woman member of the Bundestag in the B90/Gr said, "For us [Greens] it's very clear: it's never a question. It [quotas] was always like this. Anyone who joined the Greens knew it was like that."[6] Germany's Green Party is on "the left"; the party's adoption and effective implementation of this gender quota fits within conventional expectations.

Not all members of parties with longtime quotas show this convergence, however. Consider the LINKE, a party that, like B90/Gr, is unambiguously viewed as on "the left." Even while formal quotas are built into the LINKE party's nomination procedures, officeholders express grudging support for formal mechanisms for inclusion. For example, a LINKE woman member of the Bundestag told me in February 2008, "I don't really support it. Actually I find it sad, that we have a quota. . . . But I've learned over the course of years that men, due to their education and their socialization, will insist upon their political positions of power. So men must be forced to make room for women." Another LINKE woman in the Bundestag told me in November 2008, "I am not particularly in favor of them . . . because one should be elected on the basis of one's knowledge. . . . But sometimes the quota is very good." Indeed, of thirteen interviews with sitting LINKE members of the Bundestag (six with women and seven with men), more men asserted support for the quota and for efforts specifically targeting women eligibles and aspirants.

While LINKE officeholders largely express pragmatism regarding gender quota rules, the CDU has seen significant and ongoing contestation over formal mechanisms for inclusion. The CDU is unambiguously viewed as on "the right," and the party's internal debates in the 1980s and 1990s regarding a quota were acrimonious. Wiliarty (2010) argues that these early debates over "participation policy" divided party members in several senses. First, regulating candidate nomination procedures more stringently would have reduced the autonomy of regional party organizations; second, not all members, including members of the women's caucus, were in favor of quotas as such (Wiliarty 2010, pp. 126–127, 152–159). The proposal for a one-third quota was rejected by the 1995 party congress; in 1996, a working group produced the one-third "target" that remains in place today, called a quorum (Wiliarty 2010, p. 158). Indeed, voices of women and men within the party still argue against these and analogous mechanisms, such as gender quotas for corporate boards. Angela Merkel resisted corporate quotas for the first fifteen years of her tenure as chancellor, relenting finally in July 2020.[7]

Other women's voices within the CDU persist in opposition. For example, Jana Schimke, MdB representing a constituency in Brandenburg, is a CDU politician who frequently voices her opposition to quotas, and to positive discrimination more generally, over social media and in public speeches. In turn, women members of the party's *Junge Union* (youth group) are active on social media resisting quotas, including an @JUHamburg campaign reposting selfies with the caption: "I don't want to be a 'quota woman'"! (Ich möchte keine Quotenfrau sein!). At the same time, in a personal interview with me in February 2008, a woman member of the CDU in the Bundestag stated, "I wish they [quota rules] were avoidable, but as of now they are unavoidable."

Although the CDU's quorum applies both to candidacies for office and to leadership positions within the party, the statute expresses it as a "should": women should comprise at least one-third of the slots on the party lists for local, state, federal, and European Union elections ("Bei der Aufstellung von Listen für Kommunal- und Landtagswahlen, für die Wahlen zum Deutschen Bundestag und zum Europäischen Parlament soll das vorschlagsberechtigte Gremium unter drei aufeinander folgenden Listenplätzen jeweils mindestens eine Frau vorschlagen"; *Statutenbroschüre*, 2016, sec. 15, p. 5).

The FDP's repeated decision not to adopt a binding mechanism similarly mirrors the party's internally divided priorities. The FDP, arguably located at "the center" (combining economic liberalism with postmaterialism) has revisited the debate many times over the past three decades: expressing an interest in increasing women's presence among members and officeholders, rejecting institutional mechanisms for achieving this, establishing agreements to support women, and then failing to elect more women to office. Deliberations within the party, in 2019, yielded renewed agreement on establishing targets at the regional level for increasing women's presence in leadership roles and in elected office (see *ZeitOnline* 2019). These targets, akin to the CDU's quorum, address women's underrepresentation while accommodating intra-party rejection of regulating the matter. However, this 2019 agreement follows several decades of FDP explicit acknowledgment of women's underrepresentation, in particular compared to other nationally active parties. Indeed, the 2019 party congress was far from the first instance of declaring a preference for targets over quotas. In the same era when the SPD adopted its first quota, the FDP's 1986 and 1987 congresses produced a statement titled, "Putting Equal Rights into Practice."[8]

As Table 5.1 shows, those parties that formally express candidate commitments also consistently express commitments to women's presence on their leadership boards (*Vorstände*). These boards exist at local, state, and national levels. Conversely, not all parties that specify targets for women's presence on their boards also have targets for candidacy. Specifically, the CSU (on "the right") has no candidate quota, but its statute does specify a minimum presence of women on party boards. These varying combinations of tools, for various positions, reflect ongoing debates within these parties.

Importantly, the presence or absence of a quota is not the only way a party can signal whether and how seriously it acknowledges women's disproportionate absence from elected office. Numerous parties in Germany not only have not implemented a quota; they expressly reject them, arguing that they distort citizens' equal rights to vote and run for political office. These parties articulate this view in various outlets. Of the fourteen parties analyzed here, the AfD is the one that expressly rejects quotas as a vehicle for justice in its statute (rather than in other documents), in these words: "limiting the . . . right to vote through electoral rules called 'quotas' . . . is without exception not permitted" (Einschränkungen des aktiven oder passiven Wahlrechts durch sogenannte Quotenregelungen sind sowohl bei Wahlen zu innerparteilichen Ämtern als auch bei der Aufstellung von Kandidaten zu öffentlichen Wahlen ausnahmslos unzulässig; *Bundessatzung*, 2015, sec. 5, p. 2).

Six parties included in this analysis make no reference in their statutes to the presence of women in these positions (i.e., their statutes do not recognize gender as an element in their party processes). However, evidence is available elsewhere that offers insights into these parties' commitments and policies. Two parties, the ÖDP and the NPD, whose statutes make no mention of gender, nonetheless engage with the issue in recent party platforms, and they do so to assert their opposition to quotas. Like the AfD, the ÖDP asserts in its 2017 party program that quotas are undemocratic. The NPD further expresses the position that the promotion of women's equal participation in public life is itself undesirable, rejecting "gender mainstreaming ideology" as "unnatural" (*naturwidrige*) in its 2015 platform. It is important to note that members of the AfD have also voiced sentiments in other outlets that echo the NPD's contention that gender egalitarianism is at odds with the family as a fundamental (read: natural) social unit (Xydias 2020).

None of these fourteen parties expresses a target of any kind for the inclusion of ethnic-minority women. Those parties that are widely viewed as more active on behalf of disadvantaged groups include, broadly, "the left," and, more specifically, parties that express ideological commitments to social justice. None of these parties has acted formally on behalf of ethnic-minority women's presence in office.

To what extent have "the usual suspects" adopted candidate gender quotas in Germany? Table 5.2 summarizes the relationship between these fourteen political parties' implementation of a candidate gender quota and the five left-right measures: dichotomous left-right categories for (1) economic redistributionism/liberalism, (2) social progressivism/traditionalism, (3) postmaterialism/materialism, (4) multiculturalism/hegemonic-ethnic supremacy; and (5) Döring and Manow/ParlGov's (2020) aggregate left-right continuous measure. These statistical tests show whether a party's placement on the right correlates with a lower likelihood of adopting a gender quota. As in Chapter 4, the statistical test applied to pairs of categorical variables is a Fisher's exact test rather than a chi-square test, because the sample sizes are small.[9] For example, the first row presents whether a party's liberalism is correlated with its adoption of a gender quota. Table 5.2 shows that it is not, which affirms

TABLE 5.2 CANDIDATE GENDER QUOTAS × IDEOLOGICAL AXES

Ideological Axis	(Direction of Relationship) Statistical Significance of Fisher's Exact Test	Affirms Theoretical Expectations? (Y/N)
Redistributionism/Liberalism (dichotomous 0/1)	(n/a; not significant) 0.580	Y
Progressivism/Social Traditionalism (dichotomous 0/1)	(n/a; not significant) 0.627	Y
Postmaterialism/Materialism (dichotomous 0/1)	(n/a; not significant) 0.627	N
Multiculturalism/Hegemonic-Ethnic Supremacy (dichotomous 0/1)	(n/a; not significant) 1.000	N
	(Direction of Relationship) Statistical Significance of T-test	
ParlGov L-R Measure (continuous 0-1)	(−) 0.048*	

Note: These correlations were also alternately calculated with the CDU and TIER coded as lacking a quota, to see whether the adoption of a more binding mechanism might be associated with these ideological categories. Statistical significance does not change for any ideological measure.

* One-tailed t-test for whether the mean ideological placement of parties differs between the group with quotas and the group without.

the book's third theoretical expectation that redistributionist *and* liberal parties have the potential to implement gender-equity policies.

In fact, Table 5.2 shows that none of the four dichotomous ideological measures is correlated to a statistically significant degree with a party's implementation of a formal quota. This book's theoretical framework predicts that economically liberal and socially traditionalist political parties might, but are less likely, to support direct actions promoting gender equity. In turn, materialist and hegemonic-ethnic supremacist parties are expected to be outright unlikely to adopt quotas. However, statistical tests for disaggregated ideological dimensions in Table 5.2 show that, at this point in time, the adoption of a gender quota is shared across the German party system. At the same time, the Döring and Manow (2020) aggregated left-right measure is correlated with quota adoption. These simultaneous findings underscore the urgency of inspecting parties' positions more closely.

Express opposition to quotas can also be found across the German party system. The three parties that expressly reject quotas, whether in their statute or party platform, include the AfD, NPD, and ÖDP. Two of these are conventionally viewed as "on the right" (AfD and NPD), while the third is conventionally viewed as "on the left" (ÖDP). All three support state intervention in the economy (an orientation associated with the left), but the ÖDP expresses postmaterialist values in its commitments to environmental sustainability and animal rights, while the AfD's and NPD's programs emphasize materialist/existentialist values associated with heightened concern about national security. Finally, the AfD and the NPD are unambiguously hegemonic-ethnic supremacist.

This analysis suggests that the adoption of quotas has become largely unmoored from ideological orientations in contemporary Germany. Previous scholarship showing that quota adoption has diffused "from left to right" offers an account of how this unmooring occurred. However, these present findings suggest that this important early work on quotas, much of it emphasizing their adoption by parties on the left, may apply more to quotas' origins than to their subsequent development. As quota adoption becomes normalized in a political system, its attachment to other ideological commitments seems to loosen. Simultaneously, express rejection of quotas is, and has long been, found across the left-right spectrum of political parties.

Mentoring Programs

Rates of formal party membership in Germany have been on the decline for several decades (Mair and Biezen 2001; Biezen, Mair, and Poguntke 2012), and it is in this context that German political parties have developed concerted strategies for recruitment. Demuth (2004) argues that, in the early twenty-first century, parties' recruitment efforts largely addressed the aging demographics of party members and officeholders (p. 700). However, Prinz (2003) identifies the first crest of the wave of women's mentoring programs in Germany, in 1999, when Ramona Pop and Renate Künast helmed the first nationwide effort with the B90/Gr. Thus, more general programmatic training and recruitment efforts appear to have originated at the turn of the century, and efforts specifically targeting women originated with a political party that had already demonstrated its commitment to increasing women's presence in office through the early adoption of a candidate quota.

This section's analysis of mentorship programs is limited to the nationally active and successful parties, for several reasons. First, larger parties have the resources and the membership base to schedule programming on a scale that is visible and systematically searchable. Second, and relatedly, a significant source of programming consists of the national political foundations (*Parteistiftungen*), and small political parties do not have dedicated foundations. A party foundation is a nonprofit entity that is legally registered with the state as separate from but supportive of a specific party, engaged in programming and public relations. Although this analysis of larger parties' mentorship programs may not apply to parties of all sizes across the German political system, it can inform an interpretation of whether and how these efforts are grounded in parties' ideological orientations.

Ultimately, this section argues that existing training programs make the most sense when viewed in parties' historical context rather than in terms of their ideological dimensions, per se. Political parties with a longer history and more robust infrastructure are more likely to have better developed training programs, regardless of their ideological composition. The nature of these programs—which eligibles and aspirants they target, and whether they emphasize broadly civic or specifically political goals—is, in turn, related to whether the parties' origins lie more with social and community-based groups as opposed to professional or occupational groups. Thus, for example, the following discussion shows that the SPD and the CDU share in common more professionalized and institutionalized training programs geared toward candidates and officeholders, while the B90/Gr and the LINKE offer more fragmented and community-based programming. As discussed in Chapter 3, none of these parties' origins lies with the mobilization of communities marginalized by their ethnic or immigrant status, and, correspondingly, there is no evidence at this time of programmatic efforts to increase the political participation of these German voters. Wüst (2016) and Deiss-Helbig (2018) argue that the growing population of the immigrant electorate will in time pressure parties to invest in new party-group linkages.

The discussion in this section draws from a variety of sources. Collection of these data began with political foundations' websites, which were searched for evidence of mentoring programs. The most recently established foundation is, as of 2018, associated with the AfD: the Desiderius-Erasmus-Stiftung (DES; established in 2015). The other six foundations include: the Friedrich-Ebert-Stiftung (SPD, 1925), the Konrad-Adenauer-Stiftung (CDU, 1955), the Friedrich-Naumann-Stiftung (FDP, 1958), the Hanns-Seidel-Stiftung (CSU, 1966), the Heinrich-Böll-Stiftung (B90/Gr, 1986), and the Rosa-Luxemburg-Stiftung (PDS/LINKE, 1990).

Next, evidence of programming was sought with women's organizations located within or associated with each party. Parties holding seats in the state or federal legislature typically have a caucus of women members, while auxiliary women's organizations are composed of party members more broadly. The CDU and CSU have a Gruppe der Frauen (women's caucus) as well as an auxiliary organization called the Frauen Union. The FDP's women's group is called the Liberale Frauen. The SPD has the Arbeitsgemeinschaft Sozialdemokratischer Frauen. The LINKE have several more dispersed standing groups on women or gender, including a Frauenplenum. The B90/Gr have a Grüne Frauengruppe. As of early 2021, the AfD have at least one local chapter of a Frauen in der AfD group; however, participation in this organization does not appear to be restricted to AfD members. Another related setting for activities centered on supporting women and ethnic-minority women is the Bundestag's working-group structure. All party groups in the Bundestag establish working groups (Arbeitskreise and Arbeitsgruppen). The foci and titles of these working groups change with each legislative term, which offers potential insight into the parties' evolving priorities.

Results from a 2016 survey distributed to officeholding women in parties without binding quotas offer additional insights into the kinds and extents of efforts that parties may develop in lieu of formal mechanisms. This questionnaire inquired about women officeholders' awareness of and participation in mentoring opportunities. In July 2016, I contacted the 240 women holding office in the Bundestag and in German state legislatures who were members of the four parties that had either no quota or, in the case of the CDU, just a nonbinding "target" for women's candidacy: the AfD, CDU, CSU, and FDP. Of these 240 potential subjects, 16 participated in the survey, which is a response rate of 6.7 percent. Further, 2 respondents were in the CSU, 2 in the FDP, and 12 in the CDU. None of the AfD invitees participated (just 19 AfD women held a federal or state legislative office at that time). A table summarizing respondents' characteristics and the questionnaire is included in Appendix C. Although inferences drawn from these subjects' responses are constrained by the response rate, some pieces of information, in particular inconsistencies between members of the same party, offer insights about parties' implementation of mentoring as a complement to or replacement of more formalized strategies. The main finding from this survey, which the following discussion elaborates on, is that, while these parties vary in how firmly institutionalized training programs are for women, survey responses indicate that parties do not widely publicize these programs. Even within the same party, respondents expressed disagreement over these programs' very existence.

Finally, quotations are drawn from personal interviews with officeholders in these seven political parties.[10] As is the case with the 2016 survey, material from these interviews does not establish frequency or causation. However, interviewees' observations from their own experiences as candidates and officeholders contribute to contextualizing, and, to some extent, corroborating, information from other sources.

These varied sources justify placing parties into categories of *high* or *low* levels of mentorship programming. Although there is significant apparent variation in the qualities and quantities of programming across these parties, a dichotomous measure is more appropriate for two reasons: it would be difficult to substantiate finer-grained categories based on such varied forms of evidence, and parties' programming appears to vary along several dimensions. Table 5.3 summarizes parties' levels of mentorship programming in these dichotomous categories. The sections that follow are organized by party, qualitatively contextualizing their mentorship programming.

Table 5.4 shows the limitations of ideological orientations for understanding this variation. Bivariate statistical tests show that the relationship between whether a party is on the right and its extent of mentoring programs is not statistically significant for any of the following five measures of ideology: (1) economic redistributionism/liberalism, (2) social progressivism/traditionalism, (3) postmaterialism/materialism, (4) multiculturalism/hegemonic-ethnic supremacy, and (5) Döring and Manow's (2020) aggregate left-right continuous measure.

Table 5.4 shows that mentorship programs are found across ideologies in Germany. They are present in some parties that elect relatively few women

TABLE 5.3 GERMAN POLITICAL PARTIES' LEVELS OF MENTORSHIP PROGRAMMING FOR WOMEN

Party	Level of Mentorship Programming for Women (High/Low)
AfD	Low
CDU	High
CSU	Low
FDP	Low
B90/Gr	High
LINKE	Low
SPD	High

TABLE 5.4 LEVEL OF MENTORSHIP PROGRAMMING × IDEOLOGICAL AXES

Ideological Axis	(Direction of Relationship) Statistical Significance of Fisher's Exact Test	Affirms Theoretical Expectations? (Y/N)
Redistributionism/Liberalism (dichotomous 0/1)	(n/a; not significant) 0.629	Y
Progressivism/Social Traditionalism (dichotomous 0/1)	(n/a; not significant) 0.629	Y
Postmaterialism/Materialism (dichotomous 0/1)	(n/a; not significant) 0.629	Y
Multiculturalism/Hegemonic-Ethnic Supremacy (dichotomous 0/1)	(n/a; not significant) 0.629	Y
	(Direction of Relationship) Statistical Significance of *T*-test	
ParlGov L-R Measure (continuous 0-1)	(n/a; not significant) 0.252*	

Note: $N = 7$ parties
* One-tailed *t*-test for whether the mean ideological placement of parties differs between high and low levels of mentorship programming.

and absent from some parties that elect women at high rates. The following sections inspect the contours of parties' apparent efforts, and their varying levels of success. Ultimately, this discussion demonstrates that parties differ from one another in both extent and kind of mentorship and training efforts. This variation does not map onto left-right dimensions but rather appears to be rooted in those parties' origins.

AfD

Earlier sections have discussed both the AfD's low levels of expressed interest in diversifying their ranks and the party's outright rejection of electoral rules that disrupt what the party frames as "natural" rates of aspiration and candidacy. This attitude appears to extend to informal programming for encouraging women's participation. As of 2021, there was little evidence of such programming, nor are there local or regional women's organizations that might serve as sources of programming in the future. A search of AfD events in early 2021 found evidence of just one local organization of AfD women, located in the state of Nordrhein-Westfalen. Thus, little expressed interest in increasing women's presence in the party corresponds with limited infrastructure for doing so.

Like the other national political foundations, the AfD's DES receives federal funding, and it organizes regular lectures and workshops in locations across the country. Political foundations in Germany are not one and the same as the political parties with which they are affiliated, but their affiliation reflects shared broader principles and goals. The DES is the most recently established foundation (2015), and its programming and scope are relatively narrow. The DES's website makes available a calendar for 2019, which offers some insight into the foundation's priorities. This 2019 calendar includes events on media bias, migration, Jews in Germany, Islam, demographic change, sustainability, foreign policy, and finance. For instance, the DES hosted a three-day seminar titled, "Islam: On Conflict between Religious Freedom and Protection of Our Founding Principles" (ISLAM: Zum Konflikt zwischen Religionsfreiheit und einer Verteidigung unserer Grundwerte, November 4–6, 2019).

Two three-day seminars were billed as pertaining to "women's politics." These seminars took place in Gummersbach, Nordrhein-Westfalen, September 20–22, and Augsburg, Bayern, October 18–20, 2019, titled: "Women's Seminar: Equal Rights vs. Equalization" (Frauenseminar: GLEICHBERECHTIGUNG versus GLEICHSTELLUNG). Like other foundations, many of the events that the DES schedules are focused on lectures rather than practice; these seminars appear to be in that category. They do not appear to offer mentorship or training.

There is limited evidence of the emergence of local women's organizing associated with the AfD. In principle, grassroots organizations have the potential to engage in mentoring and training activities. Specifically, news coverage in January 2019 heralded the formation of a women's group associated with the AfD in the district of Siegen-Wittgenstein in North-Rhine-Westphalia: Women in the AfD (Frauen in der AfD).[11] A Facebook post by Dortmund AfD politician Matthias Helferich in January 2020 states that this regional women's group had twenty-seven members one year after its formation. Frauen in der AfD is led by former CDU-member and former Dortmund council member Regine Stephan, who left the CDU in late 2018 after supporting a controversial legislative proposal by the NPD. As of 2021, Stephan had just 209 Facebook friends, and her Facebook activity at that time consisted mostly of sharing blog posts written by Vera Lengsfeld, well-known former GDR activist who served in the Bundestag with the B90/Gr and then the CDU (1990–2005). There is no evidence of the then twenty-seven-member group Frauen in der AfD holding events for mentorship or candidacy training.

The AfD's working groups in the Bundestag, in their current and, thus far, only term (2017–present), include one on families, seniors, women, and youths that mirrors the standing legislative committee (Familie, Senioren, Frauen und Jugend) but addresses nothing more specifically about political or social equality. As noted earlier, none of the then nineteen AfD women federal or state legislators participated in the 2016 survey.

Two personal interviews with AfD women state-level legislators in May 2017 corroborate the impression that the AfD's encouragement of women candidates is idiosyncratic rather than programmatic. One of the women, an interviewee in her seventies, described choosing to attend local AfD meetings based on her concerns about German bailouts of Greece; she was the only woman at the meeting, and other attendees persuaded her to run for office. The other interviewee similarly described being drawn to the AfD on the basis of her concerns about the *Teuero Euro* (a play on words in German for the "expensive Euro"). When asked about whether the party actively sought to recruit more women as candidates, she replied that "the AfD had no quota, and no particular support for women—but also no particular support for men... Women themselves must decide that they are interested in becoming engaged" (Also es gibt keine Quote. Es gibt keinen. Keine besondere Förderung. Es gibt aber auch keine besondere Förderung für Männer.... Die Frauen, die sich entscheiden und sagen, "Ich möchte mich da gerne mehr engagieren"). Taken together, this information about the AfD places it in a "low mentorship programming" category.

CDU

The CDU is the party with a nonbinding one-third gender "quorum," discussed earlier. Intraparty debates in the 1990s that produced this quorum did not fully resolve disagreements about formal mechanisms for increasing women's rates of candidacy and officeholding. However, CDU voices that reject formal mechanisms in general simultaneously call for mentoring programs as an educational alternative to mandating presence. These calls have corresponded with the successful development of such programs, and considerable infrastructure has developed for encouraging women's candidacy. At the same time, however, interviewees and respondents to the 2016 survey were inconsistent in their awareness about these programs.

This section starts by examining activities supported by the Konrad-Adenauer-Stiftung (KAS). The KAS was founded in 1955 and now has an expansive international presence and extensive programming. Both the KAS website and the foundation's Facebook calendar publicize hundreds of scheduled events each year, and a subset of these are lectures, panels, and workshops about the importance of women's engagement in politics.[12]

The KAS Facebook calendar, specifically, listed 125 events for 2019 and 169 events for 2020. Over this time frame, these events include many lectures hosted by various regional educational forums associated with the foundation, such as the "Bildungsforum" in Baden-Württemberg, Thüringen, Bonn, and Niedersachsen. Some of these events directly addressed political engagement, though many did not. A November 6, 2019, panel and discussion titled, "Young Adults and the Language of Politics" (Sprichst Du Politik? Junge Erwachsene und die Sprache der Politik), took place in Niedersachsen. An October 6, 2020, online seminar was advertised as teaching the "fundamentals of social media communication." By contrast, Monday, October 26, 2020, launched "Twitch Week @kas," a series of regular interactive videogame sessions likely intended to engage young potential supporters.

As with other party foundations, more KAS-supported programming was *about* women than *for* women. For example, the KAS hosted a pair of events on January 14–15, 2019, marking the centennial of the first election in which German women voted. The events featured Annegret Kramp-Karrenbauer (chairwoman of the CDU, 2018–2020) and other prominent women in the CDU, who asserted: "I am a quota woman!" (Ich Bin Eine Quotenfrau!). These marquee events foreground the importance of women's participation in public life, and they explicitly embrace mechanisms that the party has adopted for encouraging this participation, even in the midst of ongoing debates about quota rules. An event on September 2, 2019, trumpeted that "democracy needs more women!" (Demokratie Braucht Frauen!).

Closer inspection of the political education forums themselves yielded more information about women's mentorship, ultimately, than the KAS calendar. These forums appear to be active at all levels. For example, the Political Education Forum (Politisches Bildungsforum) chapter in Baden-Württemberg facilitates a mentorship program specifically for encouraging women to run for local office. These events are not publicized on the KAS website calendar or on Facebook. A 2020 brochure associated with this program proclaims: "Let's get more women in city halls! Is being mayor something I want to do?" (Mehr Frauen in die Rathäuser! Bürgermeisterin—wäre das etwas für mich?).

The locations and identities of co-organizers of the KAS's programming suggest evidence of the extensive and embedded nature of these mentoring efforts. A national effort called the Frauenkolleg (Women's College), which cohosts the programming cited earlier ("Mehr Frauen in die Rathäuser!"), organizes workshops to educate women in public speaking, networking, and other skills that support professional advancement. Across Germany, local offices of the Political Education Forum help coordinate KAS and Frauenkolleg events. The Frauenkolleg also coordinates with the CDU's women's auxiliary organization, the Frauen Union.

The CDU co-organizes working groups in the Bundestag with the CSU, because they form a single party group; the party group had a Women and Children working group (Frauen und Jugend) in the 1990–1994 legislative term, and across the 1994–2021 periods the working group related to gender, more generally, covers families, seniors, women, and youth (Familie, Senioren, Frauen und Jugend). These committees, however, are focused on policy development on these issues, not on encouraging, recruiting, or training candidates and officeholders.

At the same time, CDU respondents to the 2016 survey exhibited variation in their awareness of these efforts within their party for supporting women candidates. Seven of the twelve CDU respondents indicated that their party had a mentoring program for women, and they named three: Frauen für's Mandat (Women for Political Office), Mentorenprogram (Mentors' Program), and MentoringProgramm (Mentoring Program). Half of the respondents reported that they had participated in such a program prior to winning elected office; their participation was not correlated with the timing of their entry into politics (ranging from 1990 to 2006), nor was it correlated with whether they were in the Bundestag or a state legislature at the time of the survey. Further, respondents were divided in whether they believed that their party prioritizes increasing women's presence: nine stated that their party views increasing women's presence as very important or important.

In sum, although not all women in the CDU share equal awareness of it, there is evidence of opportunities for training embedded in party infrastructure, developed and maintained over relatively long periods of time. Evidence of this programming places the CDU in a "high mentorship programming" category. There is no evidence of any programming for ethnic-minority women.

CSU

The CSU shares an auxiliary women's organization, the Frauen Union, with the CDU. However, CSU-specific efforts to train or otherwise encourage women in the party focus on Bavaria, which is the only state where the CSU elects candidates. This section, therefore, addresses CSU- and Bavaria-specific efforts. Its assessment of CSU-specific programming paints the picture of a party with a low level of activity for addressing underrepresentation.

The CSU's foundation is the Hanns-Seidel-Stiftung (HSS), established in 1966. Like the other national foundations, the HSS has an international presence, running projects in more than seventy countries. As of late February 2021, the foundation's events calendar on its website (available at hss.de) listed 114 events scheduled for the calendar year of 2021; the calendar does not include an archive of scheduled events for previous years. Six of these events in 2021, all online due to the COVID-19 pandemic, were framed for an audience of women, organized around career, finance, and, more generally, success. A three-session seminar scheduled for July 2021 was titled: "Seminar for Women on Strategies for Success: Arrogance" (Seminar für Frauen: Erfolgsstrategie: Arroganz). In turn, three events address teachers (Pädagog*innen)[13] and childcare facilities (*Kitas*).

The HSS Facebook events calendar includes both current and past years, providing more information about the breadth of programming.[14] This calendar lists 105 events for the 2020 calendar year, and 41 events for 2019. Events in 2020 were almost exclusively held remotely due to COVID-19. A subset of these events were geared for candidates or officeholders. In anticipation of local elections taking place in March 2020, the HSS organized eight gender-neutral events in late 2019 for aspiring or new public officials. For example, an event on December 12, 2019, offered a crash course in social media for local officeholders ("Social-Media: Crash-Kurs für Kommunale Mandatsträger"). On November 27, 2019, the foundation hosted a session on media training, and, on January 9, 2020, an event on avoiding invalid ballots ("Kommunalwahl 2020: Ungültige Stimmzettel vermeiden"). These are informational sessions for an undifferentiated audience. In 2020, after the local elections had taken place, the HSS scheduled training events on governance, such as an introduction to budgeting and finance for local governments. Just one event targeted the audience of women: "Women and Local Politics" (Frauen und Kommunalpolitik), on October 23, 2020.

Over the course of 2019–2020, the HSS cohosted five events with a Bavaria-based civil society organization called Starke Frauen, Starke Worte (Strong Women, Strong Words). These events featured prominent women public figures in an interview format. Starke Frauen, Starke Worte also hosts workshops for women on participating in public life. Isabelle Kürschner, a political scientist and former director with the HSS in Munich, has herself organized many of these events.

Just two CSU women participated in the 2016 survey. At that time, one of these respondents was a member of the Bavarian state legislature, and the other was a member of the Bundestag. Neither of them reported participating in a training or mentoring program prior to entering political office (both in 2006), but they both identified the Mentoring-programm der Frauen Union, a program in Bavaria founded in 2005 by Emilia Müller, then chairwoman of the Bavarian Frauen-Union (available at https://www.fu-bayern.de/ueber-uns/geschichte/). Personal interviews with CSU officeholders similarly indicate an opposition to formal measures, even when mentoring programs were not specifically mentioned. For example, in a June 2008 interview, the Bundestag office manager of a woman in the CSU, herself a young woman, expressed a preference for informal strategies: "[A quota] is always a bad reason to be elected.... The answer lies with the Frauen Union, the youth group, mentorship programs."

In sum, information from these various sources about the CSU indicates a surge of attention to promoting women candidates circa 2005 at the time when the Mentoring-programm was established, but efforts since that time have been sporadic and seemingly highly dependent on specific individual organizers. Training sessions hosted by the HSS tend to be gender neutral rather than focused on women as a group. There is no evidence of any programming for ethnic-minority women. Thus, although the party and its foundation support more generalized mentorship programming and candidate training, relatively few events target women aspirants or women candidates. This information places the CSU in a "low mentorship programming" category.

FDP

As discussed elsewhere in this chapter, the FDP has not adopted a gender quota. Instead, over the past three decades, the party has repeatedly revisited the matter of women's low rates of membership, candidacy, and election in their ranks. A small minority of party actors have favored regulatory action, but party congresses and workshops consistently assert opposition. Writing about FDP training programs for candidates and officeholders more broadly in Germany, not specifically efforts at recruiting and training women, Demuth (2004) states that no evidence is available of FDP efforts at professionalization ("Weder im Internet noch auf Anfrage der Bundesgeschäftsstelle konnten Informationen über Professionalisierungsbestrebungen der FDP gesammelt werden," p. 700). Since Demuth's (2004) study, the FDP and affiliated organizations have taken visible steps; however, the party is still placed in a "low mentorship programming" category. The locations and identities of co-organizers of the existing programming indicate that mentoring efforts are neither extensive nor embedded in party infrastructure.

This section's discussion of mentorship programming as the FDP's informal alternative to quotas draws from websites of the Friedrich-Naumann-Stiftung für die Freiheit (FNF), party documents (e.g., reports from annual party conventions), party-affiliated websites (e.g., the websites of local chapters of the Liberale Frauen, the FDP's auxiliary women's group), and from the secondary literature.

The FNF, like the other national political foundations, is highly active both in Germany and around the world. The FNF website provides only a forward-looking calendar of events, preventing data collection from this source for 2019 and 2020. However, the FNF Facebook calendar includes both current and past years' events.[15] This calendar lists 457 scheduled events in the 2019 calendar year and 376 events in 2020. Both the topics and the apparent intended audiences of this programming are wide ranging. It includes film screenings, lectures on current events or on issues such as the implications of Brexit for Germany, coverage of the United States presidential election, and so on.

Across this two-year period, some of these events can be considered efforts at candidate training or sessions for officeholders. These are overwhelmingly general in their audiences, and the modal event in this category addressed public speaking.[16] The next most frequent training events addressed the use of social media and the internet more broadly.[17] Late in the spring after the initial outbreak of COVID-19 in Germany, the FNF offered a crash course in moderating online events ("Online Crashkurse: Moderieren Digitaler Konferenzen," May 28, 2020). One workshop on running a campaign took place in early January 2020 ("Liberal Skill Camp," January 4),[18] and, in late May 2020, the FNF ran a workshop on leadership in local politics ("Verbände und Gremien gut leiten—Workshop für pol. Management," May 29, 2020). Thus, in total, the FNF publicized ten generalist training events in this two-year period, which comprises a very small percentage (just 1.2 percent) of the total events scheduled.

Exactly three events in this two-year period specifically targeted women as potential leaders or public figures with training opportunities. In 2019, the FNF hosted an Empowerment Training for "business and professional women" (February 2, 2019), and one crash course in public speech was billed for women ("Crashkurs Rhetorik für Frauen," July 6, 2019). In 2020, Women in Politics ("Frauen in der Politik," September 19, 2020) was a seminar for coaching women to succeed in men-dominated workplaces, including politics. The calendar entry for this event promised that participants would have the chance to learn about gendered communication strategies ("An diesem

Tag haben Sie Gelegenheit, die Erfolgsmomente von sogenannten männlichen bzw. weiblichen Kommunikationspräferenzen kennen zu lernen").

Another category of events covered the issue of women's presence or absence from specific occupations without being organized as training workshops. For example, a seminar titled "Women-Power-Politics" (Frauen.Macht.Politik, October 15, 2020) offered information about the prospects for increasing women's political engagement, in light of both a gendered confidence gap and difficulty balancing career and family.[19] Similarly, other events were billed as informational about challenges to the status quo.[20] Over the course of 2019, several events addressed the century anniversary of women's suffrage in Germany: 100 Jahre Frauenwahlrecht (January 12, 24, and 30, 2019; February 5, 2019; May 21, 2019), and Coffee Talk: Frauenwahlrecht und Frauenordination (November 30, 2019). Two events were organized in relation to an art exhibition of the women's suffrage movement (March 16, 2019, and May 18, 2019).

Several cultural events featured films that were, again, about women and gender rather than for a specific intended audience. On International Women's Day (March 8) 2019, the FNF hosted nationwide screenings of the Saudi Arabian–German film production *The Perfect Candidate* (2019, directed by Haifaa Al-Mansour), which features a woman candidate for political office in small-town Saudi Arabia.[21] Publicity around these screenings indicates that the film was selected as a story about persisting against the odds. February 20, 2019, featured a lecture and screening of the film *On the Basis of Sex* (2018, directed by Mimi Leder).

In short, the FNF's main calendar—the most visible site for announcing events—included copious scheduling for 2019–2020. This scheduling included many more events about women than for women aspirants, but, ultimately, these events comprised a small fraction of the total. None of them was intersectional in its attention to inequities. This programming cleaves to debates within the FDP about whether and how to address women's low numbers in leadership positions in business and politics. Women's absence in and of itself is not framed as the issue; instead, women's inclusion is billed as a source of innovation. An event titled "Female, colorful, and diverse" neatly exemplifies this message (July 2, 2019). Geared for businesses, "Weiblich, bunt, diverse" featured Thomas Sattelberger (MdB), Ursula Schwarzenbart (Diversity Management at Daimler-Benz), and Anja Ebert-Steinhübel (Learning Leadership Institute), and it emphasized diverse employees as a source of innovation. Fairness or equality does not feature in the event's focus or framing.

A limited yield of FNF-supported programming is visible beyond the main calendar. Brochure-PDFs are available on the FNF website heralding a Europe-wide program called "Empowerment," which uses the hashtag #FemaleForward to call women into political action.[22] The front page of a

2019 document trumpets: "Good Politics Needs Bold Women!" (Gute Politik Braucht Mutige Frauen!). The Empowerment-Programm includes an online form to apply to participate in the FNF's programming; however, in early 2021 the application period was closed, with the following message: "Unfortunately, the application period has concluded. We will gladly notify you when the next application period begins" (Die Bewerbungsfrist ist leider abgelaufen. Sobald die nächste Bewerbungsphase bekannt ist, informieren wir Sie gerne).[23]

The FDP's women's auxiliary organization is called the Liberale Frauen, and this is arguably the likeliest site for building infrastructure to support women aspirants, candidates, and officeholders. The Liberale Frauen organization was established in 1990, and it is firmly part of the party's national and regional infrastructure. The Liberale Frauen is, indeed, the cohost of much of the targeted programming noted earlier in the FNF events calendar.

Broadly programmatically within the FDP, several initiatives existed with the aim of increasing women's membership in the FDP and their presence among aspirants for the party by the early twenty-first century (Bieber 2018). However, contemporary versions of these initiatives largely recycle their original forms. A plan called the Women's Campaign dates to 2003 (McKay 2004), and a 2006 Plan for the Advancement of Women mirrors—two decades later—a 1987 initiative of the same name.

It could be the case that mentoring efforts are organized and taking place at the local and regional levels (i.e., they are decentralized). However, a look at local offices of the FDP indicates that mentorship programming is also not widely available or embedded in party infrastructure at local levels. There is not typically a working group (Arbeitskreise, AK) for women. At the Bundestag level, the FDP first established a working group for and about women in the nineteenth legislative period (elected 2017).

Just two FDP women participated in the 2016 survey, and their responses corroborate the characterization of "low level of programming" that has been described thus far. Both respondents were state-level legislators (see Appendix C). Neither of them had participated in a training or mentoring program prior to entering political office in 2004 and 2006, but they were divided in whether they were aware of such a program: one respondent stated that one did not exist, and the other identified a "Mentoring-Programm" even though she had not participated. Both respondents indicated that they had been expressly encouraged to run by FPD functionaries. At the same time, they shared the impression that the FDP did not view increasing women's presence at any level of government as a priority. Evidence from just two respondents is not a basis for drawing strong conclusions. However, their reported experiences corroborate the story told by other women in the party.

In a November 2007 interview, a woman member of the Bundestag with the FDP echoed her party's opposition to quotas, saying, "We have tried to find other ways to encourage women.... The idea is an active mentoring program." However, evidence suggests that these programs are not extensive. Taken together, these materials place the FDP in a "low mentorship programming" category.

B90/Gr

The German Green Party's apparatus includes extensive and institutionalized efforts to include women in the party and in the party's agenda setting. Indeed, Prinz (2003) identifies the B90/Gr as the original initiators of mentorship programming for women in Germany. The party has working groups and special interest groups with chapters across Germany. These many groups are part and parcel of the longtime success that the party has embodied at including women in decision-making roles; they represent and maintain the party's success.

In 2021, one of the pillars of the Heinrich-Böll-Stiftung (HBS) consists of a cluster of initiatives on feminism and gender ("Feminismus & Gender"), and this is not a new effort. Women in the party credit these consistent efforts for the successful inclusion of women in officeholding and leadership roles. For example, local officeholders Julia Bailey and Birgit Marenbach in Erlangen, Bavaria, argued in 2017 that women in the Greens are not just ambitious; they are well supported. The party's success in this area is the result of yearslong systematic support of women ("Die Grünen Stadträtinnen Julia Bailey und Birgit Marenbach aus der Gewinnerstadt Erlangen sagen über das erfolgreiche Abschneiden ihrer Stadt nicht nur, dass die Erlanger Stadträtinnen selbstbewusst sind und gern Verantwortung übernehmen, sondern auch, dass der Erfolg ein Resultat jahrelanger systematischer Frauenförderung ist").[24]

It may be that these events are so firmly part of the party's infrastructure that they are not visible in some venues where other parties' efforts come to the fore. Namely, the HBS Facebook events calendar for 2019–2020 shows no scheduled mentoring events of any kind, for any targeted audience.[25] This programming included 122 events on the HBS Facebook calendar for 2019 and 105 events for 2020.

Most of these events were interest-oriented and informational. For example, a lecture on May 19, 2020, addressed future of agriculture in sub-Saharan Africa ("Die Zukunft der Landwirtschaft in Sub-Sahara Afrika"). A subset of events were *about* rather than *for* women, as observed among other parties. For example, a lecture on November 10, 2020, provided information about women's rights under threat in Poland ("Polen: Frauen und Geschlechterrechte unter Druck"). Another lecture, which took place on December 9, 2020, highlighted women's participation in Belarussian political protests ("Belarus: Das weibliche Gesicht der Revolution").

The most overtly training- or encouragement-oriented HBS event featured on their Facebook calendar targeted young women. On November 10, 2020, an event with the Europäische Akademie Berlin took place called, "Jung, weiblich, und engagiert—was bleibt, wenn es politisch wird?" On October 1, 2019, the HBS hosted a training event for actively increasing gender and sexual diversity, but this event was not focused on political and public life ("Tagung: Interventionen für geschlechtliche und sexuelle Vielfalt").

Separate from individual events hosted or publicized by the HBS, B90/Gr infrastructure is well developed at local, regional, and federal levels. Locally, many districts have working groups of Green Party women (Arbeitskreis [AK] Grüne Frauen). For example, the district of Darmstadt-Dieberg, Hesse, has an AK Grüne Frauen who have an active calendar of events related to encouraging women's independence and equality in public life—not direct supports of candidates but arguably candidate-adjacent. Their website asserts that patriarchal structures require active resistance and that their women's working group exists to engage in that resistance.[26]

In a similar role, many districts have chapters of regional working groups (Landesarbeitsgemeinschäfte, LAG). Some of these LAG chapters self-identify as LAG Frauen* und Gender, widening their mandate beyond women as a group to include all genders and to address gendered issues more broadly. For example, in 2021, Berlin's chapter invites anyone interested in talking about Green politics from a feminist perspective to join their regular meetings.[27]

In personal interviews, members of the B90/Gr attested to the importance of doing more than just implement a quota for promoting women in political and public life. In February 2008, a B90/Gr woman member of the Bundestag stated, "One must do more than a quota—we must encourage women. The quota is always a crutch for addressing actual, existing disadvantages—but we need to work to ameliorate the disadvantages." A man in the Bundestag similarly cautioned in June 2007, "We should not think that this [the quota] solves all our problems—it's an instrument."

Taken together, B90/Gr infrastructure for addressing the wider issues surrounding women's rates of participation in political and public life is extensive. The locations and identities of co-organizers of this programming indicate that these efforts are embedded, stable, and distinctively community based. This is coded as a high level of programming.[28]

DIE LINKE

An intraparty quota for supporting women's equal participation in leadership and decision-making roles has long been in place with the PDS/LINKE;

this section discusses the inconsistent and limited extent of programming that is specifically for the purposes of political training. Events hosted by the Rosa-Luxemburg-Stiftung (RLS) and other auxiliary organizations are intensely focused on a combination of community and civic engagement. Events that more specifically regard women and gender highlight a feminist sensibility that is focused more on well-being and self-fulfillment than on specific political goals. As the following discussion highlights, one interpretation of these emphases lies with the party's origins in the former GDR. Scholars of women's and feminist movements have documented an "allergy against [Western] feminism" in the post-Soviet context (Einhorn 1991, p. 30). In other words, LINKE advocacy for women's rights and interests is shaped not only by a party's socioeconomic ideology but also by its historical context.

The quantity of RLS programming for 2019–2020 was very extensive compared to other party foundations: 2,359 events for 2019 and 1,573 events for 2020. The decrease in events in 2020, and more of those events taking place online, may be due to the COVID-19 pandemic.

An examination of this RLS programming evinces patterns of high levels of feminist awareness, extensive wom*n's and LGBTQ groups, and events thematically about feminism and Marxism. For example, a January 12, 2019, lecture was titled "Materializing Feminism" and an event on March 16–17, 2019, asserted that "Feminism Is Class War." A March 14, 2019, panel addressed intersectional sexual violence: "MeToo! Me Two! YouToo! WeTwo? Die Verflechtungen von Rassismus und Sexismus." Further, the RLS programs many events around queer identities, such as an August 20, 2020, event on "rainbow families" (Regenbogenfamilien). May 2019 featured the ninth annual FemFest in Würzburg, a queer feminist festival composed of lectures and workshops.

Scheduled workshops about engagement emphasize social and community activism rather than formal political activities. For example, over the 2019–2020 period the RLS in Munich offered a monthly meetup for people involved in LINKE community politics. A November 29, 2020, workshop was among the most hands-on events, offering instruction in bookkeeping for nonprofit organizations: "Grundlagen der Buchhaltung in gemeinnützigen Vereinen."

Exceptions to these more generally community-minded events include several workshops on communication strategies and social media for "politically active people," though the intended audience is not specifically candidates or officeholders, and not women or ethnic-minority women. An July 18, 2020, workshop covered directing and editing short smartphone videos for community activism ("Dreh und Schnitt von kurzen Smartphone-Videos"). A November 21, 2020, seminar offered instruction in sustainable communication strategies ("Nachhaltige Kommunikationsstrategien in der Politik"). A series of events titled "Introduction for Candidates for Local Office" (Einführung für Kandidat*innen: Das kommunale Mandat) offered candidate training, but they did not target women or ethnic-minority aspirants.

In terms of party infrastructure for networking and supporting women members and officeholders, LINKE women in the Bundestag comprise a Women's Caucus (Frauenplenum). The caucus's emphases tend to mirror the party's concern with social and economic inequalities, pointing to those issues such as poverty and the challenges of single parenting that are more commonly experienced by women as a group. At the same time, even the Frauenplenum elevates broader social goals over the specific circumstances of women or ethnic-minority women. For example, the caucus's February 2021 resolution on supporting women during the COVID-19 pandemic concluded with the line: "We don't want to return to the old normal—we want to achieve a better future for everyone. . . . Bread and roses!" (Wir wollen kein Zurück in die alte Normalität—wir können eine bessere Zukunft für alle schaffen. Her mit dem ganzen Leben: Brot und Rosen!).[29] "Bread and roses" is a phrase credited to U.S. labor protesters in the early twentieth century (Watson 2005).

Other party infrastructure more clearly focuses on women as a group, although this, too, aligns with the party's focus on the politics of labor, and there is no evidence of candidate recruitment or training. In the party's first Bundestag term (1990–1994), one of just four working groups was Feminizing Society (Feminisierung der Gesellschaft). This took the form of Feminist Politics (Feministische Politik) in the 1998–2002 legislative term. As with other parties' legislative working groups, the LINKE's Bundestag infrastructure is organized around policy production.

In personal interviews, members of the Bundestag were divided in their support of mechanisms specifically geared at promoting women candidates. Interviewees had more to say about formal mechanisms than training programs, per se (see LINKE quotations earlier in this chapter).

In sum, LINKE party and auxiliary organizations undertake broadly sociocultural programming, a subset of which showcases both feminism and queer politics. However, relatively little infrastructure appears to exist to train party or community members in formal politics. Moreover, the party's emphasis on socioeconomic and anti-capitalist priorities largely precludes intersectional policymaking for ethnic-minority women. Thus, while DIE LINKE is, literally, *the left*, it is coded as having a low level of programming for candidate recruitment and training.

SPD

In 1988, the SPD first implemented its gender quota, defined as a minimum percentage for either women or men. This section discusses evidence of the party's efforts to encourage, recruit, and train more diverse candidates alongside and in support of this quota. Available evidence paints a picture of highly professionalized efforts that dovetail with the party's long affiliation with workplaces: workers' groups and the labor movement.

The Friedrich-Ebert-Stiftung (FES) is the political foundation long associated with the SPD. As we would expect from a large and well-developed organization, the FES undertakes extensive programming within Germany and abroad. Among its standing programs, the FES supports a multiunit *Politische Akademie* (political academy).[30] Its units include workshops, lectures, and exhibitions in and on social democracy: workshops on managing nonprofits, on journalism and social media for nonprofits, and on community engagement, as well as a youth and politics forum on becoming politically engaged.

The FES Facebook calendar shows no events after February 4, 2020. However, the calendar for 2019 listed 118 events. Some of these were about women and women's rights; none of them specifically targeted women eligibles or aspirants. For example, an informational panel on March 25, 2019, was titled in English: "Feminism and Women's Rights under Attack." Another event, which took place on September 12, 2019, was billed as a "Gender Matters" event and was titled: "What Can and Should Reproductive Medicine Be Allowed to Do Today—and Tomorrow?" (Was kann und darf Reproduktionsmedizin heute—und morgen?). The training events included in this calendar were almost exclusively part of a "Nachwuchsjournalist_innen" campaign, that is, an FES effort to train and encourage the next generation of journalists, on the premise that democracy requires transparency and a free press.

The SPD's Politische Akademie has significant architecture, supporting extensive programming about civic and political engagement. The party also has a Party School at the Willy Brandt Museum (Parteischule im Willy-Brandt-Haus), which offers political party instruction hosted by the Lübeck institution and museum commemorating the late German chancellor Willy Brandt. The Party School's offerings cover the nuts and bolts of candidacy and officeholding, and they include a program specifically for supporting women aspirants and candidates, called "Women in Positions of Power!" (Die Lehrgänge 'Frauen an die Macht' unterstützen Frauen, innerhalb der Partei durchzustarten).[31] However, these events are largely not advertised on Facebook. One possible interpretation of this distinction is that when the SPD recruits, encourages, and trains women candidates, it does so along preexisting conduits between the party and workplaces. The SPD appears less likely to welcome "walk-ins," so to speak, who take the plunge on a local meeting that they saw advertised, and from that fateful choice embark on a pathway toward political officeholding.

Markedly unlike the B90/Gr, which promotes myriad small local efforts, the SPD's training academy looks professionalized and top down, and SPD programs more broadly appear to be closely intertwined with business training. As an illustration of these interconnections, the résumés of trainers with the Party School based in Lübeck show significant overlap with the world of corporate training. In turn, the Political Academy's units include a blended module called Management and Politics, on the premise that professional management of any organization (business or political office) shares the same principles. Women in the SPD may be more likely to come to candidate training through their workplace.

In terms of party infrastructure, the SPD's working groups in the Bundestag frequently include at least one that addresses women's or gender equality: Gleichstellung von Frau und Mann (1990–1998); Familie, Senioren, Frauen und Jugend (1998–2017); Gleichstellungspolitik (2009–2013). However, as with other large parties in Germany, these working groups are largely focused on policy production, not on internal training. Ultimately, the locations and identities of co-organizers of programming that this section documents indicate that these efforts are extensive, embedded, and shared across the party and across its auxiliary organizations.

Sources of Variation in Mentoring Programs

Narrative descriptions of these parties show that they vary along numerous axes in their mentorship and training efforts. This variation clearly transcends left-right dimensions and instead makes more sense in light of the parties' ages and their histories (which, if any, social groups or movements did they grow out of?) as well as in the compatibility of more corporate practices with their other principles.

The earlier discussion suggests an important distinction between singular events geared for supporting women aspirants and longer-term programming that is embedded in the parties' infrastructure at the local, state, and national levels. Parties that have developed their infrastructure over the course of many decades are likely to have more resources, overall, with which to undertake these mentorship efforts. However, a party's age is far from the only factor. The FDP, part of the original postwar "2.5 party system," does not have the embedded mentorship programming that the B90/Gr do, in spite of decades more time over which to develop the infrastructure for it. Qualitatively, parties' recruitment and training efforts make the most sense in their historical context. The SPD and LINKE, for example, are both located on "the left," but their infrastructure for supporting civil and political groups have different goals and distinctive characters. At the same time, both parties show no evidence of systematic efforts to encourage, recruit, or train ethnic-minority Germans of any gender.

Another element differentiating these parties' engagement in recruitment and mentoring programs is their roots. The character and legacy of German feminist movements help explain why programs developed by B90/Gr and LINKE are grounded in community organizations and have less directly political goals. The B90/Gr emerged out of feminist organizations; the LINKE formed from the PDS, a party forged in a context of significant distrust toward the state (the GDR). An idea that is developed in other chapters is that German women's movements do not "lean into" formal politics in the way that they do in the United States, because their goals are different. Ferree (2012) emphasizes the importance of distinguishing between feminist and women's groups, writing that "*women's movements* include conservative organizations mobilizing politically around members' gender identity, and *feminist* describes people, groups, policies, and activities that aim to enhance women's autonomy and power" (p. 19). This distinction is especially important outside the United States; in the United States, Ferree argues, "women's movement" has long implied "feminist" in a way that does not apply cross-nationally (p. 19).

Finally, the concept of "mentorship training," itself, has corporate and business roots.[32] Indeed, Kanter's (1977) *Men and Women of the Corporation* is a key early study of both mentorship practices and "token" women and the salience of gender ratios in the workplace. Kanter (1977) is widely cited by political scientists and policymakers, alike, on the concept of a critical mass. Efforts at mentorship for cultivating careers have their origin in the business world, and the parties that most closely mimic corporate programs of this kind are those that are most readily visible. This helps explain the convergence between the CDU and the SPD in the professionalized, top-down structure of their training programs: these are large promarket parties.

Die Partei Mensch Umwelt Tierschutz: The Wellbeing of Humankind, the Environment, and Animals (TIER)

Cross-national party datasets typically place Germany's TIER in a miscellaneous category (Döring and Manow 2020). As discussed in Chapter 3, this categorization indicates that a party lacks "a clear left/right position."[33] Thus, the standard approach to TIER, like other "special" parties, is to omit it from the analysis. By contrast, this book's central claim is that many political parties exhibit variation that clear left-right categories do not capture. These parties should not be omitted from the analysis, because their ideological composition still bears on other phenomena of interest. A closer inspection of TIER illustrates these implications for women's advocacy in contemporary Germany.

The TIER party was founded in 1993 in Bonn (A. Schulze 2004, pp. 72–73). Decker and Neu (2017) describe a variety of small German political parties whose names and goals include the protection of animal welfare, such as Gerechtigkeit—Umwelt—Tierschutz and Die Allianz für Menschenrechte, Tier- und Naturschutz. These smaller parties have splintered and recombined repeatedly over time (pp. xv–xviii, 153–154, 158–159). In some elections, they combine lists. Indeed, at the local and state levels, TIER works together with a variety of electoral efforts, including the Freie Wählern (Decker and Neu 2017, pp. 506–509). TIER candidates have won seats in German state legislatures and in the European Parliament.

Decker and Neu (2017) describe TIER as embodying a niche set of interests, in the sense that it advocates largely for animals rather than for human constituents (p. 45). The party combines together ecologically centered, radically democratic, and yet, in some senses, conservative ideas (p. 55). It shares some priorities with the B90/Gr in its advocacy for ecological sustainability, but Decker and Neu (2017) characterize the contemporary TIER as distinctive from the B90/Gr both in its focus on animal welfare and in its unambiguous prioritization of the environment over the economy. TIER does not appear to view sustainable development, per se, as a worthy compromise. Further, although TIER is postmaterialist in its advocacy for the environment and social justice, other values are more difficult to categorize. Like other small parties, it opposes the 5 percent minimum electoral threshold for winning seats in the Bundestag (2017 platform, p. 17). It supports raising taxes on tobacco and alcohol products (p. 16).

As discussed in Chapter 4, the party's 2017 program has little to nothing to say about women as a group, except for a clause asserting the necessity of equal pay for equal work: men and women should be treated equally in the workplace. This applies both to pay and to opportunities for professional advancement ("Männer und Frauen müssen am Arbeitsplatz gleichgestellt werden. Dies gilt für Löhne und Gehälter sowie Aufstiegschancen," p. 8). Instead, the program emphasizes equal rights, and rights against discrimination, for all genders and sexualities (p. 11). Another section emphasizes the importance of children's well-being across household arrangements (single-parent households, divorced or unmarried parents, etc.).

The party's first two federal chairpersons (*Bundesvorsitzende*) were women, Ingeborg Bingener and Gisela Bullam, and its current statute stipulates that there should be "balance" between women and men candidates for office and among party leaders. Consistently, a majority of the party's candidacies are women, sometimes by a very wide margin. At the same time, neither TIER messaging nor their actions address multiple marginalization and officeholding.

In other words, TIER performs well on multiple measures of advocacy for women's rights and interests, including a statement in favor of gender-balance in leadership positions and candidacies. However, its performance in other areas is mixed or, by some accounts, contradictory. Further, in spite of lacking "a clear left/right position," the party has survived for nearly three decades, successfully fielding candidates for office at several levels of government.

One might argue that the experiences of a small party offer limited insight into either larger parties or the party system, more generally. On the contrary, however, Germany's multiparty system affords the space for parties small and large to differentiate themselves from one another in many ideological and other directions. The variation that becomes visible under the institutional circumstances of multipartism absolutely informs our understanding of whether and how ideological orientations translate into words or actions for improving the status of all women, across subgroups. TIER abides by German laws regulating party statutes and nomination procedures. It is a party that shows a commitment to protecting the rights of creatures across species. We do not learn more about political parties by writing some of them categorically out of the conversation.

6

Rates of Election and Party Leadership

Introduction

This chapter operationalizes *advocacy for women and multiply marginalized women* as parties' level of success both at nominating and electing more women and multiply marginalized women into office and at diversifying their top party leadership. As with the strategies they employ (if any), parties vary significantly in their incorporation of women into both legislative officeholding and party leadership positions. And as with strategies for incorporation, a left-right account of this variation is insufficient. These analyses further show that the pathway between parties' acknowledgment of underrepresentation (discussed in Chapter 4) and their election and appointment of underrepresented groups is indirect. By contrast, the absence of ethnic-minority women from political office is not ideologically nuanced: parties across the left and the right neglect the matter of ethnic-minority women's absence from office. Although ethnic-minority women win office under the banners of some political parties, they do so in very low numbers at the national level. Their election is so rare, in particular when disaggregated by parties, that the sample sizes are effectively too small for statistical analysis.[1]

After a brief discussion of the literature on explaining cross-national variation in women's political incorporation, this chapter presents analyses of German candidacy data, Bundestag membership data, and information on party chairpersons. The chapter concludes with a profile of Annalena Baerbock (B90/Gr), who, in the 2021 federal elections, campaigned as the first chancellor candidate in her party's history. This concluding profile illustrates the persistence of gendered stereotypes, even as glass ceilings are cracked.

Historically Marginalized Group Members in Political Leadership Roles

A vast body of research in political science has added to our understanding of both cross-national and interparty variation in the political incorporation of historically marginalized groups, in particular, women's rates of election into legislative and executive office. These studies generally agree on the importance of both electoral and cultural systems. This discussion briefly summarizes the existing literature to set up subsequent empirical sections, which examine the salience of German political parties' ideological characteristics in the system that they share (i.e., holding context largely constant). Cross-national analyses in Chapter 8, in turn, examine parties' variation across diverging political systems.

First, studies clearly show that both specific electoral rules, which make space for newcomers and incentivize the inclusion of more varied candidates, and widely held social values that support gender equality correspond with cross-national variation in women's rates of election into political office. Institutionally, studies have identified the following electoral rules as more inclusive: proportional representation (PR) rules,[2] higher district magnitude (i.e., more representatives elected per constituency),[3] and gender quotas (i.e., the requirement to include women candidates or women officeholders), often expressed as a minimum percentage of women.[4] Research focusing on the effectiveness of gender quotas has shown that they generally correspond with greater numbers of women in political office but that their adoption is more likely in some environments than in others and, in turn, that factors such as the stringency of enforcement mechanisms moderate their effectiveness.[5] While gender quotas may be voluntarily adopted by individual political parties (as in the case of Germany), PR rules and district magnitude are shared for all parties in any given election.

Second, research on the salience of political and social values demonstrates significant cross-national variation in both these values and women's political incorporation, such that some societies are more likely to include women in leadership positions than others. For example, Alexander and Welzel (2011) and Inglehart and Norris (2003) demonstrate a strong, positive association between a society's gender equality attitudes and women's election into political office in that system. Some studies emphasize the importance of women's labor force participation (WLFP) rates, which vary cross-nationally and, in interaction with a society's social traditionalism, affect patterns in women's candidacy and election.[6] These features of the political environment are, like electoral rules, shared for all parties at a given time point.

A structural feature of systems that has received less attention in research on women and politics is multipartism, that is, whether more than two political parties regularly run for and win national legislative office. Multipartism is discussed at greater length in Chapter 2. It bears repeating here that distinctions between two- and multiparty systems are well appreciated in cross-national research on political parties, yet few studies have tested theoretical expectations about their consequences for the presentation of historically marginalized groups. That said, research has found that other features of the party system, such as electoral competitiveness, moderate women's candidacy. For example, Weeks et al. (2022) contend that right-wing parties—not expected to nominate women candidates—are more likely to do so when they are losing support and expect to do poorly. Research in this vein supports the expectation that ideologically more varied parties will incorporate women in some settings compared to others. Parties on the right are expected to respond to these pressures more so than parties on the left, because they have more room for improvement; that is, distinguishing themselves from otherwise similar parties for electoral advantage is more likely to include increasing women's presence and participation. Multipartism is measured in subsequent empirical sections as a system's effective number of parties.

Less research has addressed inclusion in party leadership positions (i.e., as party chairpersons). However, the studies that exist point to party- and system-level variables that appear to shape women's appointment in similar ways to their nomination and election. Corroborating and extending findings by O'Neill and Stewart (2009) from the Canadian context, O'Brien's (2015) study of seventy-one parties in eleven democracies over the 1965–2013 period shows that parties expecting to do poorly are more likely to appoint women leaders, in particular parties that are small or in the opposition, and O'Brien and Rickne (2016) show that the benefits of a candidate gender quota may extend to party leadership posts by expanding the pool of qualified appointees.

Electing Members of Historically Marginalized Groups in Germany (2009–2017)

This section assesses German political parties' success at promoting women toward holding national elected office and intraparty leadership positions. Candidacy data and election results are drawn from the Bundeswahlleiter (the federal returning officer), which is in charge of federal elections. Analyses of candidacies include all fourteen parties. Because of the institutional variation in state and local elections in Germany, discussed in previous chapters, variation in parties' rates of election of women is observable in this dataset only for the seven large parties that have won seats across the 2009, 2013, and 2017 Bundestag elections. An electoral threshold of 5 percent for PR elections restricts smaller parties from entry into the Bundestag; although parties may keep constituency seats that they win, this too requires a plurality vote share. These larger parties reflect arguably narrower ideological ranges than the entire party system, but they suffice for testing this book's theoretical implications.

In the time frame included in this chapter (federal elections in 2009, 2013, and 2017), election of ethnic-minority women into the Bundestag is rare, and statistical leverage is even weaker when they are disaggregated by political party. Pooling these election years together, twenty-five Migrationshintergrund candidates won seats, of whom twelve are women and thirteen are men. This presence constitutes 1.3 percent of the Bundestag's seventeenth legislative term (2009–2013), 2.2 percent of its eighteenth legislative term (2013–2017), and 2.8 percent of its nineteenth legislative term (2017–2021). Their origins include Turkey (18), Iran (2), Greece (1), India (1), Italy (1), and Senegal (1).[7] Table 6.1 lists these MdB. Because their numbers are so few, Migrationshintergrund is not included in subsequent analytical sections. Here, however, it is important to add two caveats. First, these low numbers are not surprising in light of German political parties' low apparent prioritization of recruiting, nominating, and electing ethnic-minority Germans (discussed in Chapters 4–5). Second, although these are not statistical patterns, promotion of ethnic-minority women, in particular, is more visible on what is broadly "the left."

Chapter 5 showed specifically that existing infrastructure for recruiting and training ethnic-minority aspirants is extremely limited. Indeed, the B90/Gr, CDU, and SPD were the three parties for which a high level of mentoring programming targeting women as a group is visible (see Table 5.3). While Table 6.1 may justify some speculation about these programs' success, a ready explanation may lie with a highly visible role model in the SPD: Aydan Özoğuz (SPD), who was born in Hamburg in 1967 and became a German citizen in 1989. Rising in the SPD over the 1990s and 2000s, Özoğuz has been a member of the Bundestag's *Präsidium* since the 2021 federal elections. Omid Nouripour's recent appointment (in 2022) as cochairperson of the B90/Gr party may signal future gains for the Greens, as well.

Candidacies

Table 6.2 shows that women's rates of candidacy vary significantly both among parties and between first-vote ballots (constituency candidacies) and second-

TABLE 6.1 MEMBERS OF THE BUNDESTAG WITH A MIGRATIONSHINTERGRUND (2009–2017)

Party	17th Term (2009–2013)	18th Term (2013–2017)	19th Term (2017–2021)
AfD	[party not in the Bundestag in this term]	[party not in the Bundestag in this term]	0
LINKE	3: *Sevim Dagdelen* Niema Movassat Raju Sharma	3: *Sevim Dagdelen* Niema Movassat *Azize Tank*	6: *Gokay Akbulut* *Sevim Dagdelen* Fabio de Masi *Amira Mohamed Ali* Niema Movassat *Helin (Evrim) Sommer*
B90/Gr	3: *Ekin Deligoez* Memet Kilic Omid Nouripour	4: *Ekin Deligoez* Omid Nouripour Mutlu Oezcan Cem Oezdemir	5: Danyal Bayaz *Canan Bayram* *Ekin Deligoez* Omid Nouripour Cem Oezdemir
SPD	1: *Aydan Özoğuz*	6: Karamba Diaby Metin Hakverdi *Cansel Kiziltepe* Mahmut Oezdemir *Aydan Özoğuz* *Guelistan Yueksel*	7: *Nezahat Baradari* Karamba Diaby Metin Hakverdi *Cansel Kiziltepe* Mahmut Oezdemir *Aydan Özoğuz* *Guelistan Yueksel*
CDU	0	1: *Cemile Giousouf*	0
CSU	0	0	0
FDP	1: Bijan Djir-Sarai	[party not in the Bundestag in this term]	2: Grigorios Aggelidis Bijan Djir-Sarai

Note: Women are indicated with italics.

vote ballots (party list candidacies). Across all parties and ballot types in the 2009, 2013, and 2017 federal elections, women's candidacy rates ranged from 0 percent to 85.7 percent. In this time frame, women were consistently on second-vote ballots at higher rates than on first-vote ballots, which matches historical trends for Bundestag elections (Davidson-Schmich 2014). There are five party-year exceptions to this finding: NPD (2009), ÖDP (2009), PIR (2009), TIER (2009), and TIER (2013). These are all small parties that have not yet won federal seats.

The smaller parties included in this analysis correspondingly field numerically fewer candidates, which results in large percentage-point differences in women's candidacies. Nonetheless, an assessment across these fourteen parties offers some insight into both whether any existing quotas are applied and, in turn, possible patterns underlying a party's willingness to support zero or very few women's candidacies.

Extreme values in Table 6.2 are found in parties that do not have enough electoral support to win seats: 0 percent of REP first-vote candidacies were

TABLE 6.2 WOMEN'S PROPORTION OF CANDIDACIES* FOR THE 17TH (2009), 18TH (2013), AND 19TH (2017) BUNDESTAG ELECTIONS

Party [Candidate Quota]	2009 1st-Vote Ballot	2009 2nd-Vote Ballot	2013 1st-Vote Ballot	2013 2nd-Vote Ballot	2017 1st-Vote Ballot	2017 2nd-Vote Ballot
AfD [None]	*No 1st-vote candidacies*	*No 2nd-vote candidacies*	0.114	0.156	0.105	0.128
CDU [1/3 "quorum"]	0.217	0.355	0.232	0.358	0.221	0.398
CSU [None]	0.133	0.317	0.178	0.300	0.174	0.270
FDP [None]	0.164	0.225	0.171	0.201	0.194	0.226
B90/Gr [50%]	0.358	0.495	0.405	0.509	0.419	0.515
LINKE [50%]	0.283	0.458	0.319	0.503	0.326	0.510
SPD [40%]	0.358	0.372	0.368	0.405	0.378	0.408
FW [20%]	*No 1st-vote candidacies*	0.143	0.144	0.154	0.174	0.217
MLPD [None]	0.239	0.473	0.244	0.426	0.275	0.350
NPD [None]	0.133	0.112	0.097	0.169	0.105	0.168
ÖDP [None]	0.271	0.270	0.210	0.313	0.227	0.270
PIR [None]	0.143	0.041	0.134	0.216	0.161	0.181
REP [None]	0.000	0.123	0.048	0.140	*No 1st-vote candidacies*	*No 2nd-vote candidacies*
TIER ["Balance"]	0.857	0.649	0.500	0.423	0.333	0.567

Source: *Der Bundeswahlleiter*, Sonderhefte (Special Issues) 2009, 2013, and 2017, "The Candidates for the Election to the German Bundestag" (Die Wahlbewerber für die Wahl zum Deutschen Bundestag), available at https://www.bundeswahlleiter.de/. More information is also available at https://www.bpb.de/nachschlagen/zahlen-und-fakten/bundestagswahlen/280221/gewaehlte-abgeordnete.

* A candidacy is a candidate slot. An individual person can run as both a first- and second-vote candidate; this counts as two candidacies.

women in 2009, and 85.7 percent of TIER first-vote candidacies were women (also 2009). Further, as noted earlier, these parties field small numbers of candidacies, period. In the 2009 federal election, for example, the TIER fielded first-vote candidates in just seven constituencies. Six of these were women (i.e., 85.7 percent). This party's statute expresses a commitment to balance between women and men candidates and party leaders but does not have a formal quota; this slate of candidates is not balanced, albeit it favors women.

Among nationally successful parties, the range was from lows of 10.5 percent of first-vote and 12.8 percent of second-vote candidacies (both AfD 2017) to highs of 41.9 percent of first-vote and 51.5 percent of second-vote candidacies (both B90/Gr 2017).

Table 6.3 shows the statistical relationships between women's candidacies and their left-right placements along the following axes: (1) economic redistributionism/liberalism, (2) social progressivism/traditionalism, (3) postmaterialism/materialism, (4) multiculturalism/hegemonic-ethnic supremacy; and (5) in terms of Döring and Manow's/ParlGov (2020) aggregate left-right continuous measure. For the four dichotomous ideological measures, a *t*-test discerns whether the differences in the percentages of candidacies held by women are statistically significant between left and right. A Pearson's correlation coefficient is calculated for the relationship between the aggregate, continuous left-right measure and women's candidacy rates.

For these analyses, data on parties' candidacies are pooled together across election years (i.e., up to three observations for each party). Pooling these data is justified, because electoral rules have remained sufficiently similar across this time frame that nomination and election rates can be compared.[8] Further, not all parties, in particular small parties, fielded candidates in all elections. Pooling these election years together reduces missing data points and increases the sample size for more robust analyses.

Table 6.3 shows that, in the big picture, women's rates of candidacy conform to prevailing expectations about the left versus right ideological orientation. The ParlGov left-right measure is statistically significantly correlated with candidacy rates, in a negative direction, such that parties further to "the right" nominate fewer women.

However, disaggregated ideological dimensions matter differently for first- versus second-vote candidacies. Liberal parties were hypothesized not to differ significantly from redistributionist parties in their nomination of women candidates, and this is the case for second-vote candidacies but not for first-vote candidacies. Existing research on mixed member proportional systems indicates that women are more likely to be nominated to party lists, across parties, compared to individual constituency candidacies.[9] That said, access to first-vote candidacies may be a harder nut to crack for women, in particular in parties that are more gender conservative. This interpretation is largely

TABLE 6.3 WOMEN'S RATES OF CANDIDACY (POOLED: 2009, 2013, 2017)* × IDEOLOGICAL AXES**

Ideological Axis	First-Vote Candidacies (Direction of Relationship) Statistical Significance of t-test	Affirms Theoretical Expectations? (Y/N)	Second-Vote Candidacies (Direction of Relationship) Statistical Significance of t-test	Affirms Theoretical Expectations? (Y/N)
Economic Redistributionism/ Liberalism (dichotomous 0/1)	(−) 0.013	N	(n/a) 0.108	Y
Social Progressivism/ Traditionalism (dichotomous 0/1)	(−) 0.000	Y	(−) 0.000	Y
Postmaterialism/ Materialism (dichotomous 0/1)	(−) 0.000	Y	(−) 0.000	Y
Multiculturalism/ Hegemonic-Ethnic Supremacy (dichotomous 0/1)	(n/a) 0.109	N	(−) 0.046	Y
	(Direction of Relationship) Statistical Significance Pearson's R Correlation		(Direction of Relationship) Statistical Significance Pearson's R Correlation	
ParlGov L-R Measure (continuous 0-1)	(−) 0.000		(−) 0.000	

* Pooling three election cycles yields an N of 39–40 party-years, depending on the election. The N is not 42, because several small parties did not field candidates in all election years.
** For axes 1–4, one-tailed t-tests examine whether mean candidacy rates differ in statistically significant ways between left and right. For the ParlGov continuous L-R measure, the significance of the Pearson correlation coefficient is shown.

borne out in the finding that numerous flavors of right-leaning orientations (liberalism, social traditionalism, and materialism) correspond with lower rates of women's nomination for constituency (first-vote) candidacies.

The finding that multicultural parties are not any more likely to nominate women onto first-vote ballots than hegemonic-ethnic supremacist parties does not support the book's theoretical expectations. However, it is simultaneously the case that four of the seven parties that are coded as hegemonic-ethnic supremacist are small parties (FW, NPD, REP, TIER) whose percentages tend toward extreme values due to the small number of total candidacies. When this t-test is calculated without the TIER, which is clearly an outlier party in terms of women's nomination rates, hegemonic-ethnic supremacy is statistically significantly correlated with lower rates of women's candidacy, as expected.

For second-vote candidacies, left-right differences persist across the three axes that were hypothesized to correspond with variation in actions to promote women's interests. Parties that are socially traditionalist, materialist, or hegemonic-ethnic supremacist are less likely to nominate women to their party lists. At the same time, parties that are "on the right" in a liberal sense do not differ in their second-vote candidacies from "the left" to a statistically significant degree. Aggregating these dimensions together in the ParlGov left-right measure results in the big picture story that parties on the left and right differ in their nomination of women candidates.

Finally, Table 6.4 shows the results of ordinary least squares (OLS) regression analyses. Political parties' rates of nomination of women are regressed on a series of independent variables for a more complex picture of the interplay among ideological dimensions, quota adoption, and parties' acknowledgment of the problem of women's absence from political office (see Chapter 4).

Table 6.4 largely corroborates the contention that disaggregating parties' ideological dimensions reveals more nuance in their activities promoting women's participation in public life, here in the form of political candidacy. As expected, economic liberalism does not differentiate among parties. However, socially traditionalist or hegemonic-ethnic supremacist parties do nominate women at lower rates than their progressive or multicultural counterparts, across ballot types, holding other key factors constant. At the same time, Models 2 and 4 mirror the standard account of variation in parties' nomination rates, showing the statistical significance of an aggregated left-right measure.

In Models 1–3, a party's adoption of a binding gender quota has an independent, positive correspondence with women's rates of candidacy, accounting for parties' varying ideological features. This finding affirms the importance of institutionalized commitments to increasing women's presence. Even among ideologically divergent parties, statutes' inclusion of a binding quota provision makes a difference.

Rates of Election

Analyses of women's rates of election include data only for the seven parties that have won seats in the Bundestag over this time frame (federal elections for 2009, 2013, and 2017). Table 6.5 presents these election results in tabular form (see also Figure 3.1 in Chapter 3 for a visual representation of these data). The low point across these election cycles is 11.7 percent (AfD, 2017), and the high point is 56.7 percent (B90/Gr, 2017).

TABLE 6.4 OLS REGRESSION MODELS OF WOMEN'S CANDIDACIES (POOLED: 2009, 2013, 2017)

	Women's Rates of First-Vote Candidacies		Women's Rates of Second-Vote Candidacies	
	Model 1	Model 2	Model 3	Model 4
Economic Liberalism	0.011 (0.041)	—	0.079 (0.051)	—
Social Traditionalism	−0.446 (0.062) ***	—	−0.394 (0.076) ***	—
Materialism	†	—	†	—
Hegemonic-Ethnic Supremacy	0.364 (0.063) ***	—	0.265 (0.077) **	—
ParlGov Left-Right Measure	—	−0.022 (0.007) **	—	−0.051 (0.010) ***
Gender Quota ‡	0.115 (0.044) **	0.080 (0.025) **	0.146 (0.053) **	0.037 (0.032)
Acknowledges Underrepresentation	0.026 (0.053)	0.015 (0.038)	−0.006 (0.065)	−0.103 (0.051) *
Constant	0.199 (0.036) ***	0.305 (0.063) ***	0.281 (0.045) ***	0.624 (0.085) ***
N	39	30	40	31
$P > F$	0.000	0.000	0.000	0.000
Adjusted R^2	0.649	0.766	0.467	0.740

Note: Pooling three election cycles yields an N of 39–40 party-years, depending on the election. The N is not 42, because several small parties did not field candidates in all election years. Entries are unstandardized coefficients from OLS regression models. Standard errors are noted in parentheses. The unit of analysis is the party-year. Model 1: A Breusch-Pagan test indicates some concern regarding heteroscedasticity ($Pr>X^2= 0.000$). Variance Inflation Factors (VIFs) are between 1.72 and 4.85 (mean 3.27). Model 2: A Breusch-Pagan test does not indicate concern regarding heteroscedasticity ($Pr>X^2= 0.272$). VIFs are between 1.56 and 4.64 (mean 3.37). Model 3: A Breusch-Pagan test does not indicate concern regarding heteroscedasticity ($Pr>X^2= 0.983$). VIFs are between 1.74 and 4.99 (mean 3.32). Model 4: A Breusch-Pagan test does not indicate concern regarding heteroscedasticity ($Pr>X^2= 0.191$). VIFs are between 1.46 and 4.68 (mean 3.37).

* $p < 0.10$; ** $p < 0.05$; *** $p < 0.001$

† This variable was omitted from the model due to collinearity.

‡ In these models, the CDU's quorum and the TIER's balance clause are not counted as quotas, because they are not similarly binding. Models were also run counting the CDU and TIER cases as having quotas; the one change in all four models is the coefficient for *hegemonic-ethnic supremacy* in Model 3. In the alternate model (not shown here), this coefficient is not statistically significant.

Table 6.6 shows that parties' successful election of women varies significantly between left-right categories across all measures. This finding resonates with the extensive literature showing that left-right categories are statistically significant correlates of women's presence in political office. However, it adds greater nuance regarding the ideological dimensions for which this finding holds. Indeed, the book's theoretical expectations were that economically liberal parties might well elect women at similar rates to those that are left-leaning, specifically in their state-and-the-economy orientation, but among these seven German political parties, they do not. Further, taken together with other analyses discussed in previous sections, this finding points to this final stage in the political recruitment process as the site where parties differentiate along these lines. This stark left-right ideological differentiation does not obtain at all stages.

Table 6.7 offers additional insight into the interplay between parties' adoption of gender quotas and their ideological characteristics. Collinearity between materialism and hegemonic-ethnic supremacy among these larger seven parties drops these variables from the model. Among these larger parties, it is the gender quota that is the most consistent correlate of women's rates of election. Models 5 and 7 were fit with the gender quota measure that is more stringent, only counting those quotas that are binding, while Models 6 and 8 were fit with the measure that includes the CDU's quorum and TIER

TABLE 6.5 ELECTIONS TO THE BUNDESTAG: 2009, 2013, AND 2017*			
	2009	*2013*	*2017*
Party [Candidate quota]	Party's Total Seats Won (Women)	Party's Total Seats Won (Women)	Party's Total Seats Won (Women)
AfD [None]	—	—	94 seats (11 women; 11.7%)
CDU [1/3 "quorum"]	194 seats (39 women; 20.1%)	255 seats (63 women; 24.7%)	CDU 200 seats (42 women; 21%)
CSU [None]	45 seats (6 women; 13.3%)	56 seats (15 women; 26.8%)	46 seats (8 women; 17%)
FDP [None]	93 seats (23 women; 24.7%)	0 seats	80 seats (19 women; 23.8%)
B90/Gr [50%]	68 seats (37 women; 54.4%)	63 seats (35 women; 55.6%)	67 seats (39 women; 56.7%)
PDS/LINKE [50%]	76 seats (40 women; 52.6%)	64 seats (36 women; 56.3%)	69 seats (37 women; 53.6%)
SPD [40%]	146 seats (56 women; 38.4%)	193 seats (81 women; 42.0%)	153 seats (64 women; 41.8%)
* Data drawn from election results and membership lists are on the Bundestag's website, available at bundestag.de.			

TABLE 6.6 WOMEN'S RATES OF ELECTION TO THE BUNDESTAG
(POOLED: 2009, 2013, 2007)* × IDEOLOGICAL AXES**

Ideological Axis	Women's Rates of Election	
	(Direction of Relationship) Statistical Significance of t-test	Affirms Theoretical Expectations? (Y/N)
Economic Redistributionism/ Liberalism (dichotomous 0/1)	(−) 0.0001	N
Social Progressivism/Traditionalism (dichotomous 0/1)	(−) 0.0000	Y
Postmaterialism/Materialism (dichotomous 0/1)	(−) 0.0000	Y
Multiculturalism/Hegemonic-Ethnic Supremacy (dichotomous 0/1)	(−) 0.0000	Y
	(Direction of Relationship) Statistical Significance of Pearson's R Correlation	
ParlGov L-R Measure (continuous 0-1)	(−) 0.0000	

* Pooling three election cycles yields an N of 39–40 party-years, depending on the election. The N is not 42, because several small parties did not field candidates in all election years.
** For axes 1–4, one-tailed t-tests examine whether mean election rates have statistically significant differences between left and right in the expected direction. For the ParlGov continuous L-R measure, the significance of the Pearson correlation coefficient is shown.

balance clause. In Model 5, the more stringent gender quota measure dominates the model, such that none of the ideological measures is statistically significant. This finding mirrors Chapter 5, which showed that the adoption of gender quotas extends across ideological differences in Germany; and it mirrors the finding that quotas have a distinctive, positive correlation with women's rates of candidacy.

The aggregate left-right measure is statistically significant in both Model 7 and Model 8. As elsewhere, this finding resonates with the existing literature emphasizing left-right categories, but the story is more complex when read together with data about other elements of the process of encouraging, training, and nominating women. Whether parties adopt binding quotas is technically voluntary in Germany, although quota adoption extends across ideological dimensions. Parties vary further in the extent to which they develop programs to encourage, recruit, and train more diverse candidates in support of such quotas. Finally, parties converge across ideologies in their inattention to the relative absence of migrant-background and otherwise multiply marginalized women.

TABLE 6.7 OLS REGRESSION MODELS OF WOMEN'S RATES OF ELECTION TO THE BUNDESTAG (POOLED: 2009, 2013, 2017)

| | Women's Rates of Election ||||
	Model 5	Model 6	Model 7	Model 8
Economic Liberalism	8.783 (6.726)	-8.093 (5.305)	—	—
Social Traditionalism	-3.767 (5.084)	-16.015 (4.921) **	—	—
Materialism	†	†	—	—
Hegemonic-Ethnic Supremacy	†	†	—	—
ParlGov L-R Measure	—	—	-4.239 (1.208) **	-6.516 (0.813) ***
More Stringent Gender Quota ‡	34.689 (8.302) ***	—	11.771 (5.632) *	—
Less Stringent Gender Quota ‡	—	12.156 (4.577) **	—	0.203 (4.018)
Constant	15.467 (8.039) *	36.971 (4.821) ***	49.266 (8.402) ***	65.702 (6.185) ***
N	18	18	18	18
Prob > F	0.000	0.000	0.000	0.000
Adjusted R^2	0.858	0.788	0.913	0.888

Note: Pooling three election cycles yields an N of 18 party-years. Entries are unstandardized coefficients from OLS regression models. Standard errors are noted in parentheses. The unit of analysis is the party-year.
Model 1: A Breusch-Pagan test does not indicate concern regarding heteroscedasticity ($Pr > X^2 = 0.1022$). VIFs are between 2.85 and 8 (mean 5.35). Model 2: A Breusch-Pagan test does not indicate concern regarding heteroscedasticity ($Pr > X^2 = 0.8630$). VIFs are between 1.45 and 2.16 (mean 1.80). Model 3: A Breusch-Pagan test does not indicate concern regarding heteroscedasticity ($Pr > X^2 = 0.4737$). VIFs are both 6.01. Model 4: A Breusch-Pagan test does not indicate concern regarding heteroscedasticity ($Pr > X^2 = 0.5455$). VIFs are both 2.11.
* $p < 0.10$; ** $p < 0.05$; *** $p < 0.001$
† These variables were omitted from the model due to collinearity. The sample sizes for these models are low.
‡ As discussed elsewhere, the CDU's quorum and the TIER's balance clause count as less stringent quotas.

Rates of Election and Party Leadership / 127

Inclusion in Party Leadership

All fourteen German political parties included in these analyses appoint individuals into party leadership roles. The top position on a party's executive board at the national level is generally called the federal chairperson (*Bundesvorsitzende*). Inclusion in these positions is another indicator of political incorporation. As discussed in Chapter 5, some political parties' statutes stipulate women's inclusion on these boards. In the case of the B90/Gr, the federal chairpersons comprise a pair, at least one of whom must be a woman, and the TIER has three equal chairpersons. No party statute currently requires that the federal executive board include an individual with a Migrationshintergrund.

As a parliamentary system, Germany's national head of government enters office after federal legislative elections, generally after negotiating a coalition government. The party helming this government is almost by definition the plurality seat holder, and this party will have identified a "chancellor candidate" (*Kanzlerkandidat/in*). Only those parties that expect to have a shot at helming a government coalition will campaign with a chancellor candidate. Historically, the field of likely chancellors has included almost exclusively the CDU and the SPD, and, indeed, almost all postwar FRG chancellors have hailed from these parties. The exception is Walter Scheel of the FDP, who, in 1974, served for nine days in an interim capacity after Willy Brandt's (SPD) resignation.

Table 6.8 shows that, in 2017, half of the German political parties included in these analyses were led by women. One party, the B90/Gr, had appointed an ethnic-minority man to the chair position, and no parties have ethnic-minority-women leaders. Although there has been some further diversification after 2017, this level of representation at the very top of party leadership is broadly reflective of twenty-first century inclusion, in patterns that do not immediately sort into clear left-right categories.

The ÖDP has been led by three women since its founding, including Charlotte Schmid as of 2022. As of 2022, the PIR is led by the first woman chairperson (*Vorsitzende*) in the party's relatively short history, Anna Herpertz. In the TIER, profiled in Chapter 5, three people serve simultaneously in joint leadership, and this roster includes six women over the past three decades. While no party statute stipulates that the federal executive board include an individual with a Migrationshintergrund, the B90/Gr have been cochaired by two ethnic-minority Germans: Cem Özdemir (noted in Table 6.8) and Omid Nouripour since 2022. Both are men. Özdemir was born in 1965 in Baden-Württemberg, where his parents had immigrated from Turkey as guest workers. Omid Nouripour emigrated with his family from Iran when he was

TABLE 6.8 FOURTEEN GERMAN POLITICAL PARTIES' CHAIRPERSONS IN 2017

Party	Chairpersons
AfD	*Frauke Petry*
CDU	*Angela Merkel*
CSU	Horst Seehofer
FDP	Christian Lindner
B90/Gr	*Simone Maria Peter* with **Cem Özdemir**
LINKE	*Katja Kipping* with Bernd Riexinger
SPD	Martin Schulz
FW	Hubert Aiwanger
MLPD	*Gabriele Fechtner*
NPD	Frank Franz
ÖDP	*Gabriela Schimmer-Göresz*
PIR	Carsten Sawosch
REP	Kevin Krieger
TIER	*Sandra Lück* with Matthias Ebner and Horst Wester

* Women are indicated with italics; ethnic minorities are indicated with bold text.

in his early teens, and he recounts the significant inspiration for him seeing a Turkish-German politician on television (Brenner 2018).

Annalena Baerbock: The B90/Gr Chancellor Candidate in 2021

Annalena Baerbock[10] was born in 1980 in Hannover, Germany. She completed degrees in political science and international law at the University at Hamburg and the London School of Economics. Baerbock immediately entered politics, starting where many eventual officeholders in Germany do: as legislative support staff. First, she worked as an aide to Elisabeth Schroedter, a B90/Gr member of the European Parliament (2005–2008). Baerbock's formal membership in the B90/Gr dates to 2005, as well. Baerbock next joined the B90/Gr party group in the Bundestag as a spokesperson for foreign policy and national security (*Aussen- und Sicherheitspolitik*; 2008–2009). She then served as the chairperson for the B90/Gr party of the state of Brandenburg (2009–2013), whereupon she was nominated to the party list for Constituency 061: Potsdam—Potsdam-Mittelmark II—Teltow-Fläming II, which is located in the state of Brandenburg, southwest of Berlin. Baerbock was reelected in 2017 and 2021. In the meantime, Baerbock became federal cochairperson of the B90/Gr in 2018, with Robert Habeck.

In the months before the 2021 federal elections, the B90/Gr were polling at historic highs. In the summer of 2021, public support of the Greens was even greater than for the CDU, the party of outgoing Chancellor Angela Merkel (Oltermann 2021). Even while the party had served in the government before, in coalition with the SPD in the fourteenth and fifteenth legislative terms (1998 to 2005), 2021 was noteworthy, because for the first time the B90/Gr formally campaigned with a chancellor candidate: Baerbock.

Media and public attention were mixed, focusing particular scrutiny on her capacity to mother two young children as chancellor. In a Reuters story, Nasr (2021) reports that a *Bild* editor had openly asked these questions of Baerbock: "Imagine you're chancellor in the middle of negotiations, and you suddenly get a call from your children—would you answer? Are your children ok with you wanting to be chancellor?" This kind of negative commentary on the capacity of a young mother to serve as German chancellor is disappointing yet unsurprising. As journalist Wiebke Tomescheit (2021) reflects, "A man would not be asked these questions," and Emily Schultheis (2021) similarly observes that Baerbock's "candidacy has left German political observers wrestling with the question of just how open-minded Germany actually is when it comes to women leaders."

Baerbock is quoted as reflecting on her experiences of this scrutiny in the following words: "I sense, or am often told, that it is an imposition that I, as a 40-year-old woman with young children, am standing as chancellor candidate" (quoted in Nasr 2021). The B90/Gr has long promoted women in politics. As the party's first chancellor candidate, Baerbock nonetheless received significant social and media pressure to explain how she would govern as the parent of young children. However progressive the Greens' principles and bylaws are, their candidates are subject to broadly conservative German expectations about whether and how women reconcile motherhood and career.

The B90/Gr did not perform as well as expected. However, the party joined the governing coalition (with the FDP, led by the SPD), securing important ministerial positions, including Baerbock's appointment as Germany's first woman foreign minister.

7

The Incomplete Citizen in Germany

Introduction

A single constitutional article sums up men's *categorical inclusion* in German military service in the same breath with women's *categorical exclusion*. From its insertion into the FRG's Basic Law in 1954 until its revision in 2000, article 12a stipulated both men's compulsory service and the provision that "under no circumstances may they [women] render service involving the use of arms." The 1956 Wehrpflichtgesetz (conscription law), which implemented men's compulsory service, specified that "from the age of 18, all men who are German according to the German Constitution are obligated to fulfill military service" (Wehrpflichtig sind alle Männer vom vollendeten 18. Lebensjahr an, die Deutsche im Sinne des Grundgesetzes sind). For the balance of the twentieth century, military service was thereby understood to be central to German citizenship—"der Soldat in Uniform" (the citizen soldier)[1]—yet categorically foreclosed to women.

It took so long to open combat roles to women for several reasons. Globally, women's exclusion from combat remains commonplace, because military service is so powerfully intertwined with prevailing beliefs about gender. In addition, Germany's particular history makes military service less desirable across social groups. Feminist movements that might in other settings have advocated for women's inclusion did not do so in Germany. Ultimately, neither German policymakers nor civil society advocates for women's rights were willing agents of the policy changes that allowed women to serve in combat. Instead, in 1999, the European Court of Justice (ECJ) ruled on the Bundeswehr's occupational discrimination against an individual woman, Tanja Kreil. The ECJ found that Germany's categorical exclusion solely on the basis of sex was excessively broad. This ruling precipitated revisions to the constitutional article 12a and to the policies following from it. Historically, most German political parties, across otherwise different sets of values and priorities, had long resisted including women in combat roles. Instead, parties' differing capacities to evolve on this issue offer distinctive insights into the relevance of left-right ideological axes for interpreting debates on issues of gender.

As in previous chapters, this analysis evaluates the extent to which various measures of left-right differentiation explain parties' positions and, in turn, their capacity for change. This discussion shows that society-wide commitments to patriarchy and to narrow descent-based definitions of "Germanness" transcend left-right differences. Several finer-grained ideological dimensions, however, contribute to explaining parties' capacity to change their positions over time: economic liberalism signals a greater likelihood of arguing for equal access, and hegemonic-ethnic supremacy signals an inability to reframe inclusion in terms that make it possible for the party to accept. Indeed, across these dimensions, *otherwise similar* parties differ in their capacity for change. Finally, parties' strategic roles within national legislative politics, in particular whether they were in the governing coalition at the time of the debate, contextualize parties' position taking.

Debates about women's inclusion in the military took place within the broader context of Germany's citizenship laws, which also changed over this time frame. Historically, voices on both "the left" and "the right" vigorously resisted expanding the political and social roles available to women and to ethnic minorities. In turn, these groups have either lacked or forgone direct levers on the policymaking process. Ethnic minorities in Germany have had narrow and sometimes unappealing pathways to the citizenship status that would have afforded them electoral influence. Further, and especially compared to the United States, feminist movements in both East and West Germany deeply distrusted the state. Although feminist organizations in Germany are understood to be located on the left, their "struggle is more often about women's autonomy and collective representation and less often about gender equality" per se (Ferree 2012, p. x). In other words, voices that have advocated for opening the military to women in other countries have not been in favor of it in Germany.[2]

Unlike the issues that other sections of this book address, a formal and categorical prohibition on women's participation in combat, exclusively on the basis of sex-gender, remains globally commonplace across otherwise both more traditionalist and more progressive societies, across divergent forms of government, and across many forms and sizes of the military itself. In the twenty-first century, it is still the case that significantly more countries bar women from combat than allow their participation (Addario 2019). More than half of the countries where women can serve in some or all combat roles, Germany among them, changed their policies to include women only in the twenty-first century. Exceptions to this timeline include Norway, which, in 1985, was the first NATO country to open all combat positions to women; Israel (also 1985, though not all combat services included women); Denmark (1988); and Canada (1989, excepting submarine service). Given how widely held opposition to women's inclusion is, this chapter addresses the question in terms of capacity for change: Which parties evolve on the matter of women in combat, and Why or how do they do so?

Subsequent sections first revisit the book's theoretical expectations, articulating them in terms of this chapter's attention to women's inclusion in the military. The section that follows discusses debates over citizenship laws more broadly, because they constitute essential context for interpreting the significance of opening combat roles to women: citizenship and military service were so intertwined that changes to one corresponded with changes to the other. In the end, *including* women in combat corresponded with *removing* military service from German citizens' constitutional obligations. Both of these policy changes occurred against the backdrop of gradually expanding pathways to citizenship for ethnic minorities.

The chapter's main analysis examines the opening of combat roles to women in Germany's armed forces, a series of changes that took place after decisions rendered by the ECJ in early 2000 (C-285/98, *Tanja Kreil v. Federal Republic of Germany*). A final section examines the concept of the *Innere Führung*, the "leadership principle" of the FRG's postwar military since its inception in 1954. This final discussion illustrates two important elements of this chapter's attention to the German military and citizenship. First, the *Innere Führung* as a concept conveys the centrality of democratic citizenship to the FRG's postwar Bundeswehr, developing the figure of the citizen soldier, who women categorically could not be. Second, it demonstrates how legacies imprinted on the FRG's institutional design had significant consequences for marginalized social groups.

Beyond Left, Right, and Center: Theorizing Advocacy for Expanding the Community of Political Equals

In this chapter, women's and ethnic-minority women's rights and interests take the form of inclusion in combat roles in the military, if they choose and if they meet the more general qualifications for doing so. This narrower issue unfolds within the context of these groups' claims to legal status as German citizens, period.

Many different voices have opposed expanding the community of political equals. Political science accounts of policy change in this vein, such as enfranchising more of the population, include institutional explanations, focusing on whether and how processes for change become favorable to advocates; cultural explanations, focusing on how social values change to view more individuals and groups as fellow equals; and political economy explanations, focusing on supply and demand from political parties' and other key political actors' perspectives. An example of the latter is Teele's (2018) explanation of the timing of women's enfranchisement. In the case of the United States, Teele argues that political parties in the American West faced a more competitive electoral environment compared to parties in the East and South; regionally higher rates of membership in women's suffrage movements in the West simultaneously provided infrastructure for parties to mobilize women as voters. These conditions incentivized parties to support white women's suffrage. Neither *left* nor *right* spontaneously supported expanding the franchise.

A vast multidisciplinary literature addresses the gendered and ethnicized contours of access to citizenship. The discussions that follow are not comprehensive, but rather they highlight theories and patterns in the study of military service and citizenship that inform an account of political parties beyond left, right, and center.

Kinder, Küche, Kirche, Krieg?

Goldstein (2001) argues that societies that engage in war require profoundly compelling narratives around warriors in order to contextualize and motivate individuals to participate. Historically, these narratives have been most successful when they have integrated together socially central gender beliefs with beliefs about what warriors and heroes *do*. These intertwined narratives are a site of hegemonic masculinity: a narrowly defined form of masculinity that emphasizes domination and violence (Connell and Messerschmidt 2005; Kronsell 2005).

At the same time as warrior myths are tightly bound up in beliefs about masculinity, the "full citizen" is one who has participated or can participate in national defense. In Kennedy-Pipe's (2000) words, "The modern state was born in war and consolidated through war" (p. 34). The exclusion of some social groups from participation in war is part and parcel of their exclusion from the state. When we view masculinist warrior myths next to beliefs about full citizens' obligations to participate in national defense, we see clearly that women are not full citizens when they are categorically banned from combat regardless of competency. Women's partial citizenship is even more clear when men's participation in combat is obligatory (i.e., central to their full citizenship).

Societies where women do serve in combat represent exceptions to the rule, and they highlight the extreme conditions that appear necessary for shifting public opinion and policies: women serve in combat when there is the sense of having no alternative, given the existential threats to national security. As Segal (1995) writes, profound social changes must occur to make *women* and *warrior* compatible, or "the situation has to be perceived as so dire as to require an extreme and unusual" response (p. 758). The case of Israel illustrates the exceptional circumstances that motivate political systems to include women in the military. Israeli women's compulsory military service, as well as a relatively long history of their inclusion in some or all combat roles, are a result of the country's continually heightened border tensions. Levy, Lomsky-Feder, and Harel (2007) write that, in Israel, "modern military service fulfilled a historical mechanism of defining the boundaries of citizenship by equating it with bearing arms" (p. 129).

Taken together, theoretical research on the meaning of military service and empirical research on patterns of participation indicate that women and ethnic minorities are likely to be formally excluded from this service as part of their exclusion from citizenship. This exclusion is likely to be maintained by many diverse voices, motivated by divergent principles and preferences, who nonetheless join together in opposition to greater inclusion in combat roles. Socially traditionalist parties do not view combat as appropriate or possible for women to join. Pacifist political actors would prefer that no one of any gender serve in combat. *No political parties* are particularly likely to support women's inclusion in combat roles.

In terms of the ideological dimensions that are at the center of this book's analyses, economically liberal parties are expected to be most likely to support women's inclusion in combat, all other things being equal. All other ideological dimensions are expected to motivate resistance. When forced to open combat roles to women, parties are expected to attempt to reframe the issue in terms that satisfy their ideological commitments. Social traditionalism, materialism, and existentialism will aim to reduce cognitive dissonance by changing how they interpret the military, itself, or by constructing the idea of women's participation as necessary for national security. These are the accumulated effects of pervasive patriarchy.

Pathways to Citizenship

Citizenship is a legal status associated with political and civil rights, which has historically not been available to all adults. This is because not all adults have been viewed as having either a moral claim or the ability to participate in group decision-making. As Irving (2008) writes, "Along with equality, both equity and agency are central to membership in the constitutional community, that is, the body of persons who come under, and enjoy the protection and opportunities offered by, a constitution. Even further, membership of the constitutional community entails a sense of ownership and belonging" (p. 3). The extent and kinds of rights associated with legal status as a citizen have evolved as the modern state has evolved, as has the extent to which citizenship status is available to all residents regardless of sex-gender, race-ethnicity, or level of wealth.

Political scientists distinguish broadly between two citizenship frameworks in the modern state: jus sanguinis (citizenship is by blood or heritage; a person born to citizens is a citizen) and jus soli (citizenship is associated with being born in-country). Germany historically has been an example of the former, with highly restrictive laws around access to status as a German national (Brubaker 1992). Safran (1997) refers to this as an "organic approach" to defining the community (p. 320), an approach that relies on a widely shared sense of "'folk' patrimony" (p. 314). Brubaker (2001) describes these jus sanguinis policies in later twentieth-century Germany as more specifically "differentialist," viewing culturally different migrant populations as categorically separate from the community of political equals at the same time as civil rights and social services have become more widely available (pp. 537–538).

Most receiving countries implement quotas for maximum numbers of immigrants, differentiating among origin states and among reasons for migration. While Higham ([1955] 2002) asserts that "nativism is . . . distinctively American" (p. 3), even in the United States, quota policies have evolved in their interpretation of who is or is not part of the nation, and similar restrictions have borne out in many regions of the world as well.[3] Even when "resident aliens" have legal status, pathways to full citizenship are often not available to most, in a legal limbo that persists for migrants in many otherwise different political systems.[4] Further, across many otherwise different countries, immigrant populations who are viewed as culturally different face steep barriers against integration and more specifically against the acquisition of citizenship. Thus, Germany has been similar to many other countries in implementing restrictions on access to citizenship for immigrants. At the same time, the country's long-held prohibitions against birthright citizenship were distinctively restrictive.

Historically, many countries have also implemented citizenship laws that are explicitly gendered. Women's citizenship is often tied to their relationship status: citizenship acquired or lost through marriage. These patterns are an artifact of women not having had legal status as an autonomous adult (Rürup 2016). Cross-nationally, women's lesser legal status has been most clear in the form of sex-gender restrictions on fundamental political rights such as suffrage or running for office. In addition, some countries' constitutions have included provisions regarding labor rights, household tasks, and other matters explicitly associated with women as a social group. Even after these gendered restrictions have been removed from countries' legal frameworks, citizenship policies that treat women and men differently in interaction with their marital status persist.[5]

In short, cross-nationally and historically, both racial-ethnic minorities and women have been explicitly and formally excluded from full citizenship status. Fundamentally, the explanation for expanding eligibility is that policymakers are pressured to do so in spite of their long-held opposition. However, not all parties and policymakers reverse their positions.

Recalling Chapter 2's discussion of parties' ideological dimensions, redistributionist and liberal parties are not expected to differ in their willingness to expand citizenship status; that is, parties on "the right" in these terms will not oppose a shift to jus soli, all other things being equal. By contrast, socially traditionalist parties are expected to express resistance to expanding citizenship access, especially if this expansion is framed as unsettling gender norms and German cultural identity. Materialist parties are expected to express resistance if citizenship expansion is framed as a threat to safety/security. Hegemonic-ethnic supremacist parties are expected to resist expansion wholesale and regardless of the framing, and they are expected to be unable to change this orientation without profound evolution, which would essentially amount to the transformation of this ideological position. In Safran's (1997) terms, these are parties for which "the fear that the texture of German society would be changed beyond recognition remains a constant one" (p. 323).

Subsequent sections focus on this chapter's main analysis, which addresses opening combat roles in the military to women. However, this discussion also argues that the issue of gender and the military is mutually imbricated with the matter of expanding citizenship access. Parties' evolving orientations toward these two policy issues are intertwined.

Gender and the Military in Germany

As of 2022, approximately 13 percent of soldiers in the Bundeswehr were women.[6] Although this is not a high percentage, it reflects an increase since the significant legal changes of 2000–2001 (opening combat roles to women) and 2011 (ending Wehrpflicht, compulsory military service). The CDU's Ursula von der Leyen served as Germany's first woman minister of defense from 2013–2019, navigating both significant recruitment challenges and, with Russia's 2014 invasion of Ukraine, increased pressure on the Bundeswehr's preparedness (Mushaben 2022). Recruitment remains an urgent challenge. The Ministry of Defense has undertaken efforts that even extended to a 2016–2017 web series titled *The Recruits* (*Die Rekruten*), followed by several sequels such as *The Women Recruits* (*Die Rekrutinnen*, 2019; see Kloepfer 2017).

In June 2022, the German government broke from its postwar position and committed €100 billion to expanding and modernizing its defense capabilities. This included amending article 87a of the Basic Law to permit establishing a new military fund with a "one-off credit authorization of up to 100 billion euros."[7] Taken together, these are the biggest expansions of the military since World War II.[8]

Two through lines across all of these post–World War II debates about the German armed forces intersect at the point of post-ECJ amendments to the Basic Law: (1) the role of the military in modern Germany and (2) gendered restrictions on who is a full citizen. As discussed earlier, the warrior and protector are essentially masculinist tropes at the same time as they have long symbolized the state itself. These are deeply embedded beliefs about gender, which transcend ideological dimensions that otherwise differentiate among political parties. Left, right, or center, parties are likely to resist change. Indeed, opening Germany's armed forces to women is very unlikely to have occurred on this timeline without external pressure from the European Union.

The Origins of the Bundeswehr

In Germany, enlistment in the military has remained relatively low across all social categories and all regions (Buck 2019; Knight 2019). The multigenerational tradition of military service found in some other countries is largely absent in Germany. Further, these patterns lie in part in the distinctive post–World War II development of Germany's military and public sector. As the aggressors and, ultimately, losers of the war, Germany and Japan faced both external and internal restrictions on the size and function of their militaries at the end of World War II.[9] More specifically, the terms of Germany's surrender at the end of World War II included the dissolution of the country's military. Germany's postwar occupation ended in 1949 with the division of the country into two independent states, the Federal Republic of Germany (FRG, West Germany) and the German Democratic Republic (GDR, East Germany). The FRG joined NATO in 1955, establishing the Bundeswehr as an all-defensive force, while the GDR and its Volksarmee (armed forces) were part of the Warsaw Pact. This section provides context for subsequent sections that focus on political parties' evolving orientations toward women's formal and informal roles and opportunities in Germany's military forces.

The Bundeswehr was and remains, formally, a defensive force, although its size and resources have fluctuated over time.[10] Two additional features of the Bundeswehr date to its establishment. Compulsory military service by German men was explicitly associated with the responsibilities of citizenship, while, simultaneously, women were categorically banned from all specialties in all units. Taken together, these precepts place women in a distinct and lesser category of citizen compared to men.

In 1956, the Bundestag passed the Conscription Act (*Wehrpflichtgesetz*), which specified full participation in national defense by "all men who reach 18 years of age, who are German by the definition of the Basic Law" (sec. 1). Gesley (2017) argues that the premise of this act was, in policymakers' minds, equality: to "ensure that all parts of society were represented in the armed forces and everyone was treated equally." The FRG's first president, Theodor Heuss, averred that conscription was the "legitimate child of democracy." In parliamentary documents from the time frame of the Conscription Act's development, it is clear that Bundespräsident Heuss and others viewed conscription and participation in the military as central to citizenship at the same time as it categorically excluded women. The corollary to men's general conscription was women's categorical exclusion from service with weapons, and both were added to the text of the Basic Law in 1954 (implemented in law in 1956). Until its amendment in 2000, article 12a read (emphasis added):

> If, during a state of defense, the need for civilian services in the civilian health system or in stationary military hospitals cannot be met on a voluntary basis, women between the ages of eighteen and fifty-five may be called upon to render such services by or pursuant to a law. *Under no circumstances may they render service involving the use of arms.*

In the decades after the establishment of the Bundeswehr in 1955, first the medical services opened to women (1975) and then, later, the musical corps (1991). This expansion of roles available to women strictly excluded "service involving the use of arms." Several lawsuits in the 1990s challenged this exclusionary principle, but they were unsuccessful, on the basis of article 12a. For example, Rath and Oestreich (1999) describe a case heard by the Bundesverwaltungsgericht (Federal Administrative Court), which ruled that women did not have the right to serve in the infantry due to article 12a. Earlier in the 1990s, Bettina Beggerow filed a complaint with the Truppendienstgericht Nord (Administrative Military Court of the North) regarding the refusal to transfer her from medical services to the armored division services; Beggerow had been told that, as a woman, she could not work in the armored division. The Federal Constitutional Court subsequently heard Beggerow's case, but a clerical error ended the process (Louis 2000). On other occasions, Germany's Constitutional Court maintained the position that further expanding women's inclusion in the military would require amendments to the Basic Law (Rath and Oestreich 1999).

Finally, in 1998, a nineteen-year-old electrician from Hannover named Tanja Kreil applied to work in weapons maintenance with the Bundeswehr, and her application was denied expressly in terms of the prevailing interpretation of Basic Law article 12a. Kreil contacted the office of Germany's defense minister, then Volker Rühe (CDU), who declined to act on her behalf. Her boyfriend was an enlistee in the Bundeswehr, and he suggested that she contact the Deutscher Bundeswehrverband (German Military Association, DBwV) for assistance (Rübsam 1999). With the DBwV's support, Kreil filed a legal case with the ECJ. In its defense, the German government, with supporting materials from the Italian and U.K. governments, argued that the EU did not have jurisdiction over member states' militaries. However, the ECJ found that article 12a's categorical exclusion of women was excessively broad, abrogating the European Union Council Directive 76/207/EEC on the equal treatment of men and women (1976).

Kreil is quoted as saying that her goal was simple: "I just wanted a job with the military and to learn new technical skills" (quoted in Rübsam 1999). Whatever Kreil's intentions, the ECJ's 2000 decision required Germany to change its sex-gender exclusion rule, and subsequent debate within the Bundestag led to changes to federal laws governing the military and its relationship to the state as well as to a revision of the Basic Law.[11]

The nature of men's compulsory military service also evolved in this time frame. On the one hand, the 1949 FRG's Basic Law had specified that "no person shall be compelled against his conscience to render military service involving the use of arms" (article 4). Kuhlmann and Lippert (1993), writing before the end of compulsory service, observed that "in German constitutional law, the right to object to military service for reasons of conscience takes priority over the principle of compulsory military service" (p. 98). When the Bundeswehr was established, the process by which men applied for an exemption on the basis of conscientious objection was rigorous, requiring board approval. Starting in 1973, men who would otherwise be subject to compulsory service but who were conscientious objectors could undertake an alternative civilian service (*Zivildienst*), and this introduced a shift to lesser scrutiny for men choosing to undertake civilian rather than military service (Kuhlmann and Lippert 1993, pp. 99–100). In 2011, both military and civilian compulsory service ended, and the Bundeswehr became an all-volunteer or professional force. Since that time, compulsory service has been reserved for a national security emergency, and it has not yet been reengaged.[12] Subsequent sections argue for drawing a clear line from the end of the sex-gender exclusion to the end of men's compulsory military service, such that including women in combat roles corresponded with reducing the national importance placed on service in combat. A resurgence in importance has been forced by Russia's 2022 invasion of Ukraine, and time will tell whether and how this reshapes the salience of gender and ethnicity within the Bundeswehr.

The sections that follow show that the otherwise-unexpected coalitions that formed in Germany around maintaining the sex-gender exclusion rule and eliminating it, and the constellation of attitudes they represent, are not merely random, even though they do not map cleanly onto left-right categories. Instead, these coalitions reflect that the issue of women in the military raises steep challenges to enduring, widely held beliefs about sex-gender, citizenship, and equality. Ideological dimensions that are sometimes useful for distinguishing between political parties and their attitudes toward and actions on the rights and interests of historically marginalized groups are not particularly useful for understanding the resistance to women's inclusion in the Bundeswehr. Broadly speaking, "left" and "right" largely converged in opposing women in combat in Germany, while a party at the center, the FDP, consistently supported women's inclusion.

However, debates that followed from the 2000 ECJ decision show differentiation between parties that reflects some of the book's theoretical expectations: all other things being equal, social traditionalism corresponds with significant resistance, and it motivates efforts at reframing that diminish both the masculinism of military service and its centrality to citizenship in order to reconcile women's participation in it. Economic liberalism does not preclude advocacy for women in combat. Indeed, the FDP, at the intersection of liberalism and relative social progressivism, is the one consistent advocate for women's inclusion. Ultimately, for many of these parties, post-ECJ-decision positions constitute a complete reversal compared to predecision positions.

Figure 7.1 displays German political parties' orientations toward women's inclusion in the Bundeswehr at four time points: at the time of conversations about the sustainability of the German military in the early 1980s; the early 1990s after German reunification, when the influx of soldiers from the former GDR addressed some of the country's concerns regarding lagging recruitment; late 1999/early 2000, around the time of the ECJ *Kreil* ruling, and before it was clear that policy change was legally inevitable; and the year following the *Kreil* ruling (late 2000/early 2001), when policymakers debated how to implement the ruling. This table also shows the various combinations of left-right parties based on the four finer-grained ideological dimensions examined throughout this book.[13]

Pre-2000 Positions

In the half century between the establishment of the Bundeswehr and the run-up to the ECJ's consideration of Kreil's case, public attitudes, civil society's

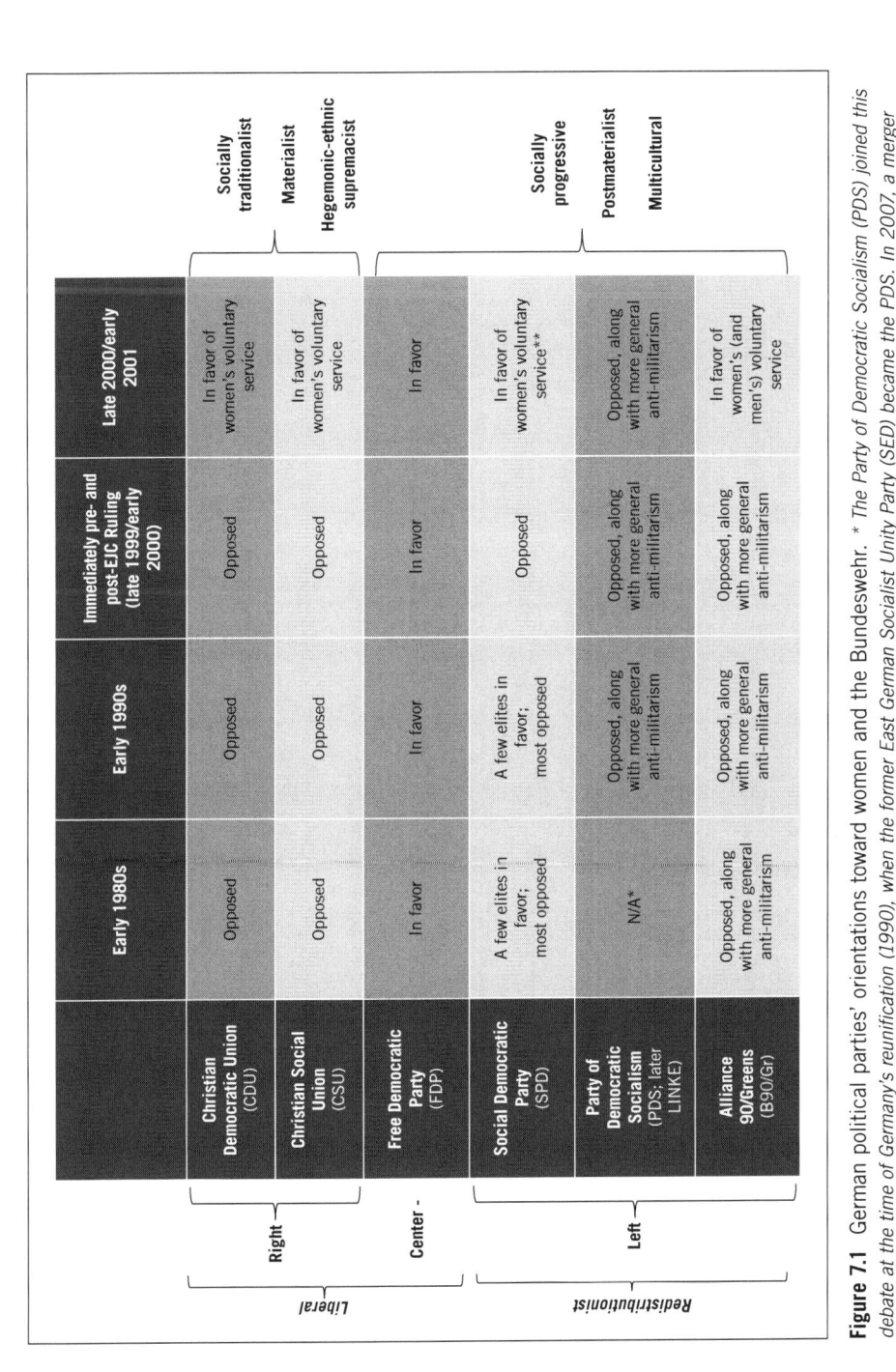

		Early 1980s	Early 1990s	Immediately pre- and post-EJC Ruling (late 1999/early 2000)	Late 2000/early 2001	
Right	**Christian Democratic Union (CDU)**	Opposed	Opposed	Opposed	In favor of women's voluntary service	⎫ ⎬ Socially traditionalist ⎪ Materialist ⎭ Hegemonic-ethnic supremacist
	Christian Social Union (CSU)	Opposed	Opposed	Opposed	In favor of women's voluntary service	
Center	**Free Democratic Party (FDP)**	In favor	In favor	In favor	In favor	
Left	**Social Democratic Party (SPD)**	A few elites in favor; most opposed	A few elites in favor; most opposed	Opposed	In favor of women's voluntary service**	⎫ ⎬ Socially progressive ⎪ Postmaterialist ⎭ Multicultural
	Party of Democratic Socialism (PDS; later LINKE)	N/A*	Opposed, along with more general anti-militarism	Opposed, along with more general anti-militarism	Opposed, along with more general anti-militarism	
	Alliance 90/Greens (B90/Gr)	Opposed, along with more general anti-militarism	Opposed, along with more general anti-militarism	Opposed, along with more general anti-militarism	In favor of women's (and men's) voluntary service	

Liberal / Redistributionist

Figure 7.1 German political parties' orientations toward women and the Bundeswehr. * The Party of Democratic Socialism (PDS) joined this debate at the time of Germany's reunification (1990), when the former East German Socialist Unity Party (SED) became the PDS. In 2007, a merger between PDS members and former SPD members created the Left Party. The Alternative for Germany (AfD) is not included in this table, because the party was not part of any of the debates on including women in the military. ** See discussion of Bundestag plenary session debates. After the January 2000 ECJ ruling, several prominent members of the SPD became vocal supporters of women's inclusion in the Bundeswehr. Other SPD MdB changed their positions more gradually. The final vote on article 12a misleadingly suggests a united perspective.

attitudes, and political parties' positions on women's participation remained relatively constant.

First, the DBwV is a civil society organization that formed in 1956 at the time when the Bundeswehr was established. In the context of Germany's corporatist system, the DBwV has been a frequent contributor to policymaking on the issue of the military and servicepeople's rights and interests, promoting laws such as the 1991 Soldatenbeteiligungsgesetz (sec. 35). Beginning in the 1980s, spokespeople associated with the DBwV voiced at least partial support for women's greater inclusion. For example, Bernhard Gertz, former head of the organization, stated in 1997 that he viewed article 12a of the Basic Law as prohibiting only nonvoluntary service by women.[14] Late in the 1990s, the DBwV's Jürgen Meinberg indicated more forcefully that the organization had been looking for opportunities to pursue legal avenues at the level of the European Union for changing policies on women's participation.[15] In fact, an internal DBwV working group called Women Soldiers (Arbeitsgruppe Weibliche Soldaten) was established in 1998, which advocated for this cause (Apelt 2015, p. 229).

The support of DBwV as an organization was also reflected in attitudes within the military, which, by the end of the 1990s, was supportive of ending a categorical sex-gender exclusion. For example, Kümmel (2002) shows April 2000 data from the Bundeswehr Institute for Social Research, in which just a small minority of survey respondents strongly opposed expanding women's roles in the Bundeswehr (15 percent), compared to a significant majority agreeing that expanding women's roles would have a "positive effect on the image of the Bundeswehr within society." Fifty-one percent of respondents supported ending all restrictions on women's participation (Kümmel 2002).

The DBwV's active efforts in the 1990s built on several short-lived efforts by the Federal Defense Ministry in the 1970s and 1980s to expand women's roles in the military, at a time when voluntary service by men was declining significantly. In spite of these voices in support, and although the DBwV as an organization supported policy changes, various vocal leaders within the Bundeswehr expressed opposition repeatedly over the two decades leading up to the ECJ's *Kreil* decision.

At the same time as various leaders within the military itself expressed resistance to change, German feminist and women's organizations also opposed women's participation in combat roles. In the 1970s and 1980s, these organizations' goals for advancing women's equal rights were tightly intertwined with anti-militarism, in both West and East Germany (Ferree 2012, p. 104). As Ferree (2012) writes, "Virtually all American feminists value the right to serve in the military, when most German feminists deplore it" (p. 16). Kaplan (1992) even credits the aforementioned Federal Defense Ministry's efforts in the 1970s and 1980s with galvanizing large anti-military protests that she argues revitalized women's movements at that time (p. 117).

As noted, the early 1980s found military personnel in Germany concerned about the organization's sustainability, because many men were choosing civilian service rather than military service (Kümmel 2002). Indeed, the coinciding issues of increasing retirements and decreasing recruitment were at the center of the 1982 Commission for Long-Term Planning of the Bundeswehr (Kommission für Langzeitplanung der Bundeswehr). The commission generated a series of solutions that included, albeit in a final bullet point, expanding the roles available to women who volunteer to serve. This item further specified that specialties disproportionately affected by retirement should be opened to women. Their emphasis on voluntary service reflected the commission's certainty that the Basic Law's prohibition on women's service with weapons was not going to change, and their emphasis on exigency reflected that this solution was not viewed particularly favorably (Konrad-Adenauer-Stiftung 1982, p. 4).

Several federal commissions on women's rights were also convened in this era. For example, the SPD and FDP coestablished a "Women and Society" commission, in 1973, aimed at assessing women's status and making policy recommendations. This commission played a role in the Marriage and Family Law Reform Act later that decade (1976–1977), and their work led to the opening of the medical services corps to women by Defense Minister Georg Leber (SPD) in 1975. German reunification, in 1990, satisfied the need for soldiers from the GDR's Volksarmee, taking the perceived urgency of including women off policymakers' agenda.

Over the course of this longer time frame (1970–2000), just one political party consistently advocated for women's inclusion in the Bundeswehr, the FDP. In addition to their participation in commissions in the 1970s and 1980s in cooperation with the center-left (SPD) and center-right (CDU), the party's FNF (see Chapter 5) organized independent events calling attention to women's exclusion. For example, an FNF seminar called "Women and the Bundeswehr" convened July 3–5, 1981, bringing together speakers from major political parties that included the CDU, CSU, and the Green Party, in addition to the FDP. In this conversation, only the FDP expressed support for opening the military to women. Although the Greens had not yet won seats in the Bundestag (they won their first national seat in 1983), Petra Kelly as a party founder participated in the seminar to voice the party's contribution to the discussion: unambiguous rejection of the militarism that women's inclusion would increase. Expressing the position that the Greens maintained until the ECJ ruling, Kelly wrote that Greens "reject any and all mandatory service or conscription" (jegliche solche Dienstpflicht und Wehrpflicht ablehnen, p. 101).

In the following decade, after Beggerow's failed 1996 lawsuit to amend the Basic Law, the FDP made several efforts within the Bundestag to address women's exclusion. The party submitted a series of formal requests for the government to lead the way on forging more equal policies during the thirteenth legislative period (1994–1998), with Guido Westerwelle (then the FDP's general secretary) referring to women's exclusion as the "final sex-specific occupational prohibition" (das letzte geschlechtspezifische Berufsverbot) (quoted in Rath and Oestreich 1999). These efforts were not successful, because the FDP alone advocated for them.

The ECJ's ruling on *Kreil v. Germany* was released nearly two decades after the FNF "Women and the Bundeswehr" seminar. In the spirit of the party's continued support, the FDP spearheaded the late 1999 proposal to implement these policies and to amend the Basic Law. Ina Lenke, a longtime force within the FDP for advancing women's rights (see Chapter 4), declared in the November 11, 1999, Bundestag debate, "It is truly shameful that a young woman had to take a case to the ECJ in order to end this last sex-specific job prohibition" (Es ist wirklich bedauerlich, dass erst eine junge Frau vor dem Europaischen Gerichtshof muss, damit endlich auch hier in Deutschland die Chance besteht, dass eines des letzten geschlechtsspezifischen Berufsverbote aufgehoben wird).[16]

Post-ECJ Ruling: Parties' Capacity to Reframe and Reform

After the ECJ ruling, women's inclusion in the German military was inevitable, and parties' responses to this inevitability illustrate both the persistence of specific ideological principles and the distinctive structural positions that parties occupy, in the following ways.

As Figure 7.1 shows, most political parties were opposed to opening combat roles to women for much of the postwar period. In 2000, the ECJ ruling on *Kreil v. Germany* produced top-down change, which many but not all parties subsequently needed to figure out how to implement; members of the governing coalition, in particular, had no choice but to do so. The SPD politician Ulla Schmidt is quoted in *Die Tageszeitung* as saying, "There wasn't any pressure on us to do so [change the policy] until now" (Oestreich 1999). By contrast, the PDS (LINKE after 2007; see Chapter 3) did not experience pressure to change their tune, because they were and remain an opposition party. Their support was not needed to implement policy changes to bring Germany into compliance with EU antidiscrimination laws. Even after the ECJ ruling in 2000, members of the PDS such as Wolfgang Gehrke insisted that the best path forward was greater disarmament,[17] or that other parties' framing of the issue was disingenuous. Heidi Lippmann (PDS), for example, scoffed that the expansion of women's occupational choice in the Bundeswehr had "nothing to do with equality."[18] We might have expected the B90/Gr to resist as well, on (German) feminist and anti-militarist grounds, but, in 2000, the B90/Gr was in the Schröder-led red-green governing coalition. The B90/Gr, then, are among the actors who reframed the issue in terms that could be supported by the party's principles.

Bundestag debates at this time reveal, simultaneously, the persistence of patriarchy and the limited role of finer-grained ideological dimensions in guiding how parties reframed the matter of women's inclusion in combat roles. In these debates, many parties and policymakers sought ways to reconcile their longtime opposition to women's inclusion in combat with inevitable, EU-led policy change. With the exceptions of the FDP, which already supported women's inclusion, and the PDS as the perennial opposition party, parties had to find a way to support inclusion. Initially, in these post-ECJ debates, some speakers insisted that women did not, in fact, wish to join the Bundeswehr. For example, in the November 11, 1999, Bundestag debate about amending article 12a of the Basic Law, the B90/Gr's Irmingard Schewe-Gerigk asserted that women's enthusiasm for enlistment was lower than people thought, specifying that even Tanja Kreil had lost interest ("Meine Letzte Informationen, die aus dieser Woche stammen, besagen, dass Frau Kreil einen Job hat, den sie auch behalten will, und kein Interesse mehr an die Bundeswehre hat").[19] Cleaving to her party's commitment to anti-militarism, Petra Bläss (PDS; later LINKE) argued that this sudden attention to women's rights "should make women suspicious," because the military "is no field of emancipation" (Das plötzliche Interesse an diesem Thema sollte Frauen stutzig machen... Die Bundeswehr ist meines Erachtens kein Bereich, in dem es zu beweisen gilt, dass Frauen gleichberechtigt sind).[20] By contrast, in the same November 11 debate, the FDP's Ina Lenke asserted that "interest among young women in the Bundeswehr has sharply increased" (Das Interesse an der Bundeswehr ist gerade bei den jungen Frauen stark angestiegen).[21] These competing claims represented a transition period between parties' longtime positions and their inevitable policy change.

As these debates evolved in 2000, policymakers' attention to the issue of women's inclusion merged with a broader conversation about reforming the Bundeswehr. The October 12, 2000, Bundestag debate about the Bundeswehr addressed several different pieces of draft legislation: a proposal by the CDU/CSU broadly addressing "The Future of the Armed Forces" (*Die Zukunft der Bundeswehr*, Drucksache 14/3775); a government coalition-led proposal to amend the Soldatengesetz (SGÄndG; Drucksache 14/4062); a proposal by the PDS to fundamentally reform the armed services through disarmament (*Zukunft durch Abrüstung*, Drucksache 14/4174); and a proposal by the FDP on ending compulsory military service for all (*Wehrpflicht aussetzen*, Drucksache 14/4256).

Speakers in the CDU and SPD who had previously opposed amending constitutional article 12a shifted to talking about modernization and improvement. For example, federal Minister of Defense Rudolf Scharping (SPD) focused on the reforms that the Bundeswehr needed to satisfy its NATO commitments, emphasizing "efficiency and economy" (Effizienz und Wirtschaftlichkeit). Minister Scharping only glancingly referred to the proximal reason for these debates in the first place (i.e., the need to integrate women).[22] Scharping, like all of the speakers in this debate, regardless of their position on the matter, avoided referring to the ECJ entirely.

Political parties' capacity to reframe women's inclusion in combat roles reflects their broader commitment to women's equality, and, to some degree, finer-grained ideological characteristics inform an interpretation of their apparent priorities. Numerous women speakers in the October 12, 2000, debate pointed to the absurdity of ignoring that policy changes to include women were the most significant, and these speakers included policymakers who had previously opposed women's inclusion. Both the B90/Gr's Angelika Beer and the SPD's Verena Wohlleben expressed this surprise, with Wohlleben asking, "How have you gone this entire time without talking about women?!"[23]

Bundestag debates about implementing the ECJ's ruling on *Kreil v. Germany* also raised numerous constitutional questions on which party groups were not agreed. First, not all party groups agreed that amending the Basic Law would be necessary to change federal statutes on women's service in the armed forces. Second, parties debated whether it was possible to allow women into voluntary combat service without simultaneously including them in the compulsory service to which German men were still (in 2000) obligated. Third, they argued over whether specifying women's voluntary service required men's voluntary service (i.e., men could claim discrimination on the basis that women could choose while they could not choose).

Ultimately, the October 2000 draft for amending article 12a was proposed collectively by the party groups of the SPD, CDU/CSU, B90/Gr, and the FDP, opening with the observation that "society has changed and now supports women's service in the armed forces."[24] However, this amendment was viewed as a frustrating compromise by some. Disagreements over the overlapping questions of women's voluntary service, men's compulsory service, and the needfulness of amending the Basic Law were evident even in the plenary session in which the Bundestag approved the amendment of 12a. For example, while the SPD had opposed women's inclusion in combat roles at earlier time frames, by late 2000, they supported it—and grudgingly agreed to amending 12a. In the October 27, 2000, Bundestag session, Anni Brandt-Elsweier (SPD) criticized the legislative process, asserting, "Our Basic Law is a legal framework and should not be a matter of horse-trading."[25]

Volker Beck's (B90/Gr) contribution to the October 27, 2000, debate emphasized equality in the workplace, but he concluded his speech with the observation that the B90/Gr party's true preference was for ending compulsory service for all, not merely for stipulating that women would not be required to serve.[26] However, the party group supported the compromise amendment. The PDS as a party group maintained their anti-militarist position more forcefully, as part of its rejection of the constitutional amendment; Petra Bläss reiterated her party's preference for both reducing the size of the Bundeswehr and getting rid of any form of compulsory service.[27]

Finally, the CDU/CSU supported amending article 12a in a way that would maintain a distinction between who could be obligated to serve. In this vein, Rupert Scholz (CDU) asserted that "the male citizen in uniform is an integral component of our society . . . it follows that the female citizen in uniform should also be eligible to share this status" (Unsere Bundeswehr ist heute integraler Bestandteil unserer Gesellschaft. Der Bürger in Uniform ist integraler Bestandteil unserer Gesellschaft. Das führt dazu, dass auch die Bürgerin in Uniform berechtiger integraler Bestandteil unserer demokratischen Gesellschaft sine muss).[28] However, he argued that they must not be required to do so.

A small number of MdB across all party groups diverged from their parties' positions, and they submitted written explanations, appended to the plenary transcript for October 27, 2000. Martin Hohmann (CDU in 2000) wrote, "In principle I support women's equality in society. . . . However, in combat zones women are in greater danger." Hohmann later joined the AfD when it was established; the AfD's social traditionalism and materialism are a better fit for Hohmann's position as he expressed it here. Seven PDS members wrote to clarify that they opposed this amendment of 12a, because it did not clarify that *neither men nor* women could be required to serve. Christine Schenk (PDS) alone spoke in the October 28, 2000, debate, identifying herself as a supporter of the 12a amendment, in contrast with her PDS colleagues. Schenk explained, "I wish there were no such thing as armies—but as long as they exist, access must be the same regardless of sex, skin color, sexual orientation, or religious affiliation" (Ich wünschte mir, es gäbe keine Armeen, aber solange es sie gibt, muss der Zugang unabhängig vom Geschlecht, von der Hautfarbe, von der sexuellen Orientierung oder der Religionszugehörigkeit möglich sein).[29]

Several individual B90/Gr legislators diverged from their party group by not supporting the amendment; Antje Vollmer, Steffi Lemke, and Franziska Eichstädt-Bohlig submitted a short statement on their position, explaining that there is "women's underrepresentation across almost all areas of society . . . and fixing these inequalities is much more important than women's inclusion in combat." These individual B90/Gr legislators were prioritizing their postmaterialism over the egalitarianism we might otherwise expect.[30]

Ultimately, the Basic Law was amended to read: "Women cannot be *forced* to perform armed military service" (emphasis added). In sum, the FDP—at the intersection of economic liberalism and social progressivism—consistently supported women's inclusion in combat. The SPD and B90/Gr, coalition partners in the 1998–2002 legislative term when these debates took place, needed to transform their positions in order to implement the ECJ's ruling, and they did so with an emphasis on workplace equity.

The CDU and CSU only grudgingly accommodated the expansion of women in combat. Although not in the governing coalition circa 2000, the CDU/CSU party group nonetheless could not simply oppose responding to the ECJ ruling as the PDS could. Until the ECJ's ruling became clear, the CDU/CSU's social traditionalism, materialism, and relative hegemonic-ethnic supremacy corresponded with unequivocal opposition to transforming the German armed forces. After the ruling, the CDU/CSU shifted to reframing the issue in terms of reforms to the armed forces that would modernize and improve it. The AfD had not yet been formed at the time when these debates took place. However, patterns across party groups in the Bundestag suggest that, unchecked by an obligation to govern, the AfD's social traditionalism, materialism, and hegemonic-ethnic supremacy would have yielded an outright inability to reframe the matter of women's inclusion in combat roles.

The End of Compulsory Military Service (2010–2011)

Previous sections addressed opening the armed forces to women in Germany. This was a policy change forced on the government, externally applied by the European justice system, because Germany's categorical exclusion of women was ruled unreasonably broad and, therefore, not in compliance with the European Union's nondiscrimination directives. In being forced to implement the *Kreil v. Germany* ruling, most German political parties worked to reframe what inclusion in combat roles meant for Germans and for Germany.

The military's symbolic and material value place it at the center of the state's identity for many countries. As discussed earlier in this chapter, this centrality has coexisted, in Germany and elsewhere, with women's exclusion from both full citizenship (particularly in periods before women's suffrage) and participation in the role of protecting the community. When women can join in playing the role of defender, what happens to the symbolism of the armed forces? Answering this question continues to follow the thread of whether and how political actors' ideological commitments help us understand their engagement in the politics of equality.

The party group that most grudgingly reframed this policy matter was the CDU/CSU. In the face of declining volunteers, the defense minister Karl-Theodor zu Guttenberg (CSU), in 2010, proposed reducing the *Wehrdienst* period to six months.[31] However, pressure from other parties was applied to eliminate it entirely. Thus, the CDU/CSU/FDP government presented the draft law *Wehrrechtsänderungsgesetz* (WehrRÄndG 2011) to the Bundestag in December 2010.[32] In March 2011, it passed with the support of the CDU/CSU, FDP, and B90/Gr, opposed by the SPD and the LINKE (see Figure 7.2).[33] These votes reflect that both political actors opposed to militarism and compulsory military service and those who remained committed to an armed forces supported this bill.

Reforming compulsory military service had been on the table for some time, so the CDU/CSU's proposal was not exclusively about resymbolizing the armed forces in light of women's participation. However, an examination of Bundestag debates on the matter offer another window into interparty differences and dynamics.

The March 2011 Bundestag plenary debate on the WehrRÄndG was the final opportunity for policymakers to voice positions and subsequently to vote on the act reforming compulsory military service, altering it into a draft for emergencies rather than an obligation for all German men. In his remarks

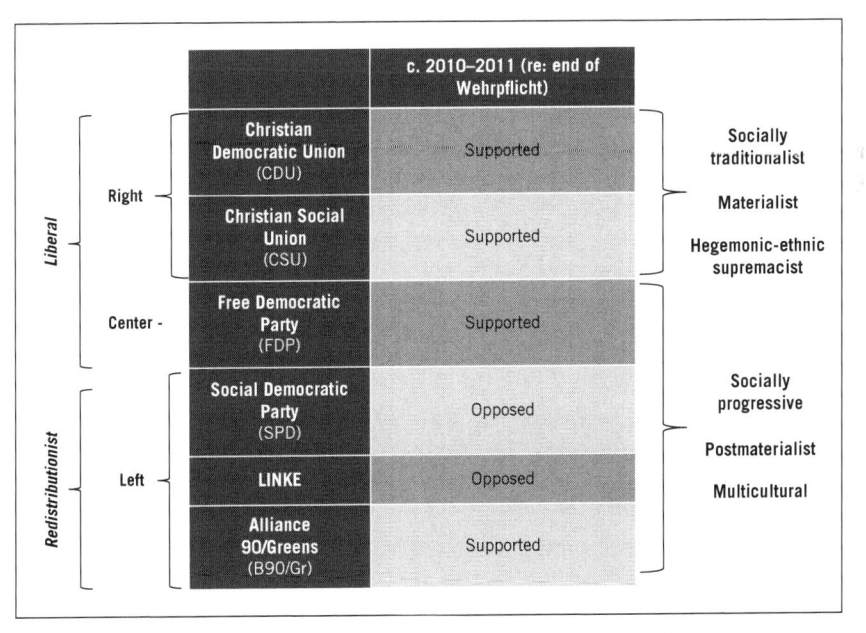

		c. 2010–2011 (re: end of Wehrpflicht)	
Liberal / Right	Christian Democratic Union (CDU)	Supported	Socially traditionalist
	Christian Social Union (CSU)	Supported	Materialist
Center -	Free Democratic Party (FDP)	Supported	Hegemonic-ethnic supremacist
Redistributionist / Left	Social Democratic Party (SPD)	Opposed	Socially progressive
	LINKE	Opposed	Postmaterialist
	Alliance 90/Greens (B90/Gr)	Supported	Multicultural

Figure 7.2 German political parties' orientations toward ending the *Wehrpflicht*.

opening this debate, CDU minister of defense Thomas de Maizière emphasized that the legislation they were discussing affirmatively implemented a voluntary armed forces—it did not simply remove compulsory service ("Ich wiederhole: Wir reden nicht nur über die Aussetzung der Wehrpflicht, wir reden gleichzeitig über die Einführung eines neuen freiwilligen Wehrdienstes").[34] In line with the CDU's greater materialism, Minister de Maizière's comments emphasized the ways in which a reformed military would better support national security: "Our country needs armed forces that are modern, powerful, and effective" (Unser Land braucht Streitkräfte, die modern, leistungsstark, [und] wirksam . . . sind).[35] He even argued that a military staffed through compulsory service was no longer justified for national security ("Eine Wehrpflichtarmee lässt sich erstens sicherheitspolitisch nicht mehr begründen").[36]

Figure 7.2 indicates that the SPD was opposed to the government coalition's proposal. In the March 2011 Bundestag debate, Hans-Peter Bartels (SPD) expressed his party's frustration at how the governing coalition in the previous legislative term (2005–2009; also helmed by the CDU/CSU party group) had rejected an SPD proposal to end compulsory military service, only to propose this later.[37] After expressing this frustration, Bartels added that the SPD would not be supporting the CDU/CSU's proposal, because its implementation was unclear; he specified further that the SPD did not want a poorly executed reform to leave Germany's armed forces unable to manage unforeseen events in the future.[38] Heckling from various other party groups followed. Later, Lars Klingbeil (SPD) accused the governing coalition of not having done their homework ("Hier haben Sie Ihre Hausaufgaben nicht gemacht").[39] SPD speakers' critiques, borne out in legislators' voting on the legislation, are potentially surprising without the added observation that they could decline to support it without endangering its passage; the CDU/CSU and FDP (coalition partners in the government) had written the bill, and the B90/Gr joined them, valuing the end compulsory military service as a step toward disarmament (evincing postmaterialism). Unlike their fellow coalition members, FDP speakers in this debate emphasized the rights of individual men not to be conscripted. In Christoph Schnurr's (FDP) words: "Compulsory military service is a massive intrusion on the fundamental rights of young men" (Die Wehrpflicht ist ein massiver Eingriff in die Grundrechte junger Männer).[40]

Finally, the LINKE opposed the government coalition's proposal, arguing that it set up the potential for a privileged occupational class of soldiers, in addition to falling short of the extent of demilitarization that the LINKE endorsed. Paul Schäfer (LINKE), asserted, "It must be absolutely unambiguous: national defense, yes; economic warfare, no. Enough" (Es muss definitiv klargestellt werden: Landesverteidigung ja, Wirtschaftskriege nein. Basta).[41]

Taken together, positions on ending compulsory military service—Heuss's "legitimate child of democracy"—do not clearly array left-right along any ideological dimension. Instead, political parties' positions can be located at the intersection between their broader attitudes toward armed conflict and how they framed the needs of national security. The content of the WehrRÄndG 2011 did "too much" for some parties and "not enough" for others. The one ideological dimension that differentiates among parties and is reflected in position taking in the March 2011 debate is social traditionalism, in the form of nostalgia about the value of service. Speakers from the CDU/CSU worked to advance reforms of the Bundeswehr in terms of the armed forces' effectiveness while still depicting service in masculinist terms. For example, Ingo Gädechens (CDU), himself a career soldier in the Bundeswehr, spoke about citizens' obligations to the state: "The state does not just give you things; it also demands things. It demands that many otherwise different men are ready to fulfill their duty in service to the state and to democracy" (Dieser Staat gibt dir nicht nur etwas, sondern er verlangt auch etwas. Er verlangte von gemusterten Männern, dass sie bereit waren, ihre Wehrpflicht abzuleisten.... Man muss bereit sein, diesem Staat zu dienen, ihn notfalls zu verteidigen, damit nicht nur die Demokratie geschützt wird, sondern auch die Gesellschaft solidarisch und mit dem notwendigen Zusammenhalt existieren kann).[42]

Ten years later, the Bundeswehr is an all-enlistees professional armed forces. It includes women, though at low rates. It is a very different armed forces in many senses compared to its 1955 origins.

Placing *Kreil v. Germany* in Broader Context

Policy changes that opened combat roles to women took place within a broader historical trajectory of German nationality and citizenship laws. This context brings into focus the significance of *Kreil v. Germany*. The trajectory of citizenship laws in German evinces the persistence of the status quo and, simultaneously, repeated reversions to earlier legal frameworks on the multiple occasions when the German state has reestablished itself after crisis. This longer history frames this chapter's conclusion: opening previously narrowly defined roles and statuses (warrior; citizen) precipitated parties' efforts to reframe them.

Citizenship Status in the German Empire

The term in Germany for citizenship/nationality is *Staatsangehörigkeit*, literally "belonging to the state."[43] This term is used rather than *Staatsbürgerschaft*, which more directly translates to "citizenship" as a legal status associated with specific rights and privileges. *Bürger* is the German term for a person with political and legal rights, etymologically deriving from *Burg* for castle (that is, an earlier form of political community in the environs of a castle or fortress, a subset of whose residents had legal standing) (Hettling 2022). English-language analysis of citizenship laws in Germany often uses the term *nationality*. Because its emphasis is on legal status, this chapter generally uses the English term *citizenship*. However, following common practice in studies of German law, it translates the *Staatsangehörigkeitsgesetz* as the Nationality Act. When the discussion is focused on orientations toward who belongs in the German polity as a full and equal member, the term *nationality* may be used.

Germany's unification in approximately its modern form dates to 1871. At this time, the German state of Prussia headed an empire that included the regions of the current *Bundesländer* as well as much of modern Poland. The earliest frameworks for legal status as a German citizen, therefore, comprise a *Reichsangehörigkeitsgesetz* (membership in the empire), and they specify that *Angehörigkeit* (membership) in a *Land* within the empire corresponds with *Angehörigkeit* in the empire. These laws define the citizenship of women explicitly in terms of their fathers and husbands, and their children's citizenship is defined in terms of the children's fathers. Further, these citizenship laws conflated German descent with German legal status.

Germany as a political system started anew multiple times over the course of the twentieth century, and, at the time of these "re-foundings," the form and content of citizenship laws have repeatedly returned to the imperial legal framework. The German Empire is typically dated 1871–1918. Within this time frame, laws regarding inclusion in and exclusion from the German polity included the *Reichsangehörigkeitsgesetz* (dated 1871); and the Nationality Act (1913). The end of World War I in Germany dovetailed with a civil war that yielded the Weimar Republic, where the 1913 Nationality Act continued to apply. Across this time frame of significant political and social change in Germany, citizenship remained grounded in shared German ethnic identity (i.e., the idea of a *Volksgeist*) (Safran 1997, pp. 320–321).

Subsequently, the Nazi regime (1933–1945) interpreted "Germanness" yet more narrowly, in terms of racial status and heteronormativity, forcibly revoking the citizenship status of groups including Jews, Roma, and Communists. The principal legal move in this direction was implemented early in the Nazi regime: the Law on the Revocation of Naturalizations and the Deprivation of German Citizenship (July 1933). Although heteronormative persons did not have citizenship revoked in this law, many were persecuted and incarcerated with perceived ethnic minorities. The revocation of various social groups' citizenship reached its apex with the Holocaust, the Nazi regime's genocide of Jews, of non-Aryans, and of dissidents. This legacy motivated the FRG, in 1949, to revert back to pre-Nazi legal frameworks, including the text of the 1913 Nationality Act (analogous to the country's reversion to the 1900 Civil Code). Over the five decades that followed, a series of amendments largely focused on whether and how a woman's marital status and her spouse's nationality affected her legal status and the legal status of her children.

Post–World War II legal changes that expanded citizenship access in Germany specifically sought to facilitate the repatriation of Germans targeted by the Nazi regime's genocide or otherwise displaced during the course of the 1933–1946 period. Article 116 of the Basic Law has, since its adoption in 1949, permitted repatriation of Germans whose citizenship was revoked by the Nazi regime, and to some degree this has applied to their descendants. This pathway to citizenship was expanded, in 2021, to include a wider range of situations, such as individuals (and their descendants) who fled Germany for their safety and acquired another citizenship before having German citizenship forcibly revoked, as well as others who resided in Germany, in 1933, without citizenship and were forced to flee.

At the same time, "non-Germans" have faced categorical exclusion from citizenship for the entirety of the twentieth century. In spite of this, the immigration of "non-Germans" into Germany was expressly a matter of national labor policy in the form of a guest worker program (*Gastarbeiterprogramm*), launched in 1955, which brought millions of mostly Southern Europeans to address labor shortages as the economy expanded postwar.[44] As Partridge (2012) writes, the very name of the program expressed "futures constructed in terms of limited stays" (p. 30). In subsequent decades, immigration into Germany from many regions of the world has expanded, and migrants from diverse sending countries have all struggled for political leverage in the context of narrow pathways to citizenship. Florvil (2020), for example, writes about Black German women's mobilization, emphasizing that many of these efforts have needed to take place well beyond formal politics.

In part because of the contradictions associated with this labor policy, the question of expanding citizenship access in Germany is often framed exclusively in terms of race-ethnicity (i.e., with an emphasis on Germany's persistent jus sanguinis). However, "even" German ethnic women legally lost citizenship through marriage to a noncitizen for much of the twentieth century, while German ethnic men, by contrast, lost their legal status through acquisition of another nationality. Gendered exclusion on the basis of family relationships, which differentially affected women and men, was largely absent from citizenship debates. As Rürup (2016) writes, "This legal inequity for married women was not among the most urgent debates" (pp. 412–413). One of the reasons for this was that "transfer of citizenship" was understood to be "through *patrilineal* ethnic membership" (p. 417, emphasis added). Very limited policy change addressed this in the immediate postwar period. In 1953, the *Reichs- und Staatsangehörigkeitsgesetz* (RuStAG) was amended so that women did not automatically lose German citizenship through marriage to a noncitizen, and, in 1957, the Bundestag adopted the Law on the Equality of Men and Women's Civil Rights, which included provisions regarding the acquisition and loss of women's citizenship through marriage or divorce (see discussion in Rürup 2016, pp. 418–419).

The establishment of the guest worker program in 1955 introduced new dimensions to this question of belonging. Between 1955 and the program's end in 1973 (the *Anwerbestopp* at the time of the 1973 oil crisis), German policymakers expected migrant laborers to return to their countries of origin, obviating the need for conversations about integration or extended residency. Subsequently, debates focused on whether and how it was possible for Migrationshintergrund residents to integrate into German society, with most policymakers agreeing that it was not possible. Initially in this period, migrants into Germany were disproportionately men, but regulations evolved to allow family members to join them after one year's residency (Martin 1981, pp. 35–36). Employers did not want to lose workers they had just trained, and they pressured the German government to allow them to stay longer than originally envisioned (Triadafilopoulos 2012, p. 3).

It was not until the 1980s that serious efforts to expand pathways to citizenship for non-German ethnics began, and it was only in the 1990s that enough political actors had come to view migrant-background populations as "here to stay" for these efforts to find success. The landmark 2000 Nationality Act represents the most significant shift in German citizenship laws, because it departs from strong inclusion/exclusion principles grounded in jus sanguinis (Hailbronner and Farahat 2015). Debates in the 1980s and 1990s leading up to this landmark act, and parties' positions taking in these debates, are the focus of the following discussion.

German Citizenship Debates in the 1980s and 1990s

H. Williams (2011) argues that the broader conversation about both immigration and *Volksgeist* needed to change "from widespread statements that Germany was not a country of immigration... to open acceptance that it is a country of immigration" before significant revisions to German citizenship laws were possible (p. 95). These changes did not happen spontaneously. Instead, several forces converged. Voices in favor of expanding citizenship access persisted and got louder—reinforced by the 1992 Maastricht Treaty, which established European citizenship and thereby legally forced some measure of jus soli on countries like Germany with more restrictive rules (Crepaz 2008, pp. 208–209). Political actors' orientations across these debates are not consistently explained by their left-right categories, and otherwise ideologically similar parties diverged from one another for other reasons.

On the one hand, many political parties' orientations toward both immigration policy and citizenship eligibility remained largely the same over the post–World War II period. The CDU and CSU have been opposed to birthright citizenship consistently; as L. Murray (1994) shows, the CDU/CSU's position in the 1980s was to encourage migrants to return to their sending countries. By contrast, the FDP proposed liberalizing citizenship laws without favoring birthright citizenship in the 1980s, but these policies did not find support with their governing coalition partner the CDU/CSU (L. Murray 1994, p. 26). In 1989, the Greens proposed citizenship rights to anyone who had resided in Germany for at least five years (Anil 2005, p. 462).

Given consistent support for greater inclusion among members of the Greens (later B90/Gr) and the FDP, the "fulcrum" for these debates was the SPD. The SPD proposed birthright (jus soli) citizenship in 1985, 1988, 1989, and 1993, and they did so from the opposition; the SPD held the chancellorship between 1969–1982[45] and then not again until 1998. However, even while some voices within the SPD clearly supported increasing accessibility, others emphatically resisted it (Anil 2005). Not only were more open citizenship laws not perceived to be electorally successful, but very public statements by SPD leaders voiced opposition (L. Murray 1994, pp. 34–35). For example, Minister of the Interior Otto Schily (SPD)[46] asserted in November 1998 in an oft quoted line, "The bounds of Germany's capacity for immigration are overrun" (Die Grenze der Belastbarkeit Deutschlands durch Zuwanderung ist überschritten; quoted in Rimscha 2001).

Political parties' orientations toward citizenship law reform in the 1980s–1990s did not map neatly onto left-right categories. At the center-right, the FDP was the earliest and most consistent proponent. Further, parties that supported expanding access did not necessarily support birthright citizenship specifically, and parties were divided on whether naturalized German citizens should be required to relinquish their previous nationality. As documented by Crepaz (2008), L. Murray (1994), and H. Williams (2011), debates in Germany largely focused on cultural differences that seemed to foreclose effective integration of "non-German" ethnic groups into broader German society.

Debate over Reforms to the Citizenship Act 1999
(Gesetz zur Reform des Staatsangehörigkeitsrechts)

The red-green coalition that came to power in 1998 under Gerhard Schröder proposed a faster track to citizenship for "non-Germans" that allowed dual citizenship (Anil 2005, p. 463). The CDU galvanized resistance to these reforms specifically in the state of Hessen, where state parliamentary elections had the potential to (and did) change the SPD-B90/Gr coalition's leverage within the Bundesrat for significant policy change. These anti-reform efforts in Hessen successfully foreclosed the government coalition's ability to enact policy change without buy-in from additional parties. Thus, the SPD and B90/Gr collaborated with the FDP.[47] The FDP did not want to allow dual citizenship, and the party's support was conditional on its removal from the proposal. The vote on the Reforms to the Citizenship Act (*Gesetz zur Reform des Staatsangehörigkeitsrechts*) took place on May 7, 1999, with 365 votes in favor, 182 votes opposed, and 39 abstentions.[48] Most members of the CDU and CSU voted no, as did two members of the PDS: Carsten Hübner and Ulla Jelpke. Hübner and Jelpke submitted to the plenary protocol their explanation that they viewed the 1999 Citizenship Act as actually making it more difficult for some people to seek citizenship, due to the language requirements.[49] Abstentions from the CDU/CSU explained their position with an emphasis on the need for citizenship law reform to more stringently require a commitment to, and integration in, Germany. In particular, they viewed potential allowances for dual citizenship to be too vague, making it difficult to predict its effects.[50] In sum: legislators' votes were not structured by a clear left-right dimensions.

Ultimately, Alba (2005) describes the 1999–2000 Citizenship Act as "provisional birthright citizenship" for second-generation German residents, because "the new citizenship law that came into force in 2000 required applicants for naturalization to renounce their existing nationality" (Faist 2015, p. 2000). Debates and policy changes in subsequent decades have adjusted restrictions on dual nationality, among other matters.

Interpreting Parties' Capacity to Evolve

Taken together, this discussion has identified enduring commitments in Germany both to a narrowly defined *Volksgeist* and to patriarchy, which largely transcend left-right political axes. Political parties of many ideological flavors have resisted the political incorporation of women, ethnic minorities, and ethnic-minority women. When forced to participate in policy change, whether by electoral pressure or because of European Union directives, many German parties have worked to reframe their orientations to maintain an illusion of continuity. In the case of women's inclusion in the Bundeswehr, this extended to the end of compulsory military service and the transformation of its meaning in German citizenship.

The primary contribution of this analysis is that parties' broader context significantly constrains their varying capacities for reframing fundamental democratic issues of political inclusion. German political parties' orientations toward expanding access to citizenship evolved alongside, and intertwined with, other debates about the community of political equals. Much work in political science argues that expansion of the electorate—a by-product of making citizenship access more inclusive—is a rational issue for political parties: when a party perceives that this expansion will benefit them, they support it. However, simultaneously, parties have ideological commitments that inform whether and how they (1) circumscribe women's citizenship by their relationships with others and (2) define nationality in racial-ethnic terms. Some parties view expanding the electorate to "others" as fundamentally at odds with their understanding of the state.

Over the entirety of the twentieth century, many otherwise divergent voices in Germany shared the sentiment that theirs was "not a country of immigration" (kein Einwanderungsland).[51] Simultaneously, and without similar fanfare, women were consistently afforded different parameters for citizenship access. Policy change became possible only when an arrangement of parties in the governing coalition (the SPD and B90/Gr) together supported a version of jus soli, with the FDP—a longtime supporter of expanding citizenship access—in the opposition. This is an account of policy change that conforms to left-right categories only if we ignore nearly a century of widely shared hegemonic-ethnic supremacy.

Die Innere Führung

The FRG did not have an armed forces in the decade following the end of World War II. As Cold War tensions increased, European and international attention to re-establishing a German military also grew. However, these conversations included significant concern about rearming the primary aggressor of World War II.

Historian Donald Abenheim writes that contemporaneous, 1950s-era explanations for the end of the Weimar Republic (1918–1933) blamed the institutions and key leaders of the military. On this basis, postwar policymakers prioritized the preservation of democratic principles in organizing and training the new Bundeswehr. Their prioritization of democratic principles required dismantling long-held military traditions that dated to the imperial *Reichswehr*, such as raising toasts to Kaiser Wilhelm, and replacing them with new practices and principles (Abenheim 1988, p. 90). This preoccupation with establishing a nonmilitaristic military mirrored other efforts by postwar framers of the FRG's political institutions to heed the lessons of history.

Motivated by these concerns, the FRG's new Bundeswehr implemented a new leadership philosophy, called the *Innere Führung*, which literally means "inner command," or "conduct."[52] Scholars and practitioners translate this phrase into English in varying ways, such as "leadership development and civic education." Kutz (2003) argues that this translation is too brief, offering instead the following: "Military leadership and conduct within a society where military forces, under civilian control, are democratically accountable to society as a whole" (p. 109). Officer training is organized around this idea of social and democratic accountability. Substantively, it denotes a specific alternative to nationalist and antidemocratic impulses within the armed forces. Writing in 2016, Bernzen, Peddinghaus, and Sieger argue that it "describes the identity of a responsible and constructively critical soldier," with the aim of "[reconciling] the functional conditions of operational armed forces with the liberal principles of a democratic constitutional state."

Building democratic accountability into the cornerstone of a national military is unusual, but it represents broader efforts in postwar West Germany to avoid repeating past mistakes. The critical proponent of this philosophy in the early 1950s was a member of the federal office tasked with planning German rearmament, Wolf Graf von Baudissin, a former officer of the Nazi regime's *Wehrmacht*.[53] Accounts of his military service during World War II indicate that he viewed the German military as having enabled Hitler. This included support of the attempted overthrow of Hitler on July 10, 1944 (Kutz 2003, p. 113).

Baudissin's philosophy was to place democratic values at the center of Germany's armed forces. Other FRG framers shared this prioritization of the protection of fundamental political and social rights; then minister of defense Theodor Blank and then *Bundespräsident* Theodor Heuss, for example, similarly underscored the need for "citizens in uniform." Heuss viewed "universal" compulsory military service as a vital component of achieving a democratic armed forces. Conscription into a military guided by democratic principles would, it was argued, "[ensure] that the military reflects all elements of society."[54] However, Heuss and others implicitly omitted from "all elements of society" the half of the population received as women, and they omitted members of social groups who were received as non-German.

Contemporary commenters about the future of the *Innere Führung* express anxiety about its continued relevance in changing times. For instance, Koltermann (2012) and others speculate that the shift to an all-volunteer force further weakens the connections between broader German society and the military (p. 19). However, simultaneously, the Bundeswehr is experiencing its most significant postwar expansion in response to Russia's 2022 invasion of Ukraine. The German military is both larger and more diverse in a global context of democratic backsliding. Indeed, recent years have seen a rise in antisystem activities within the Bundeswehr, too, raising alarm. Since 2008, the Military Counterintelligence Service (Militärischer Abschirmdienst; MAD) has identified several hundred soldiers engaged in "anticonstitutional activities," including using Nazi symbols and keeping World War II–era

Wehrmacht souvenirs such as helmets (Knight 2017). In 2019, MAD was investigating 450 suspected members of the Identitarian and *Reichsbürger* movements, respectively (Deutsche Welle 2019). These movements are essentially hegemonic-ethnic supremacist in their ideology. Thus, the contemporary Bundeswehr is paradoxically achieving greater democratic inclusion at the same time as the organization itself incubates antisystem attitudes. At this time, the military arguably needs a renewed commitment to the centrality of democratic principles, not a new leadership philosophy.

8

Political Parties across the OECD

Introduction

Angela Merkel of Germany's CDU and Marine Le Pen of France's National Rally (previously the National Front) are both women party leaders "on the right." Conventional wisdom suggests that women occupy complicated roles "on the right." However, simultaneously, most commentators and political scientists would not view Germany's CDU and France's National Rally or their leaders Merkel and Le Pen, respectively, as comparably right-leaning. In another example, a focus on the categories of "left" and "right" in Israel's party system simultaneously misses important within-country variation and makes it more difficult to understand the political behavior of Israel's ethnic minorities, in particular in global context.[1] In short, the ubiquitous labels of "left," "center," and "right" have significant limitations when thinking comparatively. This book argues that such apparent puzzlers are better interpreted with attention to finer-grained features of political parties, in their social and institutional contexts.

Thus, this chapter turns its attention to global variation between political parties, nested within their divergent cultural settings and institutional arrangements. To what extent do findings from contemporary Germany apply to other advanced-industrial political systems, and what else can we learn by juxtaposing parties across these settings? This chapter addresses these questions by looking at the 281 political parties holding national legislative seats in the member states of the OECD in 2017. These cross-national analyses address theoretical expectations about the importance of wider institutional and ideological context for understanding variation between otherwise similar political parties, and they affirm the expectation that finer-grained ideological dimensions vary in their significance across political systems.

This chapter's analyses show that the salience of left-right ideological categories is variable across the OECD. Broadly, left-leaning parties are relatively consistent across political systems in their advocacy and actions on behalf of gender and intersectional equality. By contrast, parties categorized as "on the right" vary cross-nationally in their promotion of women's rights and interests, and their variation is associated with system-wide variables, such as aggregate attitudes toward gender equality. Finally, a category of parties situated at the center, comprising 18 percent of the political parties in this cross-national dataset, showcase the importance of looking at finer-grained ideological measures. A single-dimensional arrangement obscures significant variation at the center, with particular relevance for those parties' support of proequality policies.

The most striking finding from these cross-national analyses is that a supportive pro-gender-equality context is especially influential on that subset of parties whose reputation for promoting women's rights is poor. Parties that are conventionally left-leaning in various senses are relatively consistent cross-nationally in their commitments to gender and intersectional equality. Conventionally right-leaning parties function differently depending on the setting.

At the same time, as in the case of Germany, rates of advocacy for the rights and interests of marginalized groups in society are low across parties around the world. Conventionally left-leaning parties are not particularly more active in protecting minority rights than their counterparts on the right, regardless of their reputation. Instead, we can discern patterns in parties' *active opposition* to preserving minority groups' rights. The distinguishing features of these parties are their greater (1) materialism and (2) hegemonic-ethnic supremacy. This finding is hardly surprising, as disinterest in protecting minority rights is part and parcel of hegemonic-ethnic supremacy, in particular. Although this finding is intuitive, parties widely viewed as "left," "right," and "center" are all less supportive of minority rights if they exhibit greater materialism and hegemonic-ethnic supremacy compared to their otherwise similar postmaterialist and multiculturalist counterparts.

These findings amplify two messages. First, ideological categories of "left" and "right" do not function cross-nationally to the degree that political science relies on them. Second, disrupting these expectations can improve our understanding of a fundamental issue in the practice of democracy: the inclusion in political and public decision-making of historically excluded social groups. The political, social, and economic incorporation of these groups is more successful when system-wide commitments (not individual parties) support it. A final section in this chapter profiles the country of Chile and its party system in order to illustrate the limitations of standard left-right categories for understanding many important issues.

What Can We Learn from the OECD?

Empirically, this chapter's cross-national analysis covers the thirty-five member states of the OECD in 2017.[2] The analyses of these countries make several important contributions to this book's overall argument. First, while the usage of the terms "left" and "right" is global, these ubiquitous clusters are ideologically diverse, even within a single political system. Cross-national comparisons comprise a harder test, yet, for these ideological categories. Further, the focus of preceding chapters was the single case of Germany, which is not necessarily representative of the wider advanced industrial political world. Testing theoretical expectations globally is an important counterpart to the single country analysis that comprises much of the rest of this book.

Second, attention to the varied membership of the OECD addresses several alternative, contextual explanations for variation in political parties' advocacy for historically marginalized groups. Although all OECD member states share a broad commitment to economic development as a precursor to many desirable outcomes, the OECD's Convention (signed December 14, 1960) does not specify democratic norms such as protection of minority groups' rights. This 1960 founding document mentions the concept of liberty just once, in its opening preambular clause, asserting that "economic strength and prosperity are essential for the attainment of the purposes of the United Nations, the preservation of individual liberty and the increase of general well-being." It does not mention gender or sex, race or ethnicity, indigeneity, or poverty. Member states of the OECD, and the political parties operating within these systems, are not even symbolically concerned about or committed to addressing specific problems experienced by historically marginalized groups. This leaves ample space for parties to differentiate themselves, within a shared context of relatively high levels of economic development. (See Table 8.1.)

In addition, political systems' institutional form and function vary across the OECD, which makes it possible to discern the salience of wider context for variation among parties. This book theorizes that features of the political setting matter for whether, which, and how ideological clusters of political parties engage in promoting the rights and interests of women and marginalized subgroups of women. Contextually, widely held social attitudes toward traditional gender roles vary across these countries. The structure of these party systems also varies, and the political parties within these divergent settings express a range of ideologies. Institutionally, some countries have legislated or constitutionally mandated gender quotas; in other countries, some but not all, political parties have voluntarily adopted such quotas (Weeks 2022). The single OECD country with a quota for ethnic minorities is Aotearoa/New Zealand, where there are reserved seats in the Parliament for Maori New Zealanders (Hughes 2011). Finally, OECD countries are widely studied in comparative politics, allowing this cross-national analysis both to benefit from and add to a variety of existing datasets.

Figure 8.1 plots political parties across these thirty-five systems in terms of two aggregate measures: the average percentage of women elected by par-

TABLE 8.1 VARIATION ACROSS THE OECD				
Contextual Variable	Mean	Std. Dev.	Min	Max
Presence of a national gender quota *(proportion of countries)*	0.371	0.490	0	1
Women's labor force participation (%)	54.0%	7.40	32.6	73.2
National survey respondents supportive of gender equality in public life (%)	66.9%	20.4	19.7	93.5
Effective number of parties	4.040	1.500	1.980	7.820
Control of plenary agenda* *(1–7; 1 = government determines agenda, 7 = chamber determines agenda)*	3.706	1.649	1	7

* Döring's (1995) data on control of the plenary agenda includes data for a subset of seventeen European countries, not for all OECD member states. See Appendix E.

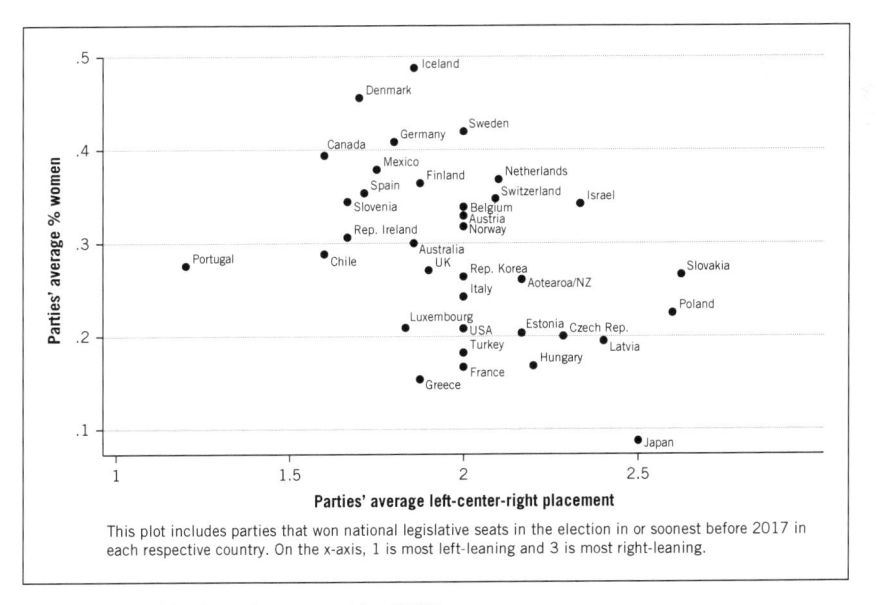

Figure 8.1 Political parties across the OECD.

ties in each country, and parties' average left-center-right placement in terms of their party families (see discussion of variables in subsequent sections). This figure offers an initial global snapshot of variation in parties' ideological placement and their success in a key area of women's political incorporation.

Parties' Ideological Commitments and Proequality Activities: Data and Methods

Cross-National Measures of Parties' Ideological Characteristics

This chapter's analyses examine the 281 parties or party groups across the OECD for 2017. In order to examine the usefulness and limitations of left-center-right categories for understanding variation in these parties' proequality activities and stances, parties are parsed in four different ways:

1. Party families (communist, social democratic, ecology/green, liberal, agrarian, conservative, Christian democratic, right wing; *sources:* Comparative Political Dataset [CPDS] and ParlGov)
2. Left, center, and right categories (based on their party families; *source:* the Database of Political Institutions)
3. An aggregate, continuous left-right measure (*source:* ParlGov)
4. Four dichotomous, finer-grained ideological left-right categories (economically redistributionist or liberal, socially progressive or traditionalist, postmaterialist or materialist, and multiculturalist or hegemonic-ethnic supremacist; *sources:* ParlGov, V-Dem)

This section discusses data collection on these parties' characteristics across the OECD. The level of detail in this discussion is important for several reasons, which is why it is not relegated to an appendix at the back of the book. At this book's heart is the contention that we must consistently view parties' ideological dimensions with greater complexity. A challenge to testing the implications of this complexity cross-nationally is that many existing datasets do not do so in the way this book argues we should. This chapter's imputations for missing data are discussed and rationalized in the following paragraphs, because they diverge from standard practices in comparative politics.

First, party family categorizations are drawn from ParlGov and from the CPDS. A small number of parties are missing from ParlGov and the CPDS, and these parties' family placements are imputed on the basis of their party programs (see Appendix E for additional details). Second, parties are categorized as left, center, or right on the basis of these families. Left-center-right designations for party families follow the Database of Political Institutions' definitions, where left is "communist, socialist, social democratic, or left-wing," center is "when party position can best be described as centrist (e.g., party advocates strengthening private enterprise in a social-liberal context)," and right is "conservative, Christian democratic, or right-wing" (Database of Political Institutions 2015 Codebook, 8). The eight agrarian parties in this dataset are coded as centrist, unless indicated otherwise. Third, ParlGov's aggregate, continuous left-right measure (used in earlier chapters on Germany) offers extensive coverage of most parties, excepting parties in Chile, Mexico, the Republic of Korea, and the United States.

Finer-grained ideological dimensions draw from varied sources, as follows. The redistributionism/liberalism variable is anchored in the ParlGov dataset because it has the overall best coverage for parties across the OECD. Missing values (parties or country-parties not included in ParlGov) were filled with the comparable V-Dem variable. Ultimately, 257 parties have a value for their position on state intervention in the economy drawing from these widely used and well-regarded cross-national datasets (91.5 percent coverage of the 281 parties across these thirty-five countries). Recall that *liberal* in this use of the term refers specifically to a party's preference for both a free market and, more broadly, a smaller government footprint.

Earlier chapters of the book developed the theoretical case for distinguishing between social traditionalism and materialism. This distinction is a departure from other cross-national studies. Empirically, three widely used comparative parties' datasets conflate these two ideologies: ParlGov's *liberty/authority* variable, CHES's *GALTAN* variable, and V-Dem's *social liberalism-conservatism* variable are all defined essentially identically, collapsing together progressive social values with libertarianism:

> "Libertarian" or "postmaterialist" parties [ParlGov and CHES] or those with liberal values [V-Dem] favor expanded personal freedoms, for example, on abortion rights, same-sex marriage, and democratic participation. Those with conservative values reject these ideas in favor of order, tradition and stability, believing that government should be a firm moral authority on social and cultural issues.[3]

The distinction between social traditionalism and materialism is important for understanding variation in advocacy for historically marginalized social groups, because these two ideological dimensions correspond with distinctive theoretical expectations. What CHES, ParlGov, and V-Dem term "liberal" or "libertarian" consists of opposition to state intervention in individuals' social lives, but this extends to inaction that may maintain social traditional norms. For example, inaction on or opposition to building childcare infrastructure is a liberal/libertarian position, at the same time as it has the effect of maintaining the social status quo; it does not expand personal freedoms for women who are traditionally responsible for childcare within the home. Previous chapters focused on contemporary Germany showed the usefulness of this conceptual distinction empirically. Cross-national analyses further highlight the significance of a political party's simultaneous *social traditionalism* with *postmaterialism*.

Distinguishing between social traditionalism and materialism is accomplished empirically in the following ways. First, the postmaterialism/materialism variable (like redistributionism/liberalism, discussed earlier) is anchored in the ParlGov dataset due to overall country coverage, in the form of the variable *liberty/authority*. For some parties omitted from ParlGov, V-Party's *GALTAN* variable filled in missing data. Between these two sources, 232 political parties (82.6 percent of the dataset) have values for this variable. As noted, CHES, ParlGov, and V-Dem collapse together social progressivism and libertarianism. Here, this variable is used to capture materialism/postmaterialism (not social traditionalism/progressivism), because the *liberty/authority* and *GALTAN* definitions emphasize a party's stance on government intervention in society and in individuals' social lives more so than they emphasize the specific content or aim of intervention.

Lacking an existing cross-national dataset that differentiates between social traditionalism and materialism, social traditionalism is coded here as the party's family, that is, the party's placement into one of the following eight categories: communist, social democratic, ecology (i.e., green), liberal, agrarian, conservative, Christian democratic, or right wing. The rationale for this choice is that it optimizes (1) distinguishing this ideological dimension from postmaterialism/materialism, (2) use of widely available shared comparative data (party family is commonly included in cross-national datasets), and (3) the breadth of meaning that progressivism and traditionalism encompass. Social traditionalism was imputed from party family categories, creating a variable coded as follows: 0 = very socially progressive (ecology/green), 1 = socially progressive (communist, socialist, liberal, and agrarian), 2 = moderate middle (liberal, agrarian), 3 = socially traditionalist (Christian democratic), and 4 = very socially traditionalist (conservative, right wing). This approach to coding parties' social traditionalism presents trade-offs. For example, it means that the trichotomous left, center, and right categorization (shown in later sections) is derived from the social traditionalism measure. Later sections address the implications of this choice for statistical analyses.

Finally, as in chapters focused on Germany, the multiculturalist/hegemonic-ethnic supremacist variable is drawn from V-Party's "cultural superiority" measure. This provides coverage on 210 parties (74.7 percent of the dataset).

Some idiosyncrasies in the dataset remain. They require discussion here because they reflect not just on the practical availability of data but also on this book's contention that we need to conceptualize ideologies more expansively in order to study political parties and their priorities cross-nationally. Namely, this chapter does not impute data for Chilean political parties, because the Chilean party system is idiosyncratic compared to other systems both in terms of party groupings and shared lists (i.e., what denominator of seat share makes sense for calculating women's rates of election) and in terms of which ideological axes differentiate among parties. Omitting these Chilean political parties from the analysis does not mean that these parties are ideologically incoherent; indeed, they offer a ready case study of the limitations of standard left-right categories for many outcomes of interest. Thus, the Chilean party system receives closer attention at the end of the chapter in order to illustrate these kinds of limitations.

Table 8.2 shows variation in finer-grained ideological dimensions across these three categories of party families: left (communist, socialist, social democratic, or left wing), center ("party advocates strengthening private enterprise in a social-liberal context"), and right (conservative, Christian democratic, or right wing).

TABLE 8.2 THE IDEOLOGICAL FEATURES OF LEFT, CENTER, AND RIGHT PARTY FAMILIES IN THE OECD

Ideological Dimension*	Left Mean (Std. Dev.) Min/Max N	Center Mean (Std. Dev.) Min/Max N	Right Mean (Std. Dev.) Min/Max N
Economic Liberalism / Redistributionism	0.299 (0.126) 0.065 / 0.712 104	0.684 (0.178) 0.167 / 0.997 45	0.693 (0.147) 0.240 / 1 102
Social Progressivism / Traditionalism*	0.188 (0.108) 0 / 0.25 93	0.494 (0.039) 0.25 / 0.5 41	0.945 (0.104) 0.75 / 1 95
Postmaterialism / Materialism	0.284 (0.121) 0.058 / 0.658 93	0.436 (0.156) 0.180 / 0.854 41	0.757 (0.134) 0.367 / 1 95
Multiculturalism / Hegemonic-Ethnic Supremacy	0.218 (0.179) 0 / 0.688 85	0.352 (0.226) 0 / 1 37	0.581 (0.279) 0 / 1 85

* See explanation in the text. Parties' social traditionalism is measured in terms of their party families.

Contextual Variables

The purpose of this cross-national analysis is to discern the relative roles of context versus party characteristics. Therefore, statistical models of inter-party variation also include a range of country-level variables. Three of these directly address the book's theoretical expectations #7, #8, and #9, respectively:

- The effective number of political parties for the legislative election included in this dataset (*source*: Gallagher 1991)
- Parliament's authority to set the plenary agenda independent of government, measured as 1 = little authority (i.e., government has extensive agenda-setting powers) and 7 = full authority (*source*: Döring 1995)
- Survey data showing the extent of pro-gender-equality attitudes. This latter variable is measured as the percentage of survey respondents disagreeing or strongly disagreeing with the following statement: "When jobs are scarce, men should have more right to a job than women" (*sources*: World Values Survey, European Social Survey, Israel Democracy Institute)[4]

In addition to these explanatory variables of particular interest, models also include, as appropriate, controls that research has shown correlate with progress in the area of women's political representation (see literature review in Chapter 6):

- Whether there is a national gender quota rule (*source:* Global Database of Gender Quotas)
- The paid labor force participation of women fifteen-plus years of age (*source:* World Bank)[5]

Many cross-national statistical analyses of women's rates of election, in particular, include the mean district magnitude and whether electoral rules are proportional. These two latter variables are not included in models shown here, because both are highly correlated with a key explanatory variable of interest, effective number of parties. Research has clearly shown that higher district magnitude and proportional electoral rules help explain higher rates of women's election, but a political system's *effective number of parties* is a direct function of these two electoral institutions. The book's theoretical expectation #7 is expressed in terms of the number of parties, not in terms of the electoral institutions that shape that party system.

Dependent Variables

Political parties' commitments to advancing the rights and interests of historically marginalized social groups are measured four ways in this chapter:

1. The percentage of national legislative seats held by women in the party (percent)
2. Whether the party's chairperson is a woman (for jointly held leadership positions: whether *at least one of them* is a woman) (0/1)
3. The party platform's level of support for "measures that promote women's equal workforce participation" (0 = strongly opposes, 1 = strongly supports; a V-Party variable)
4. Party leadership's statements on protecting minority rights against majority preferences (0 = no commitment to protecting minority social groups' rights, 1 = strong commitment; a V-Party variable)

Earlier chapters on the case of Germany discussed the significance of parties' nomination and election of women as an indicator of their commitment to advancing gender equality. Broadly, parties on "the left" elect more women than on "the right," although these patterns are disrupted by many other factors at both the party and the national level. These chapters also discussed the wealth of research on institutional explanations for women's rates of election, in particular the role of the electoral system.

In terms of women's appointment as party leaders, previous research again shows that a variety of party-level and national-level factors correspond with variation across parties and across settings (O'Brien 2015; O'Brien and Rickne 2016). O'Brien (2015) finds that political parties in specific electoral conditions appoint women leaders at higher rates: small or opposition parties, and parties attempting to redress electoral losses. O'Brien and Rickne (2016) show that a candidate gender quota has the potential to increase women's leadership appointments when this quota expands the pool of potential appointees.

Finally, this chapter's analyses look at political parties' support for two key equality policies. Policies that support women in the workplace are varied. This V-Dem variable encompasses a range of supports, such as "legal provisions on equal treatment and pay, parental leave and financial support for child care" (Lührmann et al. 2020, V-Party codebook V1, p. 28). In turn, the measure of minority rights' protection is also a V-Dem variable: "How often should the will of the majority be implemented even if doing so would violate the rights of minorities?" (V-Party codebook V1, pp. 25–26).

Table 8.3 presents variation in parties' commitments to promoting the rights and interests of women and minoritized social groups, across three

TABLE 8.3 PROEQUALITY ACTIVITIES: COMPARING PARTY FAMILIES ACROSS THE OECD*

	Women's rates of election** Mean (Std. Dev.) N	Women in party leadership positions*** Mean (Std. Dev.) N	Support for women in the workplace policies† Mean (Std. Dev.) N	Prioritization of protecting minority social group rights‡ Mean (Std. Dev.) N
Left Parties	0.348 (0.211) 108	0.325 (0.470) 105	0.882 (0.102) 66	0.820 (0.142) 66
Center Parties	0.321 (0.205) 46	0.196 (0.401) 46	0.781 (0.206) 33	0.800 (0.207) 33
Right Parties	0.217 (0.170) 102	0.162 (0.370) 99	0.653 (0.190) 71	0.633 (0.262) 71
Total	0.291 (0.203) 256	0.236 (0.425) 250	0.767 (0.194) 170	0.738 (0.229) 170

* This table includes political parties or groups in the thirty-five OECD members' national lower legislative houses (LLH) as of January 1, 2017. Sample sizes vary based on the availability of data.
** *Women's election rates:* An ANOVA shows that the differences in the means of these three party groups are statistically significant from one another, $p > F = 0.000$. Two-tailed t-tests show that left and center parties' differences are not statistically significant ($p > 0.10$), while both the left and right parties' and the center and right parties', respectively, differences are ($p < 0.05$).
*** *Women party leaders:* An ANOVA shows that the differences in the means of these three party groups are statistically significant from one another, $p > F = 0.019$. Two-tailed t-tests show that differences between both the left and center parties and the center and right parties, respectively, are not statistically significant ($p > 0.10$), while the difference between left and right parties is ($p < 0.05$).
† *Women workplace policies:* An ANOVA shows that the differences in the means of these three party groups' support for supporting women in the workplace are statistically significant from one another, $p > F = 0.000$. Two-tailed t-tests show that left, center, and right parties' differences are all statistically significant from one another ($p < 0.05$).
‡ *Protecting minority rights:* An ANOVA shows that the differences in the means of these three party groups' support for protecting minority rights are statistically significant from one another, $p > F = 0.000$. Two-tailed t-tests show that left and center parties' differences are not statistically significant ($p > 0.10$), while differences between both the left and right and the center and right are ($p < 0.05$).

left-center-right party categories (based on family parties; see earlier discussion).

This single-axis arrangement of political families is widely used in political science, and Table 8.3 offers an account of interparty variation that will be familiar to comparative political scientists: left, center, and right party families are in the aggregate different from one another, and their performance in these four areas improves monotonically moving from right to left. Nevertheless, as subsequent sections show, these bivariate analyses are limited. We learn more by inspecting multiple ideological dimensions that differentiate both between parties and within parties grouped together in families.

Further, center parties are more like the left in some areas and more like the right in others, generating varied and potentially mutually contradictory theoretical expectations about those parties' propensity to support gender and intersectional equality. Most important, subsequent analyses show that otherwise similar parties vary depending on the setting.

Modeling Attention to Rights and Interests

This chapter brings together forms of advancing the rights and interests of historically marginalized groups from the preceding empirical chapters and operationalizes them for cross-national comparisons. Each party is nested within its political system, which argues for multilevel modeling, but regression models with standard errors clustered by country estimate substantively the same results. Thus, this chapter presents and discusses OLS and logit models, as appropriate to the dependent variable, with diagnostics. Models that include only contextual variables are provided in Appendix E. These more limited models reinforce the message that contextual variables matter more for right-leaning parties than for left- or center-leaning parties.

Results

Electing Women to National Legislative Office

To what extent do parties' left-right ideological characteristics explain the rates at which they elect women to national legislative office? Focusing on the case of contemporary Germany, previous chapters showed that left-right axes contribute to but do not dominate variation among parties on this measure of women's political incorporation. Specifically, they appear to do so through other mechanisms (principally a party-level gender quota) that are now present across ideologically diverse parties.

Table 8.3 ("Proequality Activities," discussed earlier in chapter) showed that left-center-right party families offer an account of variation in four forms of proequality activities. However, parties do not operate in a vacuum, both culturally and in terms of the structural incentives that surround them. Further, these correlations are meaningful at the same time as they obscure many other dynamics. Thus, this chapter's multivariate analyses expand these findings to show that political parties' election of women is significantly moderated by their institutional and ideological context. Importantly, some parties are more sensitive to context than others. System-wide factors that are widely understood to favor higher rates of women's election appear to be more important for explaining "right" parties' success at doing so. By contrast, parties "on the left" along various dimensions are relatively consistent across po-

TABLE 8.4 ALL PARTIES' RATES OF ELECTING WOMEN

	Women's Rates of Election	
	Model 1 Coefficient (Std. Error)	Model 2 Coefficient (Std. Error)
ParlGov L-R Measure	−0.197 (0.046) ***	—
Economic Liberalism	—	0.009 (0.067)
Social Traditionalism	—	−0.075 (0.060)
Materialism	—	0.117 (0.072)
Hegemonic-Ethnic Supremacy	—	0.039 (0.049)
National Gender Quota	0.022 (0.0321)	0.017 (0.029)
Effective # of Parties	0.018 (0.007) **	0.010 (0.006) *
Pro-gender-equality Attitudes	0.002 (0.001) **	0.002 (0.001) **
WLFP	0.004 (0.003)	0.003 (0.002)
Constant	−0.059 (0.140)	0.068 (0.134)
N	231	185
$P > F$	0.000	0.000
R^2	0.185	0.322

Note: Entries are unstandardized coefficients from OLS regression models. Standard errors are clustered by country and noted in parentheses. The unit of analysis is the party-year.
Model 1: A Breusch-Pagan test indicates some concern regarding heteroscedasticity ($p > X^2 = 0.000$). Variance Inflation Factors (VIFs) are between 1.04 and 2.82 (mean 1.80).
Model 2: A Breusch-Pagan test indicates some concern regarding heteroscedasticity ($p > X^2 = 0.015$). VIFs are between 1.09 and 5.32 (mean 2.73).
* $p < 0.10$; ** $p < 0.05$; *** $p < 0.001$

litical systems in their rates of the election of women. Thus, the question is not just which parties elect more women but in which context more women are elected.

Table 8.4 juxtaposes two OLS models showing—as elsewhere in this chapter and book—that while an aggregate left-right measure corresponds with women's rates of election, disaggregated dimensions of parties' ideological characteristics do not to the same degree. The book's theoretical expectations were that all parties (left and right in various senses) *could* elect women at comparable rates, though materialist and hegemonic-ethnic supremacist parties are less likely to. Model 2 indicates that, controlling for multiple ideological dimensions, political parties' wider context (party system characteristics, and widely held pro-gender-equality attitudes) moderates women's rates of election. Even in this relatively spare OLS model, a higher effective number of parties and greater pro-gender-equality attitudes correspond with more women in elected national legislative office, while no finer-grained ideological dimension does. As of 2017 data for the OECD, otherwise similar political parties vary in their election of women based on their wider political setting.

The salience of context is the key area to which this chapter's cross-national analyses contribute. Thus, the next table subsets political parties into left, center, and right, based on their party families, in order to draw our attention closer to the ways in which otherwise similar parties vary across settings. As discussed earlier, party families are the basis for both these left-center-right categories and the social traditionalism measure; this measurement choice introduces the multicollinearity that we see indicated in Table 8.5.

Table 8.5 paints a more complex picture in several senses. First, ideological variation among parties on "the left" exists, and it matters: it corresponds with women's rates of election. Those parties otherwise viewed as left-leaning that manifest social traditionalism, and those parties that are otherwise-left that manifest hegemonic-ethnic supremacy, elect women at lower rates than their socially progressive and multiculturalist counterparts. Second, contextual variation matters for parties "on the right": a conducive environment (more political parties, and the existence of a nationally legislated or constitutional gender quota) corresponds with more women in office.

TABLE 8.5 PARTY FAMILIES' RATES OF ELECTING WOMEN

	Women's Rates of Election		
	Parties on the Left	Parties at the Center	Parties on the Right
	Model 3 coefficient (std. error)	Model 4 coefficient (std. error)	Model 5 coefficient (std. error)
Economic Liberalism	0.038 (0.145)	−0.385 (0.212)	0.185 (0.133)
Social Traditionalism	−0.438 (0.200) **	(omitted due to collinearity)	−0.060 (0.126)
Materialism	0.198 (0.179)	−0.324 (0.197)	−0.033 (0.099)
Hegemonic-Ethnic Supremacy	−0.259 (0.145) *	0.101 (0.157)	−0.048 (0.062)
National Gender Quota	−0.020 (0.043)	0.037 (0.072)	0.084 (0.045) *
Effective # of Parties	0.002 (0.001)	0.013 (0.020)	0.031 (0.007) ***
Pro-gender-equality Attitudes	0.002 (0.001) **	0.003 (0.002) *	0.001 (0.001)
Women's Labor Force Participation	0.003 (0.003)	0.006 (0.005)	0.002 (0.004)
Constant	0.122 (0.199)	0.069 (0.328)	−0.091 (0.239)
N	74	33	78
$P > F$	0.000	0.006	0.000
R^2	0.285	0.398	0.399

Note: Entries are unstandardized coefficients from OLS regression models. Standard errors are clustered by country and noted in parentheses. The unit of analysis is the party-year.
Model 3: A Breusch-Pagan test does not indicate concern regarding heteroscedasticity ($p > X^2 = 0.1551$). VIFs are between 1.09 and 3.09 (mean 1.85).
Model 4: A Breusch-Pagan test does not indicate concern regarding heteroscedasticity ($p > X^2 = 0.535$). VIFs are between 1.20 and 3.05 (mean 1.87).
Model 5: A Breusch-Pagan test does not indicate concern regarding heteroscedasticity ($p > X^2 = 0.197$). VIFs are between 1.14 and 3.39 (mean 1.90).
* $p < 0.10$; ** $p < 0.05$; *** $p < 0.001$

Otherwise similar parties, in particular on the right, elect more women in some settings than others.

Women in Party Leadership

Right-leaning parties around the globe, and even more so far-right parties, have attracted attention when one or more members of their top leadership are women. This book argues that the surprise this generates is an artifact of overstating the salience of the left-right ideological axis. We can make better sense of these apparent incongruities by inspecting finer-grained features of political parties, placing them in their social and institutional contexts.

This section's logistic regression models examine factors that correspond with women's political appointment as party leaders. Diagnostics indicate that these models fit the data well. As earlier, Table 8.6 shows that the aggregated left-right variable corresponds with women's rates of party leadership appointments, while disaggregated ideological dimensions do not. The book's theoretical expectations were that materialist and hegemonic-ethnic supremacist parties would be less likely to have women leaders, but that does not obtain in this dataset. However, as expected, higher rates of pro-gender-equality attitudes in the society where the party functions do correspond with women's leadership appointment.

Simultaneously, these results suggest that contextual factors that correspond with an increase in women's incorporation in other senses (specifically, in their election into national legislative office) instead correspond with a decrease in women's party leadership appointments. A higher effective number of parties actually corresponds with fewer women leaders. This may speak to the competitiveness of leadership positions within some multiparty systems in a way that is not captured by this model.

Next, Table 8.7 subsets political parties into left, center, and right categories, and it shows that otherwise similar political parties on "the left" are more likely to have at least one woman leader in settings where there are higher levels of pro-gender-equality attitudes. At the same time, within "the left," political parties that are more socially traditionalist are less likely to appoint women leaders. This result underscores that interparty variation within standard ideological groupings has substantive effects that disrupt expectations about "the usual suspects."

Otherwise similar parties on "the right" also differ, depending on context. As expected, higher levels of pro-gender-equality attitudes in society correspond with a broadly right-leaning party's greater likelihood of appointing a woman leader. However, these models of women's leadership also present some unexpected elements. Otherwise similar right-leaning parties vary by context but not fully as predicted: as seen previously in Table 8.6 (in which

TABLE 8.6 ALL PARTY LEADERSHIP'S INCLUSION OF WOMEN

	Women in Party Leadership	
	Model 6 Coefficient (Std. Error)	Model 7 Coefficient (Std. Error)
ParlGov L-R Measure	−1.707 (0.770) **	—
Economic Liberalism	—	0.608 (1.247)
Social Traditionalism	—	−1.041 (1.0261)
Materialism	—	−1.069 (1.952)
Hegemonic-Ethnic Supremacy	—	−0.788 (0.897)
Effective # of Parties	−0.203 (0.068) **	−0.285 (0.094) **
Pro-gender-equality Attitudes	0.037 (0.011) **	0.0531 (0.013) ***
Women's Labor Force Participation	−0.030 (0.018)	−0.065 (0.023) **
Constant	−0.575 (0.990)	0.745 (1.307)
N	224	181
$P > X^2$	0.000	0.000
Pseudo R^2	0.076	0.134

Note: Entries are unstandardized coefficients from logistic regression models. Standard errors are clustered by country and noted in parentheses. The unit of analysis is the party-year.
Model 6: A link test indicates this model is not misspecified; a Hosmer-Lemeshow test indicates that the model fits the data well ($p > X^2 = 0.190$).
Model 7: A link test indicates this model is not misspecified; a Hosmer-Lemeshow test indicates that the model fits the data well ($p > X^2 = 0.810$).
* $p < 0.10$; ** $p < 0.05$; *** $p < 0.001$

left-center-right political parties were pooled together), a higher number of political parties in the system corresponds with lower rates of women's leadership. In Table 8.7, showing subsetted models, this result obtains only for "the right." Again, this result calls for future research into the competitiveness of party leadership appointment processes.

Support for WLFP

Here, political parties' proequality commitments are measured in terms of their support for policies that encourage WLFP. Research shows that women's financial independence plays a vital role in their well-being at all stages of their lives. Having the resources to avoid poverty in older age, for example, as well as to leave an abusive relationship at any age, relies in large part on women's participation in the paid labor force.[6] WLFP has increased significantly in most countries since the mid-twentieth century, yet these rates vary cross-nationally. Indeed, this factor has been included as a control in models in previous sections, because of its importance for so many other outcomes and components of women's well-being. World Bank data from 2016 show that across the OECD, WLFP ranged from 32.6 percent (Turkey) to 73.2 percent (Iceland), with an average of 54.0 percent.[7] Another feature of gendered

TABLE 8.7 PARTY FAMILIES' LEADERSHIP'S INCLUSION OF WOMEN

	Women in Party Leadership		
	Parties on the Left	Parties at the Center	Parties on the Right
	Model 8 Coefficient (Std. Error)	Model 9 Coefficient (Std. Error)	Model 10 Coefficient (Std. Error)
Economic Liberalism	−3.053 (2.667)	3.810 (3.666)	0.810 (2.914)
Social Traditionalism	−8.955 (3.626) **	(omitted due to collinearity)	−2.571 (4.370)
Materialism	−2.188 (2.343)	−1.146 (4.593)	−2.079 (3.805)
Hegemonic-Ethnic Supremacy	1.027 (1.483)	−7.332 (3.968)	1.617 (1.638)
Effective # of Parties	−0.268 (0.200)	0.081 (0.336)	−0.914 (0.356) **
Pro-gender-equality Attitudes	0.042 (0.021) **	0.019 (0.038)	0.118 (0.036) **
Women's Labor Force Participation	−0.110 (0.036) **	0.046 (0.078)	−0.049 (0.087)
Constant	6.191 (2.401) **	−6.564 (4.542)	−1.822 (4.679)
N	72	33	76
$P > X^2$	0.001	0.000	0.022
R^2	0.209	0.304	0.303

Note: Entries are unstandardized coefficients from logistic regression models. Standard errors are clustered by country and noted in parentheses. The unit of analysis is the party-year. The inclusion of the dichotomous variable for a national gender quota does not substantively change these models, so it is omitted.

Model 8: A link test indicates that the model is not misspecified; a Hosmer-Lemeshow test does not indicate concern about the model's fit ($p > X^2 = 0.325$).

Model 9: A link test indicates that the model is not misspecified; a Hosmer-Lemeshow test does not indicate concern about the model's fit ($p > X^2 = 0.395$).

Model 10: A link test indicates that the model is not misspecified; a Hosmer-Lemeshow test indicates that the model fits the data well ($p > X^2 = 0.824$).

inequality regards differential pay: women are underrepresented in higher-paying professions and underpaid relative to men counterparts in the same professions, motivating demands for equal pay for equal work.[8] Further, across the OECD, part-time work is disproportionately done by women: 25.5 percent of employed women work part-time, compared to 9.3 percent of men.[9] These employment patterns have direct consequences for everything from day-to-day needs to pension contributions, and across all settings they are more pronounced for multiply marginalized women.[10]

In the analyses that follow, "promoting WLFP" is a V-Dem variable that ranges from "strongly opposes measures that support the equal participation of women in the labor market" to "strongly supports." This is a cache of measures that "include—but are not limited to—legal provisions on equal treatment and pay, parental leave and financial support for child care."[11] This is not an intersectional measure, and research shows that marginalized subgroups of women will not benefit to the same degree from legal frameworks that do not specifically address axes of inequality other than sex-gender.[12] At the same time, parental leave and childcare subsidies are unequivocally steps in the right direction, and this is the variable that is cross-nationally available. How do parties compare?

In the following, OLS models of parties' level of support for policies that promote WLFP include a variable for whether the party is chaired by at least one woman (the dependent variable from models in the previous section) but not a variable for whether the system includes a national gender quota. This is because while a gender quota may correspond indirectly with greater attention to women as a group (by corresponding with women's higher rates of election), it is not theorized to relate directly to the dependent variable.

Statistical results in Table 8.8 show support for many of the book's theoretical expectations. The aggregate left-right measure is statistically significant in a negative direction, but as we consistently see in other models, a party's placement on the right is significant for some but not all finer-grained ideological measures. On this crucial policy area, political parties that are right-leaning in their materialism and their hegemonic-ethnic supremacy are less supportive of WLFP policies. Left-right differentiation matters, but the explanation lies with these narrower dimensions.

To some degree, wider social and institutional factors differentiate among parties in their support for WLFP policies. As theorized, a higher number of parties in the system corresponds with greater support for proequality policies in two of these models, and higher rates of pro-gender-equality attitudes in society are statistically significant in the expected (positive) direction in one of them. Models in Table 8.8 are the first to include the measure of the legislature's agenda-setting authority, addressing the hypothesis that agenda-setting and bill initiation powers would make advocacy for historically marginalized groups more likely. This expectation applies most directly to the actual policymaking process (i.e., to the policies that the party supports). Because the Döring (1995) dataset includes only seventeen European countries rather than the entire OECD membership, models are shown with and without this variable (note the lower number of observations for models with the measure of plenary agenda-setting authority). Political parties in these seventeen countries do not appear to be differently likely to support WLFP policies depending on their legislative bodies' agenda-setting powers.

Table 8.9 subsets political parties into the categories of left, center, and right, based on their party families. These models show that parties on "the left" are consistently supportive of WLFP policies, across political and social settings, unless they manifest greater hegemonic-ethnic supremacy. As hypothesized, this ideological dimension corresponds with lower levels of WLFP support across all categories of party families. At the center, parties manifesting greater economic liberalism, greater materialism, and greater hegemonic-

TABLE 8.8 ALL PARTIES' SUPPORT FOR WLFP POLICIES

	Level of Support for WLFP Policies			
	Model 11 Coefficient (Std. Error)	Model 12 Coefficient (Std. Error)	Model 13 Coefficient (Std. Error)	Model 14 Coefficient (Std. Error)
Economic Liberalism	—	—	−0.152 (0.092)	−0.188 (0.112)
Social Traditionalism	—	—	0.066 (0.101)	0.168 (0.132)
Materialism	—	—	−0.334 (0.103) **	−0.326 (0.132) **
Hegemonic-Ethnic Supremacy	—	—	−0.229 (0.096) **	−0.410 (0.100) **
ParlGov L-R Measure	−0.458 (0.066) ***	−0.511 (0.094) ***	—	—
Woman in Party Leadership	0.017 (0.036)	0.055 (0.041)	−0.007 (0.032)	0.024 (0.037)
Effective # of Parties	0.021 (0.008) **	0.016 (0.010)	0.021 (0.011) *	−0.006 (0.010)
Plenary Agenda-Setting Authority	—	−0.018 (0.013)	—	−0.016 (0.013)
Pro-gender-equality Attitudes	−0.001 (0.001)	0.003 (0.004)	−0.002 (0.001)	0.007 (0.003) **
Women's Labor Force Participation	0.004 (0.003)	−0.001 (0.004)	0.003 (0.003)	−0.003 (0.004)
Constant	0.745 (0.158) ***	0.754 (0.266) **	0.946 (0.172) ***	0.772 (0.212) **
N	164	91	163	89
P > F	0.000	0.000	0.000	0.000
R^2	0.359	0.393	0.460	0.646

Note: Models in Table 8.8 include only parties included in the V-Dem dataset, hence lower sample sizes. Entries are unstandardized coefficients from OLS regression models. Standard errors are clustered by country and noted in parentheses. The unit of analysis is the party-year.
Model 11: A Breusch-Pagan test indicates some concern regarding heteroscedasticity ($p > X^2 = 0.016$). VIFs are between 1.07 and 1.54 (mean 1.26).
Model 12: A Breusch-Pagan test indicates some concern regarding heteroscedasticity ($p > X^2 = 0.005$). VIFs are between 1.01 and 1.67 (mean 1.30).
Model 13: A Breusch-Pagan test indicates some concern regarding heteroscedasticity ($p > X^2 = 0.000$). VIFs are between 1.10 and 4.79 (mean 2.29).
Model 14: A Breusch-Pagan test indicates some concern regarding heteroscedasticity ($p > X^2 = 0.000$). VIFs are between 1.05 and 5.00 (mean 2.30).
* $p < 0.10$; ** $p < 0.05$; *** $p < 0.001$

TABLE 8.9 PARTY FAMILIES' SUPPORT FOR WLFP POLICIES

Support for Women's Labor Force Participation Policies

	Parties on the Left		Parties at the Center		Parties on the Right	
	Model 15	Model 16	Model 17	Model 18	Model 19	Model 20
Economic Liberalism	−0.079 (0.076)	−0.074 (0.087)	−0.431 (0.162) **	−0.476 (0.160) **	−0.036 (0.155)	0.300 (0.487)
Social Traditionalism	−0.141 (0.138)	−0.080 (0.155)	(omitted due to collinearity)	(omitted due to collinearity)	0.267 (0.261)	0.248 (0.307)
Materialism	0.162 (0.140)	0.217 (0.197)	−0.505 (0.204) *	−0.294 (0.071) **	−0.301 (0.168) *	0.041 (0.287)
Hegemonic-Ethnic Supremacy	−0.184 (0.105) *	−0.294 (0.191)	−0.502 (0.155) **	−0.663 (0.113) ***	−0.125 (0.112)	−0.272 (0.111) *
Woman in Party Leadership	0.014 (0.030)	0.043 (0.029)	−0.042 (0.076)	0.033 (0.056)	−0.027 (0.074)	0.006 (0.069)
Effective # of Parties	−0.003 (0.011)	−0.016 (0.012)	0.026 (0.019)	−0.001 (0.015)	0.039 (0.014) **	0.051 (0.020) **
Plenary Agenda-Setting Authority	—	−0.004 (0.012)	—	−0.034 (0.021)	—	−0.040 (0.016) *
Pro-gender-equality Attitudes	0.001 (0.001)	0.000 (0.003)	−0.003 (0.002)	0.007 (0.005)	−0.001 (0.002)	0.008 (0.003) **
Women's Labor Force Participation	0.003 (0.003)	0.003 (0.004)	0.001 (0.005)	−0.005 (0.004)	0.006 (0.004)	−0.001 (0.003)
Constant	0.846 (0.137) ***	0.799 (0.197) ***	1.567 (0.335) ***	1.349 (0.399) **	0.299 (0.346)	−0.415 (0.543)
N	62	39	32	21	69	29
P > F	0.189	0.093	0.000	0.000	0.001	0.000
R^2	0.143	0.223	0.667	0.859	0.368	0.599

Note: Entries are unstandardized coefficients from OLS regression models. Standard errors are clustered by country and noted in parentheses. The unit of analysis is the party-year.
Model 15: A Breusch-Pagan test does not indicate concern regarding heteroscedasticity ($p > X^2 = 0.408$). VIFs are between 1.11 and 1.97 (mean 1.61).
Model 16: A Breusch-Pagan test indicates some concern regarding heteroscedasticity ($p > X^2 = 0.088$). VIFs are between 1.03 and 2.23 (mean 1.66).
Model 17: A Breusch-Pagan test does not indicate concern regarding heteroscedasticity ($p > X^2 = 0.313$). VIFs are between 1.11 and 1.63 (mean 1.33).
Model 18: A Breusch-Pagan test does not indicate concern regarding heteroscedasticity ($p > X^2 = 0.180$). VIFs are between 1.30 and 2.20 (mean 1.60).
Model 19: A Breusch-Pagan test does not indicate concern regarding heteroscedasticity ($p > X^2 = 0.981$). VIFs are between 1.21 and 1.94 (mean 1.58).
Model 20: A Breusch-Pagan test does not indicate concern regarding heteroscedasticity ($p > X^2 = 0.197$). VIFs are between 1.30 and 3.25 (mean 2.26).
* $p < 0.10$; ** $p < 0.05$; *** $p < 0.001$

ethnic supremacy are all less likely to support WLFP, but wider context does not appear to differentiate among their odds of doing so.

Ultimately, these models best fit variation among parties on "the right," reinforcing the broader finding that these parties are more sensitive to setting: where there is a higher number of political parties and where pro-gender-equality attitudes are more prevalent, "right" parties are more likely to support WLFP. Contrary to the book's theoretical expectations, however, the legislature's greater agenda-setting authority corresponds with a lower likelihood of supporting these policies. However, as noted earlier, the Döring (1995) dataset includes only seventeen European countries; parties in these systems are likely to be distinctive for other reasons not captured in these models.

Support for Protecting Minority Groups' Civil and Political Rights

Political parties also vary in their commitments to preserving the rights of marginalized social groups. In these analyses, "protecting minority rights against majority preferences" is a V-Dem variable, which is measured in terms of party leadership: "According to the leadership of this party, how often should the will of the majority be implemented even if doing so would violate the rights of minorities?" Values range from always ("the will of the majority should always determine policy even if such policy violates minority rights") to never ("the will of the majority should never determine policy if such policy violates minority rights").[13] Although this, too, is not an intersectional measure, it is in many ways a philosophical and pragmatic precursor to intersectional equality measures. If we do not see a commitment to minority rights more broadly, we are unlikely to see a commitment to the rights of multiply marginalized women.

Models that follow omit the variable for whether the system includes a national gender quota. This omission is because a national gender quota for legislative office is not theorized to relate directly to party leadership position taking (this V-Dem variable's focus).

Models in Table 8.10 show that patterns in party leaders' prioritization of minority social groups' rights largely mirror parties' support for WLFP (shown in the previous section). As before, the aggregated left-right ideological measure corresponds with some variation, but specific ideological commitments—materialism and hegemonic-ethnic supremacy—even more so. Further, and in line with the book's theoretical expectations, multipartism appears to incentivize support for the rights of marginalized groups. Although these statistical models cannot illuminate the mechanism for this, it makes prima facie sense that nonmajoritarian systems include greater attention to and advocacy for these concerns.

TABLE 8.10 ALL PARTY LEADERS' PRIORITIZATION OF MINORITY RIGHTS

	Prioritization of Minority Rights			
	Model 21	Model 22	Model 23	Model 24
ParlGov L-R Measure	−0.398 (0.067) ***	−0.336 (0.073) ***	—	—
Economic Liberalism	—	—	0.014 (0.096)	−0.038 (0.107)
Social Traditionalism	—	—	0.103 (0.077)	0.207 (0.125)
Materialism	—	—	−0.204 (0.092) **	−0.226 (0.138)
Hegemonic-Ethnic Supremacy	—	—	−0.508 (0.081) ***	−0.507 (0.119) **
Effective # of Parties	0.036 (0.011) **	0.038 (0.015) **	0.036 (0.009) ***	0.018 (0.013)
Plenary Agenda-Setting Authority	—	0.016 (0.014)	—	0.024 (0.012) *
Pro-gender-equality Attitudes	0.002 (0.002)	−0.002 (0.003)	−0.000 (0.001)	0.001 (0.002)
Women's Labor Force Participation	0.004 (0.003)	0.002 (0.004)	0.001 (0.003)	−0.001 (0.003)
Constant	0.496 (0.149) **	0.775 (0.320) **	0.759 (0.139) ***	0.721 (0.220) **
N	167	94	165	91
$P > X^2$	0.000	0.001	0.000	0.000
R^2	0.313	0.273	0.614	0.593

Note: Entries are unstandardized coefficients from OLS regression models. Standard errors are clustered by country and noted in parentheses. The unit of analysis is the party-year.
Model 21: A Breusch-Pagan test indicates concern regarding heteroscedasticity ($p > X^2 = 0.001$). VIFs range from 1.05 to 1.50 (mean 1.28).
Model 22: A Breusch-Pagan test indicates concern regarding heteroscedasticity ($p > X^2 = 0.000$). VIFs range from 1.00 to 1.65 (mean: 1.36).
Model 23: A Breusch-Pagan test indicates concern regarding heteroscedasticity ($p > X^2 = 0.000$). VIFs range from 1.10 to 4.83 (mean: 2.45).
Model 24: A Breusch-Pagan test indicates concern regarding heteroscedasticity ($p > X^2 = 0.000$). VIFs range from 1.27 to 5.04 (mean: 2.46).
* $p < 0.10$; ** $p < 0.05$; *** $p < 0.001$

TABLE 8.11 PARTY FAMILIES' LEADERS' PRIORITIZATION OF MINORITY RIGHTS

	\multicolumn{6}{c}{Prioritization of Minority Rights}
	\multicolumn{2}{c}{Parties on the Left}	\multicolumn{2}{c}{Parties at the Center}	\multicolumn{2}{c}{Parties on the Right}
	Model 25	Model 26	Model 27	Model 28	Model 29	Model 30
Economic Liberalism	0.174 (0.092) *	0.260 (0.117) **	−0.335 (0.177) *	−0.511 (0.197) **	−0.095 (0.210)	−0.132 (0.459)
Social Traditionalism	0.066 (0.089)	0.053 (0.121)	(omitted due to collinearity)	(omitted due to collinearity)	0.038 (0.208)	−0.321 (0.244)
Materialism	−0.179 (0.136)	−0.221 (0.169)	−0.406 (0.144) **	−0.299 (0.220)	−0.187 (0.168)	−0.303 (0.371)
Hegemonic-Ethnic Supremacy	−0.432 (0.127) **	−0.411 (0.255)	−0.536 (0.115) ***	−0.551 (0.151) **	−0.512 (0.112) ***	−0.326 (0.178) *
Effective # of Parties	0.020 (0.008) **	0.006 (0.011)	0.016 (0.012)	0.015 (0.011)	0.064 (0.011) ***	0.043 (0.036)
Plenary Agenda-Setting Authority	—	0.031 (0.011) **	—	0.010 (0.009)	—	0.017 (0.020)
Pro-gender-equality Attitudes	−0.000 (0.002)	0.001 (0.003)	−0.002 (0.002)	0.001 (0.003)	0.002 (0.002)	0.002 (0.003)
Women's Labor Force Participation	−0.001 (0.003)	−0.002 (0.004)	0.000 (0.002)	−0.002 (0.002)	0.003 (0.004)	0.002 (0.005)
Constant	0.921 (0.139) ***	0.840 (0.304) **	1.469 (0.211) ***	1.415 (0.324) ***	0.577 (0.302) *	0.907 (0.677)
N	63	40	32	21	70	30
$P > X^2$	0.000	0.000	0.001	0.000	0.000	0.001
Pseudo R^2	0.435	0.497	0.703	0.817	0.629	0.597

Note: Entries are unstandardized coefficients from OLS regression models. Standard errors are clustered by country and noted in parentheses. The unit of analysis is the party-year.
Model 25: A Breusch-Pagan test indicates concern about heteroscedasticity ($p > X^2 = 0.011$). VIFs range from 1.06 to 1.92 (mean: 1.58).
Model 26: A Breusch-Pagan test indicates concern about heteroscedasticity ($p > X^2 = 0.036$). VIFs range from 1.03 to 2.14 (mean: 1.64).
Model 27: A Breusch-Pagan test indicates concern about heteroscedasticity ($p > X^2 = 0.034$). VIFs range from 1.10 to 1.44 (mean: 1.27).
Model 28: A Breusch-Pagan test indicates concern about heteroscedasticity ($p > X^2 = 0.098$). VIFs range from 1.20 to 1.95 (mean: 1.52).
Model 29: A Breusch-Pagan test does not indicate concern about heteroscedasticity ($p > X^2 = 0.945$). VIFs range from 1.22 to 1.93 (mean: 1.60).
Model 30: A Breusch-Pagan test does not indicate concern about heteroscedasticity ($p > X^2 = 0.198$). VIFs range from 1.52 to 2.67 (mean: 2.16).
* $p < 0.10$; ** $p < 0.05$; *** $p < 0.001$

Next, Table 8.11 subsets political parties into left, center, and right party families.

These final models in Table 8.11 largely affirm several of this chapter's overall findings. First, materialism and hegemonic-ethnic supremacy are distinctive features of a party's ideological makeup, transcending other left-center-right categories. However, contrary to the book's theoretical expectations, economic liberalism corresponds with greater willingness to deprioritize minority rights across left and center party families. This cross-national finding is also different from the case of Germany, where the centrist FDP, largely defined in terms of economic liberalism, has historically acted earlier than other parties to remove formal barriers to political incorporation.

Second, some elements of wider context play a role in interparty variation. A higher effective number of parties in a system corresponds with greater prioritization of minority groups' rights, in particular, for parties on the left and the right. Otherwise similar parties appear largely unaffected by widely held support for socially traditional gender roles, although this may be an artifact of these attitudes not specifically addressing minoritized social categories.

Ideological Miscellanea in the Case of Chile

Cross-national analyses in this chapter have shown that a combination of party- and country-level factors explains parties' proequality actions and position taking. This finding disrupts conventional wisdom about "the left" and "the right" regarding the political inclusion of historically marginalized social groups. Another contention of the book is that because the very meaning of "left" and "right" is globally inconsistent, more cautious analyses of political parties across divergent settings is needed. A more nuanced approach is even more urgently needed in light of this chapter's statistical findings—namely, that the salience of parties' ideological commitments varies with their wider institutional and ideological context. The case of Chile illustrates these contentions about the need to examine parties' varied ideological dimensions in their historical, political, and social context.

Chile experienced a period of authoritarianism between the 1973 coup that overthrew the democratically elected socialist president Salvador Allende, and 1990, when Augusto Pinochet's right-wing military dictatorship came to an end. Political parties in Chile have, therefore, evolved over periods of profound institutional and ideological change. Prior to Pinochet's regime, the Chilean government had a long history of "highly fluid" coalitions, in a largely tripartite arrangement (Carey 2002, p. 223; see also Alemán and Saiegh [2007]). Writing in the early 2000s about Chile's post-Pinochet party system, Carey (2002) argues that coalitions increasingly functioned more like "parties composed of multiple factions" (pp. 223–224) and that the electoral system in Chile between 1990 and 2017—a system that included the world's only binominal (all two-seat districts) arrangement—incentivized parties to cluster into two loci of alliances, mirroring two political parties. This arrangement arguably contrasted with the three loci of the pre-Pinochet party system. By contrast, other scholars have contended that neither the seventeen-year Pinochet regime nor the binominal electoral system significantly disrupted the fragmented and fluid party politics of the pre-Pinochet democratic era (Siavelis 1997; Valenzuela 1994).

In all of these competing accounts of the country's electoral politics, parties in Chile have consistently faced significant incentives to form alliances. These alliances are typically categorized in left-right terms, even while parties within them are varied. Examining post-Pinochet patterns, Alemán and Saiegh (2007) identify distinct center-left and center-right party groups in Chile (1997–2000), and they observe a small, also distinct, center group. The heterogeneity of these alliances challenges left-right accounts of politics and policymaking in Chile.

The extent to which Chile's electoral institutions have reshaped party alliances also challenges the expectation that left-right structures will remain relatively stable over time. As noted, Chile's electoral rules specified two-member (binominal) districts between 1990 and 2017. As of the 2017 elections, Chileans elect the deputies of the lower legislative house from multimember districts with magnitudes ranging from three to eight representatives. The effects of this electoral law change immediately increased the system's effective number of parties from 2.09 to 3.14 (Gallagher 1991; calculated based on combined lists' seat shares in the chamber).[14]

Now in the second decade of the twenty-first century, in the wake of this electoral law change, Chile's party system is highly fragmented. This fragmentation is visible across many issue areas that relate to advocacy for historically marginalized groups and for more vulnerable populations, and we can see its effects both in the impulse toward institutional change and in countermovements against it. In 2019, massive protests against persistent social and economic inequalities led to a 2020 referendum calling for a new constitution to replace the 1980 framework that dated to the Pinochet era. One of the legacies of the Pinochet era, which has persisted across the three decades since his departure, has been the fear around expressing leftist political preferences, However, Piscopo and Siavelis (2021) describe a new "generation without fear," who played a significant role in propelling the country toward the constitutional convention that met over the course of 2020–2021. This convention was groundbreakingly inclusive (Tobar 2021), but it produced a document that was ultimately rejected in the September 2022 referendum on its adoption (Buschschlüter 2022).

The shadow of Pinochet's dictatorship is long and unambiguously persists in contemporary Chilean party politics. Institutionally, binominal electoral rules and a highly empowered president long constrained change. Culturally, a legacy of suppression of the left has preempted voices that might otherwise express their preferences. At the same time, the 2022 constitutional draft formally recognized the rights and territorial claims of Indigenous communities in Chile, it stipulated a 50 percent quota for women's inclusion in public office, and it affirmed the right to terminate pregnancy. In order to make sense of Chilean parties' and voters' orientations toward this proposed constitution, we need more than "left" and "right."

Even while finer-grained ideological dimensions may help us differentiate between political actors' reactions to the 2020–2022 constitutional project, the CPDS categorizes all political parties in Chile in its "other" (miscellaneous) category, and ParlGov omits the country and its parties entirely.

Conclusion

The main message that these analyses send is that not all parties typically grouped together in left-right terms are the same when it comes to proequality activities and commitments, and, indeed, on some matters they are highly varied. Parties otherwise viewed as on the left are, nonetheless, less proequality when they also manifest two specific ideologies that are more commonly associated with the right: materialism and hegemonic-ethnic supremacy. Parties broadly on the right are more sensitive to their wider context, across all four measures of proequality activities and commitments. Implications of these findings are numerous and significant. What we mean by "the usual suspects" does not hold cross-nationally, and potential allies for achieving greater political inclusion will depend on context.

The analyses that this chapter presents are limited in several ways that further illustrate the book's larger point. Standard comparative datasets' omission of parties that do not fit into a clear left-right arrangement, for example, curtails a systematic and global evaluation of ideological multidimensionality and its correlates and consequences. In addition, widely available measures of political incorporation are generally limited to gender-binary measures of women's seat share. Thus, future research in this vein should seek more direct attention to intersectional groups and issues.

9

Conclusion

On September 26, 2021, federal elections ushered in the twentieth post–World War II legislative term in Germany. This was a historic election in many senses. Chancellor Angela Merkel had chosen to retire at the conclusion of the term, making this the first postwar parliamentary election without an incumbent candidate for the head of government. Further, the SPD's Olaf Scholz was viewed by many as the continuity candidate for chancellor, despite his predecessor being in the rival party of the CDU.[1] One of Scholz's campaign posters even read, "Er kann Kanzlerin" (Karnitschnig and von der Burchard 2021). (See Figure 9.1.)

Polling leading into the election indicated that voters' attachment to political parties was continuing to weaken; survey respondents expressed willingness to support a diverse assortment of parties. The Green Party was on the rise, while the SPD and CDU were on the decline (Stegmaier 2022). At various points during the summer of 2021, the B90/Gr were more popular than the CDU. For the first time, the B90/Gr campaigned with a chancellor candidate: Annalena Baerbock (profiled in Chapter 6). By late September, the SPD and CDU were polling similarly—historically low but nonetheless the chief competitors for the chancellorship. Ultimately, the SPD "secured a narrow win" with 25.7 percent of the vote, while the CDU "[plunged] to historic lows" with 24.1 percent (Livingstone and Henley 2021). This has been described as "the decline of the political center in Germany" (Eriksson et al. 2021). After negotiations, a coalition consisting of the SPD (helmed by chancellor Olaf Scholz), the B90/Gr, and the FDP inaugurated the twentieth postwar parliamentary term.

Jasko @JaskoSPD · Aug 30, 2021
Replying to @Wahlrecht_de
Er kann Kanzlerin. @OlafScholz

Figure 9.1 A post on Twitter (now X) by @JaskoSPD (dated August 30, 2021) presents an image of SPD chancellor candidate Olaf Scholz against a red background. A banner of text across Scholz's midsection reads, in English translation: "He can be madam chancellor" (Er kann Kanzlerin, with the feminine ending on the word chancellor).
(Credit: Twitter: @JaskoSPD. Artwork created by Social Democratic Party of Germany.)

In the wake of this election, commentators talked about the SPD and CDU's decreasing support as heralding a "new era in party systems and party politics" (Isabelle Borucki, quoted in E. Brown 2021). Simultaneously, other commentators referred to the coexistence of "party system continuity . . . with severe challenges for German policy makers" (Dostal 2021, p. 662). With Scholz's installation as chancellor, Germany returned to leadership by both the SPD and a man; conversely, the Bundestag's leadership council, the *Präsidium*, are mostly women: led by the SPD's Bärbel Bas, with Katrin Göring-Eckardt (B90/Gr), Yvonne Magwas (CDU/CSU), Aydan Özoğuz (SPD), Petra Pau (LINKE), Claudia Roth (B90/Gr), and one man, Wolfgang Kubicki (FDP). What do we make of the contemporary party system and its key figures at this time in Germany?

This book's findings about political parties in Germany and across the OECD disrupt prevailing expectations about the salience of left-right categories for interpreting political processes, in particular regarding the political incorporation of historically marginalized groups. In the case of Germany, the 2021 federal elections and their outcome illustrate that the politics of sex-gender and race-ethnicity are not firmly anchored in classic party families or in left-right categories. Both the SPD, with Olaf Scholz, and the CDU, with Armin Laschet, returned to men chancellor candidates. Indeed, by 2021, the SPD (unambiguously on the left in many senses) is the only major chancellery-contender that has never in its history nominated a woman candidate for the position (Abels et al. 2022, p. 253).

At the same time, political parties nominated and elected record numbers of Germans with a Migrationshintergrund. These ethnic-minority legislators were elected at significantly higher rates on "the left" but at equally low rates between the hegemonic-ethnic supremacist AfD and the centrist FDP, a party shown elsewhere in this book to engage more successfully. As reported by Mediendienst Integration, as of the 2021 election, political parties' seats include the following percentages of ethnic-minority legislators: LINKE, 28.2 percent; SPD, 17 percent; B90/Gr, 14.4 percent; AfD, 7.2 percent; FDP, 6.3 percent; and the CDU/CSU party group, 4.1 percent. Although these percentages are broadly higher on the left than on the right, they are not arrayed monotonically, and all but the LINKE's proportions are notably below Germany's ethnic-minority population. Thus, as earlier chapters in the book show, these rates of election offer a left-right account, but closer inspection indicates that more complicated dynamics are at work. Even those parties with a gender quota lack a formal quota for ethnic minorities; even those parties that successfully elect women and ethnic minorities at higher rates lack significant recruitment and mentoring programs (see discussions in Chapters 5–6). Greater rates of nomination by the LINKE, in particular, are being generated by other processes that are less visible.

While various hallmark ideologies associated with "the left," in particular social progressivism and postmaterialism, did not signal parties' particularly active advocacy in their 2021 federal campaigns, some parties distinguished themselves in their *active opposition to* equality policies. Abels et al. (2022) note that campaigns leading up to the 2021 election, across parties, largely ignored "gender issues such as gender gaps in pay, pensions, care work and leadership positions or the massive gendered effects of the COVID-19-pandemic" (p. 254). Parties from which we would have expected greater attention did not place social justice at the top of their agendas. Instead, the ideological dimension that persists across these campaigns and the election is *hegemonic-ethnic supremacy*. While parties across the left and right converged in some ways, the AfD and the CSU, both distinguished by hegemonic-ethnic supremacism, actively denigrated efforts at gender and social equality. For example, these parties' spokespeople emphasized critiques of "the gender asterisk" (i.e., the spelling practice in German of inserting an asterisk in the plural form of a word to make it more gender-inclusive; see discussion in Abels et al. 2022, p. 262).

The coalition-building process, in 2021, further illustrates the ways in which an election's broader context matters for all parties and may contribute to transcending left-right politics. The AfD and LINKE were highly unlikely coalition partners at any point, but even the inclusion of both the B90/Gr and FDP in coalition negotiations presented the necessity of compromise across significant differences. Indeed, FDP leader Christian Lindner quipped that "the only two things the FDP and the Greens could agree on was 'the legalisation of cannabis'" (quoted in Livingstone and Henley 2021). Nonetheless, Abels et al.'s (2022) analysis of these three parties' coalition contract shows their collective prioritization of a range of issues in support of inclusion. The governing contract to which the SPD, B90/Gr, and FDP agreed addresses gender mainstreaming, citizenship, LGBT rights, and antidiscrimination frameworks (Abels et al. 2022, p. 260). Although this coalition contract is clearly different from the agreement that a CDU/CSU-led government would have produced, the FDP was not as far away on proequality goals as the party is often portrayed.

Finally, *Er kann Kanzlerin* represents an enormous shift in the public face of German federal politics. Scholz and the SPD's campaign for the chancellery balanced an acknowledgment of Merkel's sixteen years of service with their electoral efforts against Merkel's own party, the CDU. As Robinet-Borgomano (2021) phrases it, Olaf Scholz's chancellor candidacy offered "change without disruption." When Merkel first ascended to her party's leadership, and subsequently began what would be a sixteen-year tenure as chancellor, Germany had no role model like her. Mushaben (2017) and others persuasively argue that Merkel created a *Leitbild* (model) for Germany and German politics at the intersection of east/west differences, financial crises, and gendered leadership stereotypes. By the time of Merkel's retirement, most political commentators agreed that she embodied what many German voters wanted, across otherwise ideologically different preferences: consistently "unpretentious, unruffled, and pragmatic" (Romaniec 2021).

Avenues for future research are many. In the case of Germany, increases in the Migrationshintergrund population who are both full citizens and voters will surely pressure more political parties to respond to calls for greater representation, both descriptive and substantive.[2] To what extent will socially traditionalist, materialist parties be able to reframe integration in terms that provide continuity in their policies? In terms of the policymaking process, qualitative analyses of additional, varied policy domains will contribute to a more nuanced understanding of the interplay between parties' ideological commitments and their strategic and electoral environment. In terms of comparative analyses, other cross-national institutional differences may further improve our understanding of rights expansions—for instance, whether systems with lower party discipline make it more likely for individual pioneers within parties to successfully expand the agenda.

Appendix A

German Political Parties' Names and Abbreviations

This appendix summarizes the abbreviations used for German political parties' names throughout the book.

TABLE A.1 GERMAN POLITICAL PARTIES' NAMES AND ABBREVIATIONS

Party Name	Party Abbreviation
Alternative für Deutschland	AfD
Bündnis 90/Die Grünen	B90/Gr
Christlich Demokratische Union Deutschlands	CDU
Christlich-Soziale Union in Bayern	CSU
Freie Demokratische Partei	FDP
Freie Wähler	FW/FWD
Partei des Demokratischen Sozialismus / Die Linke	PDS/LINKE
Marxistisch–Leninistische Partei Deutschlands	MLPD
Nationaldemokratische Partei Deutschlands	NPD
Ökologisch-Demokratische Partei	ÖDP
Piratenpartei Deutschland	PIR
Die Republikaner	REP
Sozialdemokratische Partei Deutschlands	SPD
Partei Mensch Umwelt Tierschutz	TIER

Appendix B

Categorizing Small Political Parties

This appendix displays documentation and quotations that substantiate the placement of political parties into ideological categories, for those parties not included in existing comparative politics datasets. The seven small German political parties in the book's analyses are often omitted from such existing datasets.

TABLE B.1 DOCUMENTATION* FOR IMPUTING GERMAN POLITICAL PARTIES' IDEOLOGICAL PLACEMENTS

Elements of the Wahlprogramm (WP, Election Program)

Party Name (Abbreviation)	Economic Redistributionism (L) or Liberalism (R)	Social Progressivism (L) or Traditionalism (R)	Postmaterialism (L) or Materialism (R)	Multiculturalism (L) or Hegemonic-Ethnic Supremacy (R)
Freie Wähler (FW/FWD)	L, on the basis of support for taxing financial transactions; emphasis on preventing child poverty; financial regulations; "kostenfreie Kinderbetreuung" (WP p. 7).	R, on the basis of elements of the WP that emphasize traditional values: "in der Tradition der Werte aus den Anfängen unserer Republik Antworten auf die Veraenderungen unserer Zeit biete . . . haben wir diese Werte konserviert . . . Sicherheit, Stabilität und Ordnung" (p. 5); "Die Familie ist der Ort der Sicherheit und Geborgenheit und gibt im Alltag einen festen Halt" (p. 7).	R, on the basis of elements of the WP that prioritize safety and security: "Sicherheit, Stabilität und Ordnung" (p. 5); the section on Sicherheit & Stabilität is tied (15 pages) for longest with the section on "Ehrlichkeit & Fleiss."	R, on the basis of the WP's expressions of nationalism and opposition to immigration.
Marxistisch–Leninistische Partei Deutschlands (MLPD)	L, on the following basis: it is unambiguously a communist party in favor of significant redistributionism and state intervention in the economy.	L, because the WP mentions nothing about protecting traditional families and nothing about any specific form of culture being best.	L, because the WP expresses support for recycling and reducing trash and tightening environmental regulations, opposition to nuclear power, antimilitarism, and open borders.	L, because the WP expresses support for open borders; "Gleiche Rechte für Migranten und Deutsche!"
Nationaldemokratische Partei Deutschlands (NPD)	L, on the basis of the WP's emphasis on socially responsible entrepreneurialism, its support of limits on financial "speculation" (i.e., regulations), and its opposition to global capitalism.	R, on the basis that the WP itself is titled, "Arbeit. Familie. Vaterland"; "Schutz von Familie und Ehe. Homosexuelle Lebenspartnerschaften bilden keine Familie und dürfen nicht gefördert werden" (p. 12).	R, because the WP emphasizes concerns about safety and security; Integration ist Voelkermord; "Wir Nationaldemokraten halten am Humboldtschen Ideal einer klassischen Hochschulbildung fest, die in der deutschen Geistestradition wurzelt" (p. 40).	R, because the WP expresses nationalism; "Trennung von Deutschen und Ausländern" (p. 40); WP is expressly opposed to multiculturalism.

(*continued*)

TABLE B.1 DOCUMENTATION* FOR IMPUTING GERMAN POLITICAL PARTIES' IDEOLOGICAL PLACEMENTS *(continued)*

Elements of the Wahlprogramm (WP, Election Program)

Party Name (Abbreviation)	Economic Redistributionism (L) or Liberalism (R)	Social Progressivism (L) or Traditionalism (R)	Postmaterialism (L) or Materialism (R)	Multiculturalism (L) or Hegemonic-Ethnic Supremacy (R)
Ökologisch-Demokratische Partei (ÖDP)	L, on the basis of the following elements of the WP: "Bei einem hohen Einkommen ist ein höherer Steueranteil gerechtfertigt als bei einem niedrigen Einkommen" (p. 49); "Die ÖDP steht dem gegenwärtigen kapitalistischen Wirtschaftssystem kritisch gegenüber" (p. 63); "Nachhaltige und soziale Kriterien können nicht mehr berücksichtigt werden, wenn dem Markt absolute Freiheit zugesprochen wird" (p. 63).	L, on the basis of the following elements of the WP: "Alle Versuche, Frauen, Männer und Familien bei der Wahl ihres Lebensmodells zu bevormunden und zu diskriminieren, lehnen wir ab" (sec. 2.9).	L, because it is unambiguously a postmaterialist ecology party.	L, on the basis of the following elements of the WP: "Nur ein friedliches Zusammenleben aller Gruppen der Gesellschaft kann ein gutes Leben für alle möglich machen" (sec. 5.7.3); WP expresses support for helping everyone across cultures, not disadvantaging migrants.
Piratenpartei Deutschland (PIR)	L, because the WP supports raising the maximum tax, reintroducing property taxes.	L, on the basis of the following elements of the WP: Platform expressly says the party wants to reject/overcome traditional gender roles; "Wir setzen uns dafür ein, die einseitige Bevorzugung traditioneller Rollen-, Familien- und Arbeitsmodelle zu überwinden. Echte Wahlfreiheit besteht erst, wenn längere berufliche Auszeiten oder Teilzeitarbeit unabhängig vom Geschlecht gesellschaftliche Normalität sind" (sec. 12.1, Präambel); WP favors rejecting the monogamous hetero model of Lebenspartnerschaften: "Nicht klassischen Familienbildern" (sec. 12.1.2).	L, on the basis of the following elements of the WP: "Nachhaltigkeit ist unser Massstab" (p. 37), i.e., proenvironmental sustainability; WP mentions animal rights: "Tiere können als Lebewesen nicht selbst für ihre Rechte eintreten, daher sind sie auf eine Vertretung in Form von Verbänden angewiesen" (p. 38).	L, on the basis of the following elements of the WP: "Wir PIRATEN stehen für eine offene, freie und pluralistische Gesellschaft ein, in der verschiedene Kulturen, Weltanschauungen und Religionen friedlich gemeinsam leben können" (sec. 2.1.1).

Die Republikaner (REP)	R, on the basis of interest in reducing taxes, support for strong separation between economy and the state.	R, on the basis of the following elements of the WP: "Wir stehen in der Tradition aller derjenigen Deutschen, die Patriotismus mit dem Streben nach Freiheit und Demokratie verbunden haben" (p. 7).	R, on the basis of the following elements of the WP: "Behauptung Europas als Hort des christlichen Abendlandes und dessen Werte" (p. 14); "Keine rechtliche Anerkennung gleichgeschlechtlicher Partnerschaften und kein Adoptionsrecht für Homosexuelle" (p. 25); "Wir fordern Augenmaß statt blindem, fanatischem Eifer. Deshalb müssen alle Entscheidungen zum Umweltschutz auf der Grundlage möglichst objektiver wissenschaftlicher Erkenntnisse getroffen werden" (p. 48); "Mindestanteil der deutschsprachigen Musiktitel von 50% in Hörfunksendungen" (p. 19).	R, because the WP expresses nationalism: "Bewahrung der deutschen Heimat, keine multikulturelle Gesellschaft, kein Vielvölkerstaat!" (p. 19).
Partei Mensch Umwelt Tierschutz (TIER)	R, because the WP expresses support for regulations on economic transactions, and it criticizes Merkel's "neo-capitalism."	L, on the basis of the following elements of the WP: "Gleichstellung von Homosexuellen, Bisexuellen, Trans- und Intersexuellen" (sec. 8, p. 11); WP supports full equality, ending restrictions on adoptions and blood donation.	L, on the basis of the following elements of the WP: "Gleichstellung von Homosexuellen, Bisexuellen, Trans- und Intersexuellen" —in support of full equality, ending restrictions on adoptions and blood donation (sec. 8, p. 11); WP's emphasis on animals' well-being; "Die Umwelt geht uns alle an" (pt. D); "Demokratie statt Lobbykratie" (pt. F); "Unsere Zielsetzungen sind vielmehr sozial, ökologisch, tierfreundlich und nachhaltig, getreu unseres Leitgedankens: Partei ergreifen für Mensch, Tier und Umwelt!" (p. 4).	R, on the basis of the following elements of the WP: Section 3 (p. 18) is called: "Menschliche Asylpolitik;" "Es müssen höhere Investitionen in Sprach- und Integrationskurse vorgenommen werden" (p. 18); WP emphasizes assimilation, language acquisition, and proper funding for localities that are receiving migrants.

* Page numbers refer to the party's 2017 or otherwise current Bundestag election program. REP and NPD did not have programs specific to 2017. WP = Wahlprogramm (election program).

Appendix C

Survey of German Women Officeholders "on the Right"

This appendix discusses a 2016 survey of women in parties "on the right" (AfD, CDU, CSU, and FDP) holding office in state- and national-level legislatures in Germany at that time.

DESCRIPTION OF THE QUESTIONNAIRE

This was a questionnaire for women holding legislative office at the federal or state level in Germany. It posed questions about respondents' career history and demographic characteristics as well as substantive questions about their pathways to candidacy and election. The survey launched on June 9, 2016. Potential subjects included the 240 women then holding legislative office at the federal (Bundestag) or state level (Landtag) in the following political parties: the AfD, the CDU, the CSU, and the FDP. Functioning email addresses (i.e., messages were not returned to sender) were available for all but five of these officeholders. Three weeks after initial contact, potential subjects received a follow-up invitation, excepting the eleven who had requested to opt out of the study.

TABLE C.1 SNAPSHOT OF 2016 SURVEY RESPONDENTS	
240 Invited Subjects $N = 16$	
Party	12 – CDU
	2 – CSU
	2 – FDP
Level of Government	7 – Bundestag (federal)
	9 – Landtag (state)
Year of Birth	Range: 1952–1985
Year of Entry into Politics	Range: 1990–2006
East German?	3 born and raised in former E. Germany

RELEVANT ITEMS FROM THE QUESTIONNAIRE (ENGLISH TRANSLATION)

1. What is your year of birth? _____
2. What is your party affiliation? _____
3. In what year did you first run for political office at any level? _____
4. What was your motivation for this first effort at running for office?
   - I had been interested in entering politics for a while.
   - I wanted to address a specific issue or problem in my community.
   - What was the issue/problem that motivated you to run for office? _____
   - Someone encouraged or invited me to run for office.
   - My spouse/family member passed away, and I was appointed to fill the seat.
   - Other: _____
5. Did any of the following individuals suggest that you run for office? Please select all that apply.
   - An official from a political party
   - A coworker or business associate
   - An elected official
   - A friend or acquaintance
   - A spouse or partner
   - A member of your family (other than your spouse or partner)
   - A nonelected political activist
   - Other: _____
6. Did you participate in any training for running for office (e.g., did your local or other party organization provide information about running for office)?
   - Yes
   - No
7. What form did this training take? Please select all that apply.
   - Networking/social events
   - Media training
   - Debate training
   - Fundraising training
   - Informational sessions on specific issues
   - Training in parliamentary procedures
   - Webinar/online or video instruction
   - Other: _____
8. If you wish to elaborate on any training you participated in, please do so in the space below.
9. Year first entered current office/seat: _____
10. Does your party have a mentorship program to support female candidates?
    - Yes
    - No
11. If answer to #10 is yes: does the program have a name or title? _____
12. If answer to #10 is yes: how often does this program organize events?
    - Weekly or more frequently
    - Monthly
    - Every couple of months
    - Annually

13. If answer to #10 is yes: how effective do you think this program is at supporting female candidates?
    - Very effective
    - Somewhat effective
    - Neither effective nor ineffective
    - Somewhat ineffective
    - Very ineffective
    - Don't know
14. If you wish to elaborate on your responses to these questions on the mentorship of female candidates in your party, please do so in the space below.
15. Does your party have a mentorship program to support female officeholders?
    - Yes
    - No
16. If answer to #15 is yes: does the program have a specific name or title? _____
17. If answer to #15 is yes: how often does this program organize events?
    - Weekly or more frequently
    - Monthly
    - Every couple of months
    - Annually
18. If answer to #15 is yes: what form do these events take?
    - Networking/social events
    - Media training
    - Informational sessions on specific issues
    - Informational sessions on specific parliamentary procedures
    - Webinar/online or video mentorship content
    - Other: _____
19. If answer to #15 is yes: how effective do you think this program is at supporting female officeholders?
    - Very effective
    - Somewhat effective
    - Neither effective nor ineffective
    - Somewhat ineffective
    - Very ineffective
20. If you wish to elaborate on your responses to these questions on the mentorship of female officeholders in your party, please do so in the space below.
21. Some political parties have a formal rule for including women among candidates (this is sometimes referred to as a "quota"). Are you aware of your party having a formal rule (a quota) of this kind?
    - Yes
    - No
22. If answer to #21 is yes: how effective do you think this quota is at increasing women's presence in office?
    - Very effective
    - Somewhat effective
    - Neither effective nor ineffective
    - Somewhat ineffective
    - Very ineffective
23. If answer to #21 is yes: what is your opinion of this quota? Please select all that apply.

- I fully support this quota.
- I think that a quota is a just solution to the problem of women's smaller presence in political office.
- In principle, I do not agree with the idea of a quota, but I am committed to increasing women's presence in office, and a quota is a good way for accomplishing this goal.
- I think that election to office should be based on merit and qualifications alone, not on gender.
- I do not support this quota.
- This quota is a problem when there are not enough qualified female candidates.
- I think this quota elects women who are less qualified.
- I think this quota implies that women are less qualified.
- I think this quota is not fair to men.

24. Some political parties have a formal rule for including women among party officials. Here, I refer to this as an "intraparty quota." Are you aware of your party having an intraparty quota regarding the presence of women among party officials?
    - Yes
    - No

25. If answer to #24 is yes: how effective do you think this intraparty quota is at increasing women's presence in leadership positions?
    - Very effective
    - Somewhat effective
    - Neither effective nor ineffective
    - Somewhat ineffective
    - Very ineffective

26. If answer to #24 is yes: what is your opinion of this intraparty quota? Please select all that apply.
    - I fully support this quota.
    - I think that the quota is a just solution to the problem of women's smaller presence in leadership positions.
    - In principle, I do not agree with the idea of a quota, but I am committed to increasing women's presence in leadership positions, and a quota is a good way for accomplishing this goal.
    - I think that appointment to a leadership position should be based on merit and qualifications alone, not on gender.
    - I do not support this intraparty quota.
    - This intraparty quota is a problem when there are not enough qualified female candidates for leadership positions.
    - I think this intraparty quota results in the placement of less qualified women into leadership positions.
    - I think this intraparty quota implies that women are less qualified for leadership positions.
    - I think this intraparty quota is not fair to men.

27. Sometimes party officials are motivated to invite or encourage women to run for office by informal rules. These informal rules are not part of the party's bylaws, but they are nonetheless known and they are often followed. Would you say that your party has informal commitments to increasing the number of female candidates?

- Yes
- No
- Comments: _____

28. Informal commitments to increasing women's presence in office can be expressed in many different ways. Would you say that party officials talk about the need to recruit more women to run for office
    - Frequently
    - Occasionally
    - Rarely
    - Never
    - Other: _____
29. Would you say that party officials talk about ways in which more female officeholders in the party might improve the party's success in elections
    - Frequently
    - Occasionally
    - Rarely
    - Never
    - Other: _____
30. Would you say that party officials talk about ways in which more female officeholders in the party might help the party succeed in its policy goals (advancing policies that are important to the party, passing legislation, etc.)
    - Frequently
    - Occasionally
    - Rarely
    - Never
    - Other: _____
31. Would you say that your party's informal documents (memos, emails) discuss the need to recruit more women to run for office
    - Frequently
    - Occasionally
    - Rarely
    - Never
    - Other: _____
32. Would you say that your party's informal documents (memos, emails) discuss ways in which more female officeholders in the party might improve the party's success in elections
    - Frequently
    - Occasionally
    - Rarely
    - Never
    - Other: _____
33. Would you say that your party's informal documents (memos, emails) discuss ways in which more female officeholders in the party might help the party succeed in its policy goals (advancing policies that are important to the party, passing legislation, etc.)
    - Frequently
    - Occasionally
    - Rarely

- Never
- Other: _____
34. If yes to question #27: would you say that your party followed this informal rule at the time when you first entered politics?
    - Yes
    - No
    - I first entered politics with a different party from the one I am currently a member of (if so: did that party follow an informal rule at the time when you first entered politics? Y/N)
    - Other: _____
35. If answer to #34 is yes: how effective do you think these informal strategies for increasing women's presence in office are?
    - Very effective
    - Somewhat effective
    - Neither effective nor ineffective
    - Somewhat ineffective
    - Very ineffective
36. If you wish to elaborate on your responses to questions on informal practices for increasing the number of female candidates in your party, please do so in the space below.

Appendix D

Interviews with German Legislators

*T*his appendix summarizes personal interviews with German state- and national-level legislators (or their staff, where indicated in Table D.2). All interviews were conducted by the author.

TABLE D.1 INTERVIEWS CONDUCTED 2007–2008

Political Party	Party's # Seats in the 16th Bundestag	Women's Presence in the 16th Bundestag: # (% of Party)	# Interviews: Women	# Interviews: Men
LINKE	54	26 (49.1%)	6	7
B90/Gr	51	30 (58.8%)	5	3
SPD	222	79 (36.0%)	7	4
CDU	180	38 (21.1%)	5	6
CSU	46	9 (19.6%)	1	2
FDP	61	15 (24.6%)	4	4

Source: IPU Archive of Statistical Data for August 2009, available at http://www.ipu.org/wmn-e/arc/classif 310809.htm.

Note: The total number of legislators at the end of the sixteenth legislative period was 612, including 197 women.

TABLE D.2 INTERVIEWS CONDUCTED 2014 AND 2017	
2014	2017
7 women officeholders in the CDU: 6 – Bundestag (federal) 1 – Berliner Abgeordnetenhaus (state)	**10 women officeholders/party staff:** 2 – AfD (state legislators) 5 – CDU (state legislators) 1 – CDU (staff with the Frauen Union) 1 – FDP (state legislator) 1 – FDP (staff with the Liberale Frauen)

Appendix E

Cross-National Analyses

This appendix displays the political parties included in Chapter 8's cross-national analyses.

TABLE E.1 COUNTRIES AND PARTIES IN THE CROSS-NATIONAL DATASET

Country	Election Year	Left Parties	Center Parties	Right Parties
Australia	2016	Australian Greens, Australian Labor Party, Katter's Australian Party	Liberal National Party of Queensland, Nick Xenophon Team	Liberal Party of Australia, Nationals
Austria	2013	Social Democratic Party, The Greens	NEOS, Team Stronach	Austrian People's Party, Freedom Party
Belgium	2014	Green, ECOLO, Socialist Party Differently, Socialist Party, Workers' Party of Belgium	Francophone Democratic Front, Party of Liberty and Progress, Reformist Movement	Flemish Christian People's Party, Flemish Interest, Humanist Democratic Center, N-VA/V&W, Parti Populaire
Canada	2015	Green Party, New Democratic Party, Québec Bloc	Liberal Party	Conservative Party
Chile	2013	Communist Party, Democratic Revolution, Ecological Green Party, Humanist Party, Party for Democracy, Social Democrat Radical Party, Social Green Regionalist Federation, Social Convergence, Socialist Party of Chile	Liberal Party of Chile	Christian Democratic Party, Independent Democratic Union, National Renewal, Political Evolution

TABLE E.1 COUNTRIES AND PARTIES IN THE CROSS-NATIONAL DATASET (continued)

Country	Election Year	Left Parties	Center Parties	Right Parties
Czech Republic	2013	Communist Party of Bohemia and Moravia, Czech Social Democratic Party	Yes 2011	Christian Democratic Union/People's Party, Civic Democratic Party, Dawn of Direct Democracy, Tradition Responsibility Prosperity
Denmark	2015	Alternative, Red-Green Alliance, Republican Party, Social Democrats, Socialist People's Party	Danish Social-Liberal Party/Radical Liberal Party, Liberal Party, New Liberal Alliance	Conservative People's Party, Danish People's Party
Estonia	2015	Estonian Centre Party, Social Democratic Party/Moderates	Estonian Reform Party	Estonian People's Party, Free Party, Union of Pro Patria and Res Publica
Finland	2015	Green League, Left Alliance, Social Democratic Party of Finland	Agrarian Union/Centre Party, Finnish Party/True Finns, Swedish People's Party	Christian Democrats, National Coalition Party
France	2012	French Communist Party/Left Front, Greens, Miscellaneous Left (DVG), Radical Party of the Left, Socialist Party	—	Democratic Movement, Miscellaneous Right (DVD), National Front, Union for a Popular Movement, Union of Democrats and Independents
Germany	2013	Bündnis 90/Greens, Social Democratic Party, The Left	—	Christian Democratic Union, Christian Social Union
Greece	2015	Coalition of Radical Left (SYRIZA), Communist Party, Panhellenic Socialist Movement/Democratic Alignment, The River	Union of Centrists	Independent Greeks (ANEL), New Democracy, Golden Dawn
Hungary	2014	Hungarian Socialist Party, Politics Can Be Different	—	Christian Democratic People's Party, Hungarian Civic Alliance, Movement for a Better Hungary
Iceland	2016	Left-Green Movement, Pirate Party of Iceland, Social Democratic Alliance	Bright Future, Progressive Party	Independence Party, Reform Party
Ireland	2016	People before Profit, Labour Party, Sinn Fein, Social Democrats	—	Fianna Fail, Fine Gael

(continued)

TABLE E.1 COUNTRIES AND PARTIES IN THE CROSS-NATIONAL DATASET (continued)

Country	Election Year	Left Parties	Center Parties	Right Parties
Israel	2015	Alignment, Meretz	All of Us, There Is a Future	Israel Is Our Home, Jewish Home, Likud, Shas, United Torah Judaism
Italy	2013	Articolo 1, Democratic Party, Left Ecology Freedom	Centre-Right Coalition, Civic Choice	Brothers of Italy, Forward Italy, North League
Japan	2014	Japan Communist Party, Social Democratic Party	—	Clean Government Party, Democratic Party of Japan, Japan Restoration Party, Liberal Democratic Party, Party for Future Generations, Putting People's Lives First
Latvia	2014	Harmony Centre	Green and Farmers' Union	Latvian Association of Regions, National Alliance/Fatherland and Freedom/LNNK, Unity
Luxembourg	2013	Luxembourg Socialist Workers' Party, The Greens, The Left	Democratic Party	Action Committee Pensions/Alternative Democratic Reform Party, Christian Social People's Party
Mexico	2015	Convergence, Ecologist Green Party of Mexico, National Regeneration Movement, Party of the Democratic Revolution	Institutional Revolutionary Party, New Alliance	National Action Party, Social Encounter
Netherlands	2012	Green Left, Labour, Socialist Party	Democrats 66, Party for People over 50, People's Party for Freedom and Democracy	Christian Democratic Appeal, Christian Union, Party for Freedom, Reformed Political Party
New Zealand	2014	Green Party, Labour Party	ACT New Zealand	National Party, New Zealand First Party, United Future
Norway	2013	Green, Norwegian Labour Party, Socialist Left Party	Centre Party, Liberal Party of Norway	Christian Democratic Party, Conservative Party, Progress Party
Poland	2015	—	Modern, Polish People's Party	Civic Platform, Kukiz '15, Law and Justice
Portugal	2015	Left Bloc, Party for People, Animals, and Nature, Social Party, Unified Democratic Coalition	Popular Democratic Party/Social Democratic Party	—
Republic of Korea	2016	Justice Party	Democratic Party, People's Party	Liberty Korea Party

TABLE E.1 COUNTRIES AND PARTIES IN THE CROSS-NATIONAL DATASET (continued)

Country	Election Year	Left Parties	Center Parties	Right Parties
Slovakia	2016	Direction—Social Democracy	Freedom and Solidarity	Most-Hid, Network, Ordinary People and Independents, People's Party Our Slovakia, Slovak. National Party, We Are Family—Boris Kollar
Slovenia	2014	Alliance of Alenka Bratusek, Party of Miro Cerar/Modern Center Party, Social Democrats/ United List of Social Democrats	—	New Slovenia—Christian People's Party, Slovenian Democratic Party
Spain	2016	Compromise, Spanish Socialist Workers' Party, United We Can, Left Alliance	Citizens	Basque Nationalist Party, People's Alliance Party/ People's Party
Sweden	2014	Greens, Left Party/ Communist Party, Social Democrats	Farmers' League/ Centre Party, Liberals/People's Party	Christian Democrats, Right Party/Moderate Party, Sweden Democrats
Switzerland	2015	Green Liberal Party, Green Party, Social Democratic Party of Switzerland, Swiss Labor Party	The Liberals, Swiss People's Party	Catholic Conservative/ Christian Democratic Party, Conservative Democratic Party of Switzerland, Evangelical People's Party, Geneva Citizens' Movement, Ticino League
Turkey	2015	Peoples' Democratic Party, Republican People's Party	—	Justice and Development, Nationalist Movement Party
United Kingdom	2015	Greens, Labour, Scottish National Party, Sinn Fein, Social Democratic and Labour	Liberal Democratic Party	Conservatives, Democratic Unionists, Ulster Unionist Party, United Kingdom Independence Party
United States	2016	Democratic Party	—	Republican Party

Note: The first column lists the thirty-five countries that were OECD members in 2017. Subsequent columns categorize families of parties that won seats in their national lower legislative house in the election closest to and before January 1, 2017. Parties that did not win seats in that election are not included in the dataset.

TABLE E.2 DESCRIPTIVE STATISTICS FOR VARIABLES IN CROSS-NATIONAL ANALYSES

Variable	Unit of Analysis	N Parties	Mean	Std. Dev.	Min	Max
Proportion of party's seats held by women *Countries' electoral commission websites*	Political party	281	0.295	0.2185	0	1
Whether one or more party leaders are women *Parties' websites*	Political party	261	0.234	0.424	0	1
Left-Center-Right party family category *CPDS, V-Dem, ParlGov*	Political party	256	1.973	0.909	1	3
Hegemonic-ethnic supremacy (0–4, where 0 = least ethnic supremacist and 4 = most ethnic supremacist) *V-Dem*	Political party	210	1.561	1.139	0	4
Mean district magnitude *DPI, ESCE*	Political system	281	20.148	34.640	0.9	150
Whether there is a national quota rule *GDGQ*	Political system	281	0.406	0.492	0	1
Whether electoral rules are proportional *DPI, IPU*	Political system	281	0.897	0.305	0	1
Effective number of political parties *CPDS, Gallagher and Mitchell*	Political system	281	4.438	1.812	1.98	8.84
Pro-gender-equality attitudes (% of survey respondents) *WVS, ESS, IDI*	Political system	281	75.333	14.020	45	94
Women's paid labor force participation (% of women 15+ years) *WB*	Political system	281	53.985	6.985	32.6	73.2

Source: Comparative Political Database (CPDS), Database of Political Institutions (DPI), Electoral System Change in Europe since 1945 (ESCE), European Social Survey (ESS), Gallagher and Mitchell (2008), Global Database of Gender Quotas (GDGQ), Israel Democracy Institute (IDI), ParlGov, Varieties of Democracy (V-Dem), World Bank (WB), World Values Survey (WVS).

TABLE E.3 PARTIES' RATES OF ELECTING WOMEN ACROSS LEFT–CENTER–RIGHT FAMILIES

	Women's Rates of Election		
	Parties on the *Left*	Parties at the *Center*	Parties on the *Right*
	Model 3 Coefficient (Std. Error)	Model 4 Coefficient (Std. Error)	Model 5 Coefficient (Std. Error)
National Gender Quota	0.066 (0.043)	−0.005 (0.065)	0.085 (0.037) **
Effective # of Parties	−0.001 (0.013)	−0.001 (0.022)	0.035 (0.011) **
Pro-gender-equality Attitudes	0.001 (0.001)	0.004 (0.002) **	0.000 (0.001)
WLFP	0.005 (0.003) *	0.001 (0.007)	0.005 (0.004)
Constant	−0.032 (0.143)	−0.001 (0.038)	−0.249 (0.165)
N	108	46	102
$P > F$	0.083	0.027	0.001
R^2	0.045	0.155	0.197

Note: The model displayed includes only contextual variables, not features of specific political parties (except for the subsetting within the dataset). This more limited model reinforces the message that contextual variables affect right-leaning parties more so than left- or center-leaning parties.

Entries are unstandardized coefficients from OLS regression models. Standard errors are clustered by country and noted in parentheses. The unit of analysis is the party-year.

Model 3: A Breusch-Pagan test does not indicate concern regarding heteroscedasticity ($P > X^2 = 0.583$). Variance Inflation Factors (VIFs) are between 1.32 and 2.66 (mean 1.97).

Model 4: A Breusch-Pagan test indicates some concern regarding heteroscedasticity ($P > X^2 = 0.087$). VIFs are between 1.26 and 2.78 (mean 2.01).

Model 5: A Breusch-Pagan test indicates some concern regarding heteroscedasticity ($P > X^2 = 0.001$). VIFs are between 1.12 and 2.56 (mean 1.84).

* $p < 0.10$; ** $p < 0.05$; *** $p < 0.001$

TABLE E.4 WHETHER PARTY LEADERSHIP INCLUDES WOMEN: LEFT—CENTER—RIGHT

	Women's Party Leadership		
	Parties on the *Left*	Parties at the *Center*	Parties on the *Right*
	Model 3	Model 4	Model 5
Effective # of Parties	−0.041 (0.100)	0.251 (0.206)	−0.620 (0.181) **
Pro-gender-equality Attitudes	0.007 (0.014)	−0.025 (0.032)	0.034 (0.015) **
WLFP	−0.003 (0.030)	0.038 (0.050)	0.020 (0.043)
Constant	−0.860 (1.269)	−2.960 (2.375)	−2.600 (2.041)
N	105	46	99
$P > X^2$	0.951	0.597	0.000
Pseudo R^2	0.002	0.031	0.127

Note: This model displayed includes only contextual variables, not features of specific political parties (except for the subsetting within the dataset).

Entries are unstandardized coefficients from logistic regression models. Standard errors are clustered by country and noted in parentheses. The unit of analysis is the party-year. The inclusion of the dichotomous variable for a national gender quota does not substantively change these models.

Model 3: A link test indicates that the model is not misspecified; a Hosmer-Lemeshow test indicates that the model fits the data well ($p > X^2 = 0.767$).

Model 4: A link test indicates that the model is not misspecified; a Hosmer-Lemeshow test indicates that the model fits the data well ($p > X^2 = 0.404$).

Model 5: 7: A link test indicates that the model is not misspecified; a Hosmer-Lemeshow test indicates that the model fits the data well ($p > X^2 = 0.797$).

* $p < 0.10$; ** $p < 0.05$; *** $p < 0.001$

Notes

CHAPTER 1

1. Caul (2001) finds that gender quotas originate in party systems on the left. Swers (1998) finds that, controlling for sex-gender, members of the Democratic Party are more likely than Republicans to support "women's issues bills," especially on reproductive issues and women's health. Xydias (2014) finds that women German legislators on the left are more active in promoting women's economic and political rights (more feminist), while their women counterparts on the right are active in women's family-related rights (more traditionalist). Celis and Erzeel (2015) explicitly look "beyond the usual suspects," at non-left and nonfeminist legislators, for sources of women's advocacy. Similarly, Celis and Childs (2012) refer to "an unstated conflation between the substantive representation of women and the substantive representation of (leftist/liberal/progressive) feminist interests" (p. 216).

2. "Women's Rights Organizations," Womankind Worldwide, available at https://www.womankind.org.uk/policy-and-campaigns/women's-rights/women's-rights-organisations.

3. See, for example, *Deutsche Welle*, "Merkel and the Female Question," September 1, 2005, available at http://www.dw.com/en/merkel-and-the-female-question/a-1697967.

4. Women disproportionally supported right-leaning parties through the 1970s. See Box-Steffensmeier, de Boef, and Lin (2004); Duverger (1955); Inglehart and Norris (2000); and Kaufmann (2002). Attitudinal surveys show that women shifted to supporting the left at higher rates than their men counterparts in the 1970s–1980s. This is known as realignment; see Inglehart and Norris (2000) and Norris (1996).

5. Attention to this variation is a growing research program in political science. Recent work on explaining global and within-U.S. variation in the promotion of women's rights includes Barnes and Cassese (2017) and Htun and Weldon (2018).

6. As subsequent sections and chapters discuss at greater length, this book generally refers to "sex-gender" as a nexus of biological and social forces. It takes the position that

the extent to which we can view women as a coherent social group is a product of both. On the argument that shared labor, and shared *expectations* of labor, "create" women as a group, see K. Jones and Jónasdóttir (1988); Phillips (1998); and Sapiro (1981).

7. By "majority ethnic status," I refer to the ethnic group that embodies the highest socioeconomic status. In the contemporary United States, for example, this is white Americans of European heritage.

8. Celis and Childs (2012); Celis and Erzeel (2015); Webb and Childs (2012); De Geus and Shorrocks (2020); O'Brien (2018); Och and Shames (2018); Plumb (2016); Shames, Och, and Cooperman (2020); Xydias (2022).

9. See O'Brien (2018) for attention to "righting the conventional wisdom" regarding variation among party families.

10. On Germany, see Ferree (2012). On provisions within Germany's Basic Law in comparative perspective, see McDonagh (2009, pp. 38–39).

11. McDonagh (2009) categorizes Germany among those countries that have made an affirmative commitment to protecting its residents' social welfare. Similarly, Krook, Lovenduski, and Squires (2009) categorize Germany as having a consociationalist-corporatist model of citizenship, by which community members "share a philosophical commitment to social partnership" (p. 789) and "place the onus for unequal outcomes on broader social structures" (p. 790).

12. See also Xydias (2014), which disaggregates attention to women's interests in order to observe interparty variation.

13. Goldstein (2001); Sjoberg (2016); Stiehm (1982); Tickner (1992); Young (2003).

14. See Anthias (2012); Dhamoon (2011); Duerst-Lahti (2008); and Nash (2008) on how intersectionality as a methodology must not treat indicators of marginalization as discrete and unchanging, because this ignores how power relationships are created (and, therefore, how they might change).

15. See Reingold and Smith (2012); Strolovitch (2006); and Walsh and Xydias (2014).

16. See Hancock (2007) on trade-offs among empirical approaches to intersectionality.

17. The World Economic Forum reports in 2017 that the ratio of women's to men's pay ranges from 0.67 in lower-middle income countries to 0.72 in high-income countries, with considerable variation within each country category. See "The Global Gender Gap Report 2017," World Economic Forum, available at http://reports.weforum.org/global-gender-gap-report-2017/.

18. Inter-parliamentary Union Women in National Parliaments, data reported for March 2, 2018. These data are available at http://archive.ipu.org/wmn-e/world.htm.

19. WHO, "Violence against Women—Fact Sheet," 2017, available at http://www.who.int/mediacentre/factsheets/fs239/en/.

20. See Gunnarsson (2011); Rifkin (1980); and Walby (1989). Patriarchy is discussed at greater length in Chapter 2 as a source of theoretical expectations regarding political actors' engagement in promoting women's rights and interests.

21. See Celis and Childs (2012).

22. See, for example, Swers (2002) and Thomas (1994). Reingold, Haynie, and Widner (2020) update this attention to incorporate intersectional policies, i.e., those policies that are "intentional in addressing distinct challenges these [multiply marginalized] groups face by offering culturally or group appropriate specialized programs and services" (p. 121).

23. Diamond and Hartsock (1981); Jónasdóttir (1988); Walby (1989).

24. R. Brown (2016a). On the European context, see Shutes and Chiatti (2012) and Simonazzi (2008).

25. Celis and Childs (2012, p. 215). See Celis (2006); Pitkin (1967); Swers (2002); and Xydias (2014). Women's substantive representation consists of "acting for or on behalf of" women, though these actions' content and their consequences are wide ranging. Celis and Childs (2020) refer to the "affected representative" as an advocate who accurately invokes social groups' perspectives, conditions, and needs.

26. See Budge et al. (2006); Camia and Caramani (2012); and Hooghe, Marks, and Wilson (2002).

27. See Huber and Inglehart (1995); Imbeau, Petry, and Lamari (2001); and Ross (2000).

28. Quantitative analyses in existing research almost universally control for ideological placement on the left or right. When this variable is statistically significant, this result is taken for granted. When it is not statistically significant, the author typically observes that it must be confounded by the effects of other variables.

29. Original presentations of this concept include Duverger (1954); Seiler (1980); and Beyme (1984).

30. Marks, Wilson, and Ray's (2002) nine party-family categories include extreme right, conservative, liberal, Christian democratic, social democratic, green, regionalist, protestant, and agrarian.

31. Celis, Schouteden, and Wauters's (2015) party family categories include Christian democratic, conservative, extreme right, green, liberal democratic, social democratic, regionalist, and a residual category.

32. Goldstein (2001); Sjoberg (2016); Stiehm (1982); Tickner (1992); Young (2003).

CHAPTER 2

1. Walsh and Xydias (2014). See also Htun and Ossa (2013) on the case of Bolivia, where an intersectional lens clarifies why a gender quota was implemented but Indigenous rights stagnated.

2. See N. Brown and Banks (2014); Jordan-Zachery (2017); Reingold and Smith (2012); and Strolovitch (2006).

3. See work in social psychology on the congruence of social roles, such as Eagly and Johanessen-Schmidt (2001) and Eagly and Karau (2002). On the cross-national persistence of gendered political leadership, specifically, see Duerst-Lahti (1997); Duerst-Lahti and Kelly (1996); and Jalalzai and dos Santos (2021).

4. See discussion of the wide range of definitions that political scientists provide for *ideology* in Gerring (1997) and Xydias (2021). Gerring asserts that the commonality across all of these definitions is that ideology is viewed as consisting of a stable set of principles. Putnam (1971) similarly defines ideology as "an explicit, consciously held belief system" (p. 655).

5. See, for example, Green-Pedersen (2007) and Green-Pedersen and Mortensen (2015) on system-wide factors shaping issue competition.

6. Gerring (1997) argues that "political culture" is more amorphous than "ideology." See also Krook, Lovenduski, and Squires (2009) on, alternatively, "models of political citizenship."

7. Framing xenophobia in terms of "hegemonic-ethnic supremacy vs. multiculturalism" has a basis in existing research. See, for example, Yuval-Davis (1997) on how a multitiered (ethnicity-disaggregated/intersectional) model of citizenship is needed to understand women's citizenship and their rights. On disaggregated/hierarchical models of citizenship, see also Dietz (1987); Peleg (2007); and Sasson-Levy (2013).

8. Budge (2006); Camia and Caramani (2012); Hooghe, Marks, and Wilson (2002).

9. See Koenker (1995) on the persistence of patriarchy on the Soviet shop floor, Jaquette and Wolchik (1998) on Soviet failure to resolve the "woman question" (i.e., worsened double burden), and Lapidus (1975) on the ineffectiveness of women's integration into political leaderships in the Soviet Union.

10. The World Values Survey is available at https://www.worldvaluessurvey.org/wvs.jsp.

11. See Mushaben (2009); and Schreurs (2003, p. 156).

12. See Blee (2003); Rogers and Litt (2003); and Xydias (2020).

13. See also Jacobs and Skocpol (2005); Lindblom (1968); and Strolovitch (2006).

14. See Cox (2000, p. 170), who argues that rules may be effectively exogenous if it is too costly for political actors to change them. See also the discussion in Shepsle and Weingast (1984), who argue that most rules are endogenous.

CHAPTER 3

1. See Ferree (2012, p. 18). Pfau-Effinger (2004) offers an explanation for the development of Germany's Hausfrau social and economic model.

2. UN Refugee Agency, UNHCR, available at https://www.unhcr.org/en-us/germany.html.

3. Das Präsidium des Deutschen Bundestages, available at https://www.bundestag.de/parlament/praesidium/praesidium-196416.

4. Twelve of the fourteen parties in this analysis (all but the REP and NPD) have election programs updated for 2017.

5. See discussions in Gerhard (1990); Meyer (2003); Schiller (2003); and Xydias (2014).

6. See discussion in Chandler (1995, pp. 344–346).

7. Chandler (1995, pp. 347–348).

8. See McFadden (2019, p. 72).

9. See Laurence and Maxwell (2012, pp. 13–31).

10. Bonn was the seat of the West German capital from 1949; after reunification, the Bundestag moved back to Berlin in 1999. See Cullen (1999, pp. 66–78).

11. Petra Pau and Gesine Lötzsch won direct mandates in Berlin. They served in the Bundestag without a party group (*fraktionslos*).

12. For more English-language detail on state-level electoral and legislative institutions, see Gunlicks (2003).

13. For a lengthier historical treatment of these political parties and their origins and development, see Gunlicks (2003, pp. 267–273) and Bergsträsser (1965). In the 2021 federal election, the regionalist party, the *Südschleswigscher Wählerverband* (SSW), won a single seat in the Bundestag and was represented at the national level for the first time since 1953.

14. Germany united into the German Empire, a federated, partially democratic parliamentary system, at the end of the Franco-Prussian War in 1871. See MacGregor (2016) and H. Schulze (1998).

15. These parties are *liberal* in the European sense of the term: prioritizing individual rights and a free market.

16. On the FDP's formation out of wider ranging and locally rooted liberal parties, see Dittberner (1987).

17. Boutwell (1983, pp. 78, 80); Summers (2015); Xydias (2013).

18. For a more extensive discussion of the Left Party's emergence, see Hough, Koß, and Olsen (2007).

19. Formally, joint efforts by the AfD and PEGIDA have been limited, but they share broader goals. See *Deutsche Welle*, "AfD, PEGIDA Hold Side-by-Side Events in Dresden," May 9, 2017, available at https://www.dw.com/en/afd-pegida-hold-side-by-side-events-in-dresden/a-38761338.

20. Arzheimer (2015); Franzmann (2016); Grimm (2015); Schmitt-Beck (2017); and Wüst (2016).

21. Döring and Manow (2020). Information is available at the ParlGov project's website: https://parlgov.org/data/codebook.pdf.

22. Döring and Manow (2020). Information is available at the ParlGov project's website: https://parlgov.org/data/codebook.pdf.

23. Castles and Mair (1984); the Chapel Hill expert surveys.

24. Gabel and Huber (2000, pp. 94–95); Mair and Mudde (1998, p. 218).

25. Benoit and Laver (2007, pp. 94–95); Laver (2001).

26. Döring and Manow (2020). Information is available at the ParlGov project's website: https://parlgov.org/data/codebook.pdf.

27. Lührmann et al. (2020). The V-Party codebook is available at https://www.V-Dem.net/data/the-V-Dem-dataset/.

CHAPTER 4

1. Suffrage expanded to include women twenty years of age and older in 1918. Occupational and other restrictions on women increased during the Nazi regime (1933–1945), but, subsequently, article 3 of the FRG's Basic Law (1949) states that all persons (women and men) are equal before the law and that men and women have equal rights. An additional sentence formulated after Germany's reunification in 1990 states: "The state shall promote the actual implementation of equal rights for women and men and take steps to eliminate disadvantages that now exist." Other formal inequalities written into the German Civil Code were removed in the 1950s and 1970s. See Kolinsky (1993) and Xydias (2014).

2. See Bjarnegård (2013); Norris and Lovenduski (1995); Piscopo (2019); Shames et al. (2021).

3. In Israel, Itzkovich-Malka and Friedberg (2018); in Switzerland, Lloren (2015); in the United States, Swers (2013); and in Germany, Xydias (2013, 2014).

4. On the tendency of policymaking to favor majority-status group members, see N. Brown (2014); Reingold, Haynie, and Widner (2020); Reingold and Smith (2012); Strolovitch (2006); and Walsh and Xydias (2014).

5. See, for example, Mansbridge and Tate (1992) for a discussion of attention to inequalities that are inflected by both race-ethnicity and gender.

6. Countries where women nominally gained suffrage in the 1990s–2000s also include Afghanistan, Brunei, Kuwait, Oman, Qatar, Saudi Arabia, and the United Arab Emirates. However, these are all settings where suffrage rights are sufficiently ineffectual for all citizens, regardless of gender. This makes it difficult to meaningfully refer to women's empowerment in a democratic political sense. Other, authoritarian countries, such as the People's Republic of North Korea, do not formally discriminate on the basis of sex-gender, and yet we would similarly not describe North Korean women as empowered by their political rights.

7. An extensive research program exists showing the salience of electoral system rules for accounting for variation in women's rates of election. Because these rules are held constant for all political parties in Germany, this literature is not addressed in this chapter.

8. See Bjarnegård (2013); Kenny (2013); and Bjarnegård and Kenny (2016).

9. More specifically, on the choice to frame the issue as a matter of men's overrepresentation, see also Bjarnegård and Murray (2018); Clayton, O'Brien, and Piscopo (2019); and Davidson-Schmich (2016, p. 1).

10. See Inglehart and Norris (2003); Paxton, Hughes, and Barnes (2020); and Sanbonmatsu (2002).

11. See Burns, Schlozman, and Verba (1994, 1997); Paxton, Hughes, and Barnes (2020, chapters 5–6); and Bernhard, Shames, and Teele (2021).

12. The exceptions are the NPD and the REP, for which platforms for 2017 could not be located. In the case of the REP, the federal program posted on their website (https://www.die-republikaner.net/) is undated. In the case of the NPD, the version widely circulated appears to be most recently revised in 2010.

13. Plenarprotokolle 15/141, November 24, 2004, p. 13099.

14. Plenarprotokolle 15/141, November 24, 2004, p. 13104.

15. Plenarprotokolle 16/55, September 29, 2006, p. 5356.

16. Plenarprotokolle 16/55, September 29, 2006, p. 5356.

CHAPTER 5

1. See Waylen (2017) for a compilation of essays showing the application of feminist institutionalism to understanding political recruitment across a diverse range of political systems worldwide. See Lowndes (2020) for an analysis of the persistence of gendered inequalities in spite of gender equality policies.

2. See Krook and Norris (2014) for an overview of strategies "beyond quotas."

3. Dahlerup and Freidenvall (2005); Davidson-Schmich (2006, 2016); Krook (2009, chapter 3); M. Jones (1994); R. Murray (2007).

4. See also Krook (2009, chapter 2).

5. Exceptions include Clover et al. (2011), which compares training programs in Canada and India, and Ruf (2021), which examines parties' nonquota strategies to promote women candidates for local elections in the German state of Baden-Württemberg.

6. See Appendix D for additional detail regarding these personal interviews with German officeholders.

7. Reuters (2020).

8. See discussion in Kittilson (2006, pp. 94–95, 100).

9. See Agresti (2002, p. 91) and Larntz (1978).

10. These personal interviews took place between 2007 and 2017, with officeholders primarily at the federal level. See Appendix D for more details.

11. Reported in the *SZ-Siegen*: "Kreis-AfD gründet Frauengruppe," available at https://afd-siegen-wittgenstein.de/aktuelles/2019/01/frauengruppe-gegruendet/.

12. The KAS website is available at www.kas.de; the KAS Facebook events calendar is available at https://www.facebook.com/kasfb/.

13. Nouns in the German language are gendered. Over the last ten years, a variety of typographical options for achieving gender-inclusive language has come into common use. This includes the "'gender star,' an asterisk placed within a noun to indicate it refers to men, women and nonbinary people alike" (Nicholson 2021).

14. The HSS Facebook events calendar is available at https://www.facebook.com/HannsSeidelStiftung/.

15. The FNF Facebook events calendar is available at www.facebook.com/FriedrichNaumannStiftungFreiheit/events.

16. These included a breakfast time event on participating in debates ("Frühstückstraining," November 20, 2020) and several iterations of a crash course in public speech ("Crashkurs Rhetorik—Die Kunst der freien Rede," November 1 and October 31, 2020; "Politische Rhetorik Grundlagen," January 26, 2020).

17. These included Social Media for Political Activists ("Social Media für politische Aktivisten," October 19, 2019), Storytelling on Instagram ("Social Media #ThursDate: Storytelling bei Instagram," May 28, 2020), and Getting Followers ("Follower gewinnen," June 28, 2020).

18. The calendar entry reads: "Das LIBERAL SKILL CAMP gibt Ihnen die Gelegenheit sich innerhalb eines Nachmittags zentrale Fertigkeiten für politische Kampagnen anzueignen: Sie rotieren alle 45 Minuten zwischen den vier Modulen und bekommen so Einblicke in politische Rhetorik, in Tricks & Kniffe politischer Kommunikation durch Social Media, in Kampagne- und Fundraisingstrategien für politische Verbände."

19. "Sind es die Vorurteile, Frauen seien weniger selbstbewusst als Männer und können sich nicht richtig durchsetzen? Oder doch Schwierigkeiten bei der Vereinbarkeit von Karriere und Familie? Welche politischen Themen treiben Frauen eigentlich um und wofür würden sie sich einsetzen?"

20. These included: "More Women in Leadership Positions" (Mehr Frauen in die Chefetagen, February 6, 2020) and Women in Media (February 8, 2020). An event called "Overqualified and Underrepresented?" addressed the career opportunities of well-educated women (Überqualifiziert und unterrepräsentiert? July 12, 2020).

21. Information is available at https://www.freiheit.org/de/deutschland/film-die-perfekte-kandidatin.

22. Information is available at https://www.freiheit.org/empowerment.

23. Information is available at https://www.freiheit.org/form/empowerment-interessenten.

24. Information is available at https://www.boell.de/de/2017/04/26/mehr-macht-fuer-frauen-der-weg-fuehrt-ueber-die-quote?dimension1=ds_feminismus.

25. The HBS Facebook events calendar is available at https://www.facebook.com/boellstiftung/events/.

26. "Patriarchale Strukturen und offene oder versteckte Diskriminierung in der Arbeitswelt oder im Alltag müssen analysiert, aufgebrochen und verändert werden. Deswegen empowern und stärken wir uns im Frauen-Arbeitskreis auch gegenseitig. Wir arbeiten generationenübergreifend, sprechen mit Feministinnen der zweiten Frauenbewegung, lernen voneinander und entwickeln gemeinsam Visionen für das 21. Jahrhundert als feministisches Jahrzehnt," available at https://gruene-darmstadt.de/kreisverband/ueber-uns/arbeitskreis/arbeitskreis-gruene-frauen/.

27. "Alle Interessierten laden wir ein, zu unseren Sitzungen zu kommen, mit uns zu diskutieren und grüne Politik aus feministischer Perspektive zu gestalten," available at https://gruene.berlin/ueber-uns/wer-wir-sind/landesarbeitsgemeinschaften/lag-frauen-und-gender.

28. The finding that the B90/Gr are particularly active in their mentorship and training programs corroborates Ruf's (2021) findings for the state of Baden-Württemberg.

29. Information is available at https://www.die-linke.de/partei/parteidemokratie/parteitag/siebenter-parteitag/frauenplenum/resolution-des-frauenplenums/.

30. Information is available at https://www.fes.de/stiftung/politische-bildung-und-beratung/arbeitseinheiten-politische-akademie.

31. The Party School at the Willy-Brandt-Haus has a wiki, which is available at https://parteischule-wiki.spd.de/.

32. Hunt and Michael (1983) offer a review of early scholarship on organizational behavior on this topic.

33. Information is available at https://parlgov.org/data/codebook.pdf.

CHAPTER 6

1. See discussions in Wüst (2016) and Wüst and Faas (2018), which focus on the share of the voting population who migrated to Germany and are ethnic minorities (termed Migrationshintergrund, meaning a "migrant background").

2. See Matland (1993); Matland and Studlar (1996); Norris (2004); and Rule (1987).

3. Matland (1993); Matland and Taylor (1997).

4. Dahlerup and Freidenvall (2005); Franceschet, Krook, and Piscopo (2012); Kittilson (2005).

5. Davidson-Schmich (2016); R. Murray (2007); Schwindt-Bayer (2009); Valdini (2019); Weeks (2018).

6. See Iversen and Rosenbluth (2008); and Kenworthy and Malami (1999).

7. This biographical information is drawn from MdB biographical pages, available at Bundestag.de.

8. The exception is the 2008 Federal Constitutional Court ruling that found overhang seats unconstitutional. Thus, as of the 2013 Bundestag election, the overall allocation of seats must remain proportional with the distribution of second votes. (See discussion in Chapter 3.) Other changes have gone into effect that affect elections after this book's time frame, such as an amendment that applies to the 2021 federal election and temporarily lowers the number of supporting signatures required to validate a constituency nomination (the provision expires at the end of 2021). Some changes apply into the future, such as the 2020 amendment reducing the number of districts from 299 to 280.

9. See Coffé and Davidson-Schmich (2020) comparing women's candidacies in the systems of New Zealand and Germany, Davidson-Schmich (2014) on Germany, and Fortin-Rittberger and Eder (2013) on Germany.

10. Basic details of Baerbock's curriculum vitae are available at Bundesregierung.de, the web page for the foreign ministry; Baerbock has been the foreign minister since 2021. A more extensive CV is in her MdB bio, available at https://www.bundestag.de/abgeordnete/biografien/B/baerbock_annalena-857150.

CHAPTER 7

1. General Wolf Graf von Baudissin, a significant influence on the formation of the FRG military in the 1950s and the creator of the concept of the *Innere Führung*, emphasized the figure of the "citizen soldier" (Baudissin 1969, p. 195).

2. See discussion in Chapter 3. Also, see Ferree (2012); and Wiliarty (2010).

3. See Ngai (1999) for additional analysis of race-based restrictions implemented in the United States.

4. See, for example, Baban, Ilcan, and Rygiel (2017) on the limited options for Syrian refugees in Turkey, who have some social citizenship rights but are not full citizens, and Yeoh et al. (2021) on the partial citizenship of "marriage migrants" in Singapore.

5. See Irving (2008, chapter 4).

6. "Frauen in der Bundeswehr: Europa Machte Es Möglich," available at https://www.bundeswehr.de/de/ueber-die-bundeswehr/selbstverstaendnis-bundeswehr/chancengerechtigkeit-bundeswehr/frauen-bundeswehr.

Notes to Chapter 7 / 219

7. "100 Billion Euros for a Powerful Federal Armed Forces," June 3, 2022, available at https://www.bundesregierung.de/breg-en/service/special-fund-federal-armed-forces-2047910.

8. *Deutsche Welle*, February 27, 2022.

9. See Berger (2003); and Meiers (2005, pp. 160–161).

10. The Bundeswehr was reduced in size significantly after the end of the Soviet Union and the reunification of Germany; information is available at https://www.bundeswehr.de/en/about-bundeswehr/history/reforms-bundeswehr. As noted earlier, June 2022 marked a significant increase in funding for the Bundeswehr in response to Russia's invasion of Ukraine.

11. For discussions of ECJ rulings and EU member states' armed forces, see Liebert (2004); Schwarze (2002); Slagter (2006); and Xydias (2017).

12. See "Wehrpflicht soll zum 1. Juli ausgesetzt werden," FAZ, November 24, 2010, available at https://www.faz.net/aktuell/politik/inland/bundeswehr-wehrpflicht-soll-zum-1-juli-ausgesetzt-werden-1577622.html.

13. Figure 7.1 and the discussion of it draw from Xydias (2017).

14. Quoted, in 1997, "Ich will Soldatin sein! Bettina Beggerow klagt als erste Frau gegen das letzte Berufsverbot," *EMMA*, September–October.

15. *Die Welt*, "Europa-Richter?" October 27, 1999.

16. BT-Plenarprotokoll, 14/69, 11.11.99, p. 6246.

17. BT-Plenarprotokoll, 14/124, 12.10.00, p. 11890.

18. BT-Plenarprotokoll, 14/131, 10.11.00, p. 12671.

19. BT-Plenarprotokoll, 14/69, 11.11.99, p. 6251.

20. BT-Plenarprotokoll, 14/69, 11.11.99, p. 6253.

21. BT-Plenarprotokoll, 14/69, 11.11.99, p. 6246.

22. BT-Plenarprotokoll, 14/124, 12.10.00, pp. 11870–11874.

23. BT-Plenarprotokoll, 14/124, 12.10.00, p. 11885.

24. BT-Plenarprotokoll, 14/128, 27.10.00, and Drucksache 14/4380.

25. BT-Plenarprotokoll, 14/128, 27.10.00, p. 12339.

26. BT-Plenarprotokoll, 14/128, 27.10.00, p. 12341.

27. BT-Plenarprotokoll, 14/128, 27.10.00, p. 12343.

28. BT-Plenarprotokoll, 14/128, 27.10.00. p. 12340.

29. BT-Plenarprotokoll, 14/128, 27.10.00, p. 12347.

30. BT-Plenarprotokoll, 14/128, 27.10.00, p. 12385.

31. BT-Plenarprotokoll, 17/47, 11.6.10.

32. Bundesrat-Drucksache 859/10; Bundestag-Drucksachen 17/4821, 17/5239.

33. BT-Plenarprotokoll, 17/99, 24.3.11, p. 11342.

34. BT-Plenarprotokoll, 17/99, 24.3.11, p. 11342.

35. BT-Plenarprotokoll, 17/99, 24.3.11, p. 11342.

36. BT-Plenarprotokoll, 17/99, 24.3.11, p. 11343.

37. BT-Plenarprotokoll, 17/99, 24.3.11, p. 11343.

38. BT-Plenarprotokoll, 17/99, 24.3.11, pp. 11345–11346.

39. BT-Plenarprotokoll, 17/99, 24.3.11, p. 11352.

40. BT-Plenarprotokoll, 17/99, 24.3.11, p. 11353.

41. BT-Plenarprotokoll, 17/99, 24.3.11, p. 11348.

42. BT-Plenarprotokoll, 17/99, 24.3.11, p. 11350.

43. See Faist (2015, p. 193); and Hailbronner and Farahat (2015).

44. See Ireland (2004, pp. 28–29); and Triadafilopoulos (2012, pp. 2–3).

45. With the exception of Walter Scheel's (FDP) brief tenure as chancellor in May 1974.

46. Schily was a founder of Germany's Green Party in 1980. He switched to the SPD in 1989.
47. Hailbronner (2006, pp. 229–230); Ingram and Triadafilopoulos (2010, p. 375).
48. Bundestag-Drucksache 14/533.
49. BT-Plenarprotokolle 14/40, May 7, 1999, p. 3475.
50. BT-Plenarprotokoll, 14/128, May 7, 1999, p. 3475.
51. See discussions in, among others, Joppke (1999, chapter 3); Triadafilopoulos (2012, p. 2); and H. Williams (2014, p. 57).
52. See discussions in Koltermann (2012, p. 4); and Kutz (2003, p. 17).
53. See Abenheim (1988, chapter 4); Kucera (2017, p. 47); and Kutz (2003, pp. 113–114).
54. Gesley (2016) discusses Heuss's perspective on this subject.

CHAPTER 8

1. For example, Doron (2005) discusses the inadequacy of conventional left-right categories for understanding Israeli coalition building, and Haklai and Rass (2022) show that Arab Israeli voters are not monolithic (p. 37).
2. As of January 2017, the OECD had thirty-five member states. Colombia, Costa Rica, and Lithuania have joined since that time. Officeholding data in this chapter's analyses refer to the elections closest and prior to January 1, 2017 (e.g., women's presence in Australia's House of Representatives as of the country's July 2016 elections). See Xydias (2022), which offers an analysis of the 281 seat-holding parties across these thirty-five countries with attention to hegemonic-ethnic supremacy as a key factor in interparty variation on women's rights and interests.
3. ParlGov data are available at: https://parlgov.org/; V-Dem data are available at https://www.V-Dem.net/; and CHES data are available at https://www.chesdata.eu/.
4. World Values Survey available at https://www.worldvaluessurvey.org/wvs.jsp; European Social Survey available at https://www.europeansocialsurvey.org/; and Israel Democracy Institute available at https://en.idi.org.il/.
5. See Kunovich and Paxton (2005); and Paxton and Kunovich (2003). The Database of Gender Quotas is available at https://www.idea.int/data-tools/data/gender-quotas-database. Data on gendered patterns from the World Bank are available at https://genderdata.worldbank.org/.
6. Research about this broader matter exists on many issues and in many disciplines. For example, on the feminization of poverty, see Goldberg (2010). On the need for financial resources to exit abusive relationships, see Showalter (2016).
7. Data on the labor force participation of women fifteen years of age and older are from the World Bank for 2016.
8. Information on World Bank (2022) is available at https://www.worldbank.org/en/news/press-release/2022/03/01/nearly-2-4-billion-women-globally-don-t-have-same-economic-rights-as-men.
9. Information on the OECD (2022) part-time employment rate (indicator) was accessed on August 1, 2022, and is available at https://doi.org/10.1787/f2ad596c-en.
10. Information on the International Labor Organization (2022) is available at https://www.ilo.org/wcmsp5/groups/public/---ed_protect/---protrav/---travail/documents/publication/wcms_849209.pdf.
11. Lührmann et al. (2020, p. 28).
12. See discussion in Chapters 1–2.
13. Lührmann et al. (2020, pp. 25–26).

14. Gallagher (1991) and Gallagher and Mitchell (2008). Updated election indices are available at https://www.tcd.ie/Political_Science/about/people/michael_gallagher/ElSystems/Docts/ElectionIndices.pdf.

CHAPTER 9

1. Merkel herself disputed this characterization, although Scholz campaigned on their shared record. See Bennhold and Eddy (2021); and Oltermann (2021).

2. See Wüst (2016); and Wüst and Faas (2018).

References

Abels, Gabrielle, Petra Ahrens, Anne Jenichen, and Malliga Och. 2022. "The 2021 Federal German Election: A Gender and Intersectional Analysis." *Politics* 42 (3): 249–266.

Abenheim, Donald. 1988. *Reforging the Iron Cross: The Search for Tradition in the West German Armed Forces*. Princeton, NJ: Princeton University Press.

Adams, James, Michael Clark, Lawrence Ezrow, and Garrett Glasgow. 2004. "Understanding Change and Stability in Party Ideologies: Do Parties Respond to Public Opinion or to Past Election Results?" *British Journal of Political Science* 34 (4): 589–610.

Addario, Lynsey. 2019. "On Today's Battlefields, More Women Than Ever Are in the Fight." *National Geographic* 236 (5): 132–151.

Agresti, Alan. 2002. *Categorical Data Analysis*. 2nd ed. New York: Wiley Interscience.

Alba, Richard. 2005. "Bright vs. Blurred Boundaries: Second-Generation Assimilation and Exclusion in France, Germany, and the United States." *Ethnic and Racial Studies* 28 (1): 20–49.

Alemán, Eduardo, and Sebastián M. Saiegh. 2007. "Legislative Preferences, Political Parties, and Coalition Unity in Chile." *Comparative Politics* 39 (3): 253–272.

Alexander, Amy, and Christian Welzel. 2011. "Empowering Women: The Role of Emancipative Beliefs." *European Sociological Review* 27 (3): 364–384.

Althusser, Louise. 1971. *Lenin and Philosophy and Other Essays*. New York: Monthly Review.

Anil, Merih. 2005. "No More Foreigners? The Remaking of German Naturalization and Citizenship Law, 1990–2000." *Dialectical Anthropology* 29 (3–4): 453–470.

Anthias, Floya. 2012. "Transnational Mobilities, Migration Research and Intersectionality." *Nordic Journal of Migration Research* 2 (2): 102–110.

Apelt, Maja. 2015. "Der Lange Abschied von der männlichen Organisation: Geschlechterverhältnisse zwischen Formalität und Informalität am Beispiel des Militärs." In *Formalität und Informalität in Organisation*, edited by Victoria von Groddeck and Sylvia Marlene Wilz. Wiesbaden: Springer VS.

Arzheimer, Kai. 2015. "The AfD: Finally a Successful Right-Wing Populist Eurosceptic Party for Germany?" *West European Politics* 38 (3): 535–556.

Atchison, Amy L., and Ian Downs. 2019. "The Effects of Women Officeholders on Environmental Policy." *Review of Policy Research* 36 (6): 805–834.

Baban, Feyzi, Suzan Ilcan, and Kim Rygiel. 2017. "Syrian Refugees in Turkey: Pathways to Precarity, Differential Inclusion, and Negotiated Citizenship Rights." *Journal of Ethnic and Migration Studies* 43 (1): 41–57.

Bacchi, Carol. 2009. *Analysing Policy: What's the Problem Represented to Be?* Frenchs Forest, NSW: Pearson.

Bale, Jeff. 2017. "Gendering the Controversy over Education Policy Reform in Hamburg, Germany." In Davidson-Schmich 2017, 145–172.

Barker, Fiona, and Hilde Coffé. 2018. "Representing Diversity in Mixed Electoral Systems: The Case of New Zealand." *Parliamentary Affairs* 71 (3): 603–632.

Barnes, Tiffany D., and Erin C. Cassese. 2017. "American Party Women: A Look at the Gender Gap within Parties." *Political Research Quarterly* 70 (1): 127–141.

Baudissin, Wolf Graf von. [1969] 1970. *Soldat für den Frieden: in Politik - Strategie - Führung von Streitkräften.* Munich: R. Piper.

Bennhold, Katrin, and Melissa Eddy. 2021. "Merkel Departs, Opening a New Chapter for Germany and Europe." *New York Times*, December 8, 2021. Available at https://www.nytimes.com/2021/12/08/world/europe/germany-merkel-scholz-chancellor-government.html.

Benoit, Kenneth, and Michael Laver. 2007. "Estimating Party Policy Positions: Comparing Expert Surveys and Hand-Coded Content Analysis." *Electoral Studies* 26: 90–107.

Berger, Thomas. 2003. *Cultures of Antimilitarism: National Security in Germany and Japan.* Baltimore: Johns Hopkins University Press.

Bergsträsser, Ludwig. 1965. *Geschichte der Politischen Parteien in Deutschland.* Munich: Wilhelm Mommsen.

Bernhard, Rachel, Shauna Shames, and Dawn Teele. 2021. "To Emerge? Breadwinning, Motherhood, and Women's Decisions to Run for Office." *American Political Science Review* 115 (2): 379–394.

Bernzen, Enno, Dirk Peddinghaus, and Robert Sieger. 2016. "*Innere Führung*—Leadership Culture in Camouflage." Available at http://www.ethikundmilitaer.de/en/full-issues/2016-innere-fuehrung/zentrum-innere-fuehrung-innere-fuehrung-leadership-culture-in-camouflage/.

Beyme, Klaus von. 1984. *Politische Parteien in Westeuropa.* Munich: Piper.

Bieber, Ina E. 2018. "Frauen in der FDP- Mehr Chancen durch Vielfalt." Mannheim: GESIS—Leibniz-Institut für Sozialwissenschaften.

Biezen, Ingrid van, Peter Mair, and Thomas Poguntke. 2012. "Going, Going, . . . Gone? The Decline of Party Membership in Contemporary Europe." *European Journal of Political Research* 51:24–56.

Bjarnegård, Elin. 2013. *Gender, Informal Institutions and Political Recruitment: Explaining Male Dominance in Parliamentary Representation.* Springer.

Bjarnegård, Elin, and Meryl Kenny. 2016. "Comparing Candidate Selection: A Feminist Institutionalist Approach." *Government and Opposition* 51 (3): 370–392.

Bjarnegård, Elin, and Rainbow Murray. 2018. "Revisiting Forms of Representation by Critically Examining Men." *Politics and Gender* 14 (2): 265–270.

Blee, Kathleen M. 2003. *Inside Organized Racism: Women in the Hate Movement.* Berkeley: University of California Press.

———. 2007. "Ethnographies of the Far Right." *Journal of Contemporary Ethnography* 36 (2): 119–128.
Bobbio, Norberto. 1994. *Left and Right: The Significance of a Political Distinction*. Chicago: University of Chicago Press.
Böhme, Irene. 1983. *Die da drüben: Sieben Kapitel DDR*. Berlin: Rotbuch.
Boix, Carles. 1999. "Setting the Rules of the Game: The Choice of Electoral Systems in Advanced Democracies." *American Political Science Review* 93 (3): 609–624.
Boutwell, Jeffrey. 1983. "Politics and the Peace Movement in West Germany." *International Security* 7 (4): 72–92.
Box-Steffensmeier, Jan, Suzanna de Boef, and Tse-min Lin. 2004. "The Dynamics of the Partisan Gender Gap." *American Political Science Review* 98 (3): 515–528.
Brenner, Yermi. May 2, 2018. "When Refugees Lead: Conversation with German Politician Omid Nouripour." *New Humanitarian*. Available at https://deeply.thenewhumanitarian.org/refugees/community/2018/05/02/when-refugees-lead-conversation-with-german-politician-omid-nouripour/.
Brown, Erik. 2021. "Interpreting the 2021 German Federal Election Results." Brookings Institution. October 28, 2021. Available at https://www.brookings.edu/events/interpreting-the-2021-german-federal-election-results/.
Brown, Nadia. 2014. *Sisters in the Statehouse: Black Women and Legislative Decision Making*. New York: Oxford University Press.
Brown, Nadia, and Kira Hudson Banks. 2014. "Black Women's Agenda Setting in the Maryland State Legislature." *Journal of African American Studies* 18 (2): 164–180.
Brown, Rachel H. 2016a. "Four Years, Three Months: Migrant Caregivers in Israel/Palestine." Ph.D. diss., City University of New York.
———. 2016b. "Multiple Modes of Care: Internet and Migrant Caregiver Networks in Israel." *Global Networks* 16 (2): 237–256.
Brubaker, Rogers. 1992. *Citizenship and Nationhood in France and Germany*. Cambridge, MA: Harvard University Press.
———. 2001. "The Return of Assimilation? Changing Perspectives on Immigration and Its Sequels in France, Germany, and the United States." *Ethnic and Racial Studies* 24 (4): 531–548.
Buck, Tobias. 2019. "German Army Struggles to Attract Much-Needed Recruits." *Financial Times*, January 29, 2019. Available at https://www.ft.com/content/ffc33796-23ce-11e9-8ce6-5db4543da632.
Budge, Ian. 2000. "Expert Judgements of Party Policy Positions: Uses and Limitations in Political Research." *European Journal of Political Research* 37:103–113.
———. 2001. "Validating Party Policy Placements." *British Journal of Political Science* 31 (1): 210–223.
———. 2006. "Identifying Dimensions and Locating Parties: Methodological and Conceptual Problems." In *Handbook of Political Parties*, edited by Richard S. Katz and William J. Crotty. Sage.
Budge, Ian, Hans-Dieter Klingemann, Andrea Volkens, and Judith Bara. 2006. *Mapping Policy Preferences, 1984–2004: Eastern Europe and the OECD*. Oxford: Oxford University Press.
Der Bundeswahlleiter (Sonderhefte). 2009. *Die Wahlbewerber für die Wahl zum Deutschen Bundestag* (The Candidates for the Election to the German Bundestag), available at https://www.bundeswahlleiter.de.
———. 2013. *Die Wahlbewerber für die Wahl zum Deutschen Bundestag* (The Candidates for the Election to the German Bundestag), available at https://www.bundeswahlleiter.de.

———. 2017. *Die Wahlbewerber für die Wahl zum Deutschen Bundestag* (The Candidates for the Election to the German Bundestag), available at https://www.bundeswahl leiter.de.

Buschschlüter, Vanessa. 2022. "Chile Constitution: Voters Overwhelmingly Reject Radical Change." BBC, September 5, 2022. Available at https://www.bbc.com/news/world-latin-america-62792025.

Butler, Judith. 1990. *Gender Trouble: Feminism and the Subversion of Identity*. New York: Routledge.

Camia, Valeria, and Daniele Caramani. 2012. "Family Meetings: Ideological Convergence within Party Families across Europe, 1945–2009." *Comparative European Politics* 10: 48–85.

Campbell, Angus, Philip E. Converse, Warren P. Miller, and Donald E. Stokes. 1960. *The American Voter*. New York: Wiley.

Caramani, Daniele, and Simon Hug. 1998. "The Literature on European Parties and Party Systems since 1945: A Quantitative Analysis." *European Journal of Political Research* 33 (4): 497–524.

Carey, John. 2002. "Parties, Coalitions, and the Chilean Congress in the 1990s." In *Legislative Politics in Latin America*, edited by Scott Morgenstern and Benito Nacif, 222–253. Cambridge: Cambridge University Press.

Carmines, Edward G., and James A. Stimson. 1993. "On the Evolution of Political Issues." *Agenda Formation* 151:151–152.

Cassese, Erin C., and Tiffany Barnes. 2018. "Reconciling Sexism and Women's Support for Republican Candidates: A Look at Gender, Class, and Whiteness in the 2012 and 2016 Presidential Races." *Political Behavior* 35 (3): 677–700.

Cassese, Erin C., and Mirya R. Holman. 2017. "Religion, Gendered Authority, and Identity in American Politics." *Politics and Religion* 10 (1): 31–56.

Castles, Francis G., and Peter Mair. 1984. "Left–Right Political Scales: Some Expert Judgements." *European Journal of Political Research* 12:73–88.

Caul, Miki. 2001. "Political Parties and the Adoption of Candidate Gender Quotas: A Cross-National Analysis." *Journal of Politics* 63 (4): 1214–1229.

Celis, Karen. 2006. "Substantive Representation of Women: The Representation of Women's Interests and the Impact of Descriptive Representation in the Belgian Parliament (1900–1979)." *Journal of Women, Politics and Policy* 28 (2): 85–114.

Celis, Karen, and Sarah Childs. 2012. "The Substantive Representation of Women: What to Do with Conservative Claims?" *Political Studies* 60:213–225.

———. 2020. *Feminist Democratic Representation*. New York: Oxford University Press.

Celis, Karen, Sarah Childs, Johanna Kantola, and Mona Lena Krook. 2008. "Rethinking Women's Substantive Representation." *Representation* 44 (2): 99–110.

Celis, Karen, and Silvia Erzeel. 2015. "Beyond the Usual Suspects: Non-Left, Male and Non-Feminist MPs and the Substantive Representation of Women." *Government and Opposition* 50 (1): 45–64.

Celis, Karen, Anke Schouteden, and Braum Wauters. 2015. "Cleavage, Ideology, and Identity: Explaining the Linkage between Representatives and Interest Groups." *Parliamentary Affairs* 69 (2): 348–365.

Chandler, William M. 1995. "Immigration Politics and Citizenship in Germany." In *The Federal Republic of Germany at Forty-Five: Union without Unity*, edited by Peter H. Merkl, 344–356. Washington Square: New York University Press.

Chapel Hill Expert Survey (CHES), available at https://www.chesdata.eu/.
Clayton, Amanda, Diana Z. O'Brien, and Jennifer M. Piscopo. 2019. "All Male Panels? Representation and Democratic Legitimacy." *American Journal of Political Science* 63 (1): 113–129.
Clover, Darlene E., Catherine McGregor, Martha Farrell, and Mandakini Pant. 2011. "Women Learning Politics and the Politics of Learning: A Feminist Study of Canada and India." *Studies in the Education of Adults* 43 (1): 18–33.
Coffé, Hilde, and Louise K. Davidson-Schmich. 2020. "The Gendered Political Ambition Cycle in Mixed-Member Electoral Systems." *European Journal of Politics and Gender* 3 (1): 79–99.
Collins, Patricia Hill. 2000. "Gender, Black Feminism, and Black Political Economy." *Annals of the American Academy of Political and Social Science* 568:41–53.
Connell, R. W., and James W. Messerschmidt. 2005. "Hegemonic Masculinity: Rethinking the Concept." *Gender and Society* 19 (6): 829–859.
Converse, Philip E. 1964. "The Nature of Belief Systems in Mass Publics." In *Ideology and Discontent*, edited by David E. Apter. New York: Free Press.
Cotgrove, Stephen, and Andrew Duff. 1981. "Environmentalism, Values, and Social Change." *British Journal of Sociology* 32 (1): 92–110.
Cox, Gary W. 2000. "On the Effects of Legislative Rules." *Legislative Studies Quarterly* 25 (2): 169–192.
Crenshaw, Kimberlé. 1989. "Demarginalizing the Intersection of Race and Sex: A Black Feminist Critique of Antidiscrimination Doctrine, Feminist Theory, and Antiracist Politics," 1989: 139–167. *University of Chicago Legal Forum*.
Crepaz, Markus M. L. 2008. *Trust beyond Borders: Immigration, the Welfare State, and Identity in Modern Societies*. Ann Arbor: University of Michigan Press.
Crowder-Meyer, Melody. 2020. "Baker, Bus Driver, Babysitter, Candidate? Revealing the Gendered Development of Political Ambition among Ordinary Americans." *Political Behavior* 42:359–384.
Cullen, Michael S. 1999. *The Reichstag: German Parliament between Monarchy and Federalism*. Berlin-Brandenburg: be.bra.
Curry, Jane, and Joan Urban, eds. 2003. *The Left Transformed in Post-Communist Societies: The Cases of East-Central Europe, Russia, and Ukraine*. Washington, D.C.: Rowman and Littlefield.
Dahlerup, Drude, and Lenita Freidenvall. 2005. "Quotas as a 'Fast Track' to Equal Representation for Women: Why Scandinavia Is No Longer the Model." *International Feminist Journal of Politics* 7 (1): 26–48.
Database of Political Institutions. 2015. Codebook. Available at https://publications.iadb.org/en/database-political-institutions-2015-dpi2015.
Davidson-Schmich, Louise K. 2006. "Implementation of Political Party Gender Quotas: Evidence from the German Laender 1990–2000." *German Politics* 12 (2): 211–232.
———. 2014. "Closing the Gap: Gender and Constituency Candidate Nomination in the 2013 Bundestag Election." *German Politics and Society* 32 (2): 86–105.
———. 2016. *Gender Quotas and Democratic Participation: Recruiting Candidates for Elective Offices in Germany*. Ann Arbor: University of Michigan Press.
———, ed. 2017. *Gender, Intersections, and Institutions: Intersectional Groups Building Alliances and Gaining Voice in Germany*. Ann Arbor: University of Michigan Press.
Decker, Frank, and Viola Neu. 2017. *Handbuch der Deutschen Parteien*. 3rd ed. Wiesbaden: Springer Fachmedien Wiesbaden.

De Geus, Roosmarijn A., and Rosalind Shorrocks. 2020. "Where Do Female Conservatives Stand? A Cross-National Analysis of the Issue Positions and Ideological Placement of Female Right-Wing Candidates." *Journal of Women, Politics and Policy* 41 (1): 7–35.

Deiss-Helbig, Elisa. 2018. "Within the Secret Garden of Politics: Candidate Selection and the Representation of Immigrant-Origin Citizens in Germany." Ph.D. diss., Institut für Sozialwissenschaften der Universität Stuttgart.

Demuth, Christian. 2004. "Neue Rekrutierungs- und Professionalisierungsstrategien der Parteien: Fort- und Weiterbildung der Mitglieder." *Zeitschrift für Parlamentsfragen* 35 (4): 700–716.

Deutsche Welle. 2005. "Merkel and the Female Question." September 1, 2005. Available at http://www.dw.com/en/merkel-and-the-female-question/a-1697967.

———. 2017. "AfD, PEGIDA Hold Side-by-Side Events in Dresden." May 9, 2017. Available at https://www.dw.com/en/afd-pegida-hold-side-by-side-events-in-dresden/a-38761338.

———. 2019. "More Right-Wing Extremists Found in German Military." September 3, 2019. Available at https://www.dw.com/en/germany-more-right-wing-extremist-soldiers-uncovered-than-previously-reported/a-47838341.

———. 2021. "Germany's Incoming Government Signs Three-Party Coalition Deal." December 7, 2021. Available at https://www.dw.com/en/germanys-incoming-government-signs-three-party-coalition-deal/a-60039455.

———. 2022. "Germany Commits €100 Billion to Defense Spending." February 27, 2022. Available at https://www.dw.com/en/germany-commits-100-billion-to-defense-spending/a-60933724.

Dhamoon, Rita Kaur. 2011. "Considerations on Mainstreaming Intersectionality." *Political Research Quarterly* 64 (1): 230–243.

Diamond, Irene, and Nancy Hartsock. 1981. "Beyond Interests in Politics: A Comment on Virginia Sapiro's 'When Are Interests Interesting? The Problem of Political Representation of Women.'" *American Political Science Review* 75 (3): 717–721.

Dietz, Mary G. 1987. "Context Is All: Feminism and Theories of Citizenship." *Daedalus* 116 (4): 1–24.

Dittberner, Jürgen. 1987. *FDP—Partei Der Zweiten Wahl: Ein Beitrag zur Geschichte der Liberalen Partei und Ihrer Funktion im Parteiensystem der Bundesrepublik*. Opladen: Westdeutscher.

Donovan, Barbara. 2007. "'Minority' Representation in Germany." *German Politics* 16 (4): 455–480.

———. 2017. "Migrant Women and Immigrant Integration Policy." In Davidson-Schmich 2017.

Döring, Holger, ed. 1995. *Parliaments and Majority Rule in Europe*. Mannheim Centre for European Social Research (MZES), University of Mannheim.

———. 2001. "Parliamentary Agenda Control and Legislative Outcomes in Western Europe." *Legislative Studies Quarterly* 26 (1): 145–165.

Döring, Holger, and Philip Manow. 2020. *Parliaments and Governments Database (Parlgov): Information on Parties, Elections and Cabinets in Modern Democracies*. Development version.

Doron, Gideon. 2005. "Right as Opposed to Wrong as Opposed to Left: The Spatial Location of 'Right Parties' on the Israeli Political Map." *Israel Studies* 10 (3): 29–53.

Dostal, Jörg Michael. 2021. "Germany's Federal Election of 2021: Multi-Crisis Politics and the Consolidation of the Six-Party System." *Political Quarterly* 92 (4): 662–672.

Dubrow, Joshua K. 2008. "How Can We Account for Intersectionality in Quantitative Analysis of Survey Data? Empirical Illustration for Central and Eastern Europe." *ASK* 17:85–100.
Duerst-Lahti, Georgia. 1997. "Reconceiving Theories of Power: Consequences of Masculinism in the Executive Branch." In *The Other Elites*, edited by MaryAnne Borelli and Janet M. Martin, 11–32. Boulder, CO: Lynne Rienner.
———. 2008. "'Seeing What Has Always Been': Opening Study of the Presidency." *PS: Political Science and Politics* 41 (4): 733–737.
Duerst-Lahti, Georgia, and Rita Mae Kelly, eds. 1996. *Gender, Power, Leadership and Governance*. Ann Arbor: University of Michigan Press.
Duverger, Maurice. 1954. *Political Parties: Their Organization and Activity in the Modern State*. Hoboken: John Wiley & Sons.
———. 1955. *The Political Role of Women*. Paris: UNESCO.
Eagly, Alice H., and Mary C. Johanessen-Schmidt. 2001. "The Leadership Styles of Women and Men." *Journal of Social Issues* 57 (4): 781–797.
Eagly, Alice H., and Steven J. Karau. 2002. "Role Congruity Theory of Prejudice toward Female Leaders." *Psychological Review* 109 (3): 573–598.
Edinger, Lewis Joachim, and Brigitte Lebens Nacos. 1998. *From Bonn to Berlin: German Politics in Transition*. New York: Columbia University Press.
Eijk, Cees van der, Hermann Schmitt, and Tanja Binder. 2005. "Left-Right Orientations and Party Choice." In *The European Voter: A Comparative Study of Modern Democracies*, edited by Jacques Thomassen. Oxford: Oxford University Press.
Einhorn, Barbara. 1991. "Where Have All the Women Gone? Women and the Women's Movement in East Central Europe." *Feminist Review* 39 (1): 16–36.
Elger, Katrin, Ansbert Kneip, and Merlind Theile. 2009. "Survey Shows Alarming Lack of Integration in Germany." *Der Spiegel*, January 26, 2009. Available at https://www.spiegel.de/international/germany/immigrant-survey-shows-alarming-lack-of-integration-in-germany-a-603588.html.
Erenz, Benedikt. 2005. "Die Kampagne 'Du bist Deutschland' hat einen historischen Vorläufer." *ZeitOnline*, November 30, 2005. Available at https://www.zeit.de/online/2005/48/denn_du_bist_deutschland?utm_referrer=https%3A%2F%2Fen.wikipedia.org%2F.
Eriksson, Anton, Jana Konle, Malina Aniol, Nikki Shure, and Thomas Fröhlich. 2021. "The Decline of the Political Center in Germany." American-German Institute, September 23, 2021. Available at https://www.aicgs.org/2021/09/the-decline-of-the-political-center-in-germany/.
Erzeel, Silvia, and Karen Celis. 2016. "Political Parties, Ideology and the Substantive Representation of Women." *Party Politics* 22 (5): 576–586.
Erzeel, Silvia, and Ekaterina R. Rashkova. 2017. "Still Men's Parties? Gender and the Radical Right in Comparative Perspective." *West European Politics* 40 (4): 812–20.
Escobar-Lemmon, Maria C., and Michelle Taylor-Robinson. 2016. *Women in Presidential Cabinets: Power Players or Abundant Tokens?* New York: Oxford University Press.
European Social Survey, available at https://www.europeansocialsurvey.org/.
Faist, Thomas. 2015. "Shapeshifting Citizenship in Germany: Expansion, Erosion, and Extension." In *The Human Right to Citizenship: A Slippery Concept*, edited by Rhoda E. Howard-Hassmann and Margaret Walton-Roberts, 193–208. Philadelphia: University of Pennsylvania Press.
Falkenhagen, Frédéric. 2013. "The CSU as an Ethno-Regional Party." *German Politics* 22 (4): 396–420.

Federici, Silvia. 2020. *Revolution at Point Zero: Housework, Reproduction, and Feminist Struggle*. Binghamton, NY: PM Press.
Ferree, Myra Marx. 2012. *Varieties of Feminism: German Gender Politics in Global Perspective*. Redwood City, CA: Stanford University Press.
Florvil, Tiffany. 2020. *Mobilizing Black Germany: Afro-German Women and the Making a Transnational Movement*. Champaign: University of Illinois Press.
FOCUS Magazin. 2005. "Mehr Liberale Frauen an die Macht." Available at https://www.focus.de/politik/deutschland/mehr-liberale-frauen-an-die-macht-fdp_id_2037914.html.
Fortin-Rittberger, Jessica, and Christina Eder. 2013. "Towards a Gender-Equal Bundestag? The Impact of Electoral Rules on Women's Representation." *West European Politics* 36 (5): 969–985.
Fox, Richard L., and Jennifer L. Lawless. 2010. "If Only They'd Ask: Gender, Recruitment, and Political Ambition." *Journal of Politics* 72 (2): 310–326.
Franceschet, Susan, Mona Lena Krook, and Jennifer M. Piscopo, eds. 2012. *The Impact of Gender Quotas*. Oxford: Oxford University Press.
Franzmann, Simon T. 2016. "Calling the Ghost of Populism: The AfD's Strategic and Tactical Agendas until the EP Election 2014." *German Politics* 25 (4): 457–479.
Fredriksson, Per, and Le Wang. 2011. "Sex and Environmental Policy in the U.S. House of Representatives." *Economics Letters* 113 (3): 228–230.
Gabel, Matthew T., and John D. Huber. 2000. "Putting Parties in Their Place: Inferring Party Left-Right Ideological Positions from Party Manifestos Data." *American Journal of Political Science* 44 (1): 94–103.
Gallagher, Michael. 1991. "Proportionality, Disproportionality and Electoral Systems." *Electoral Studies* 10:33–51. Updated indices available at https://www.tcd.ie/Political_Science/about/people/michael_gallagher/ElSystems/Docts/ElectionIndices.pdf.
Gallagher, Michael, and Paul Mitchell, eds. 2008. *The Politics of Electoral Systems*. New York: Oxford University Press.
Gemenis, Kostas. 2012. "Proxy Documents as a Source of Measurement Error in the Comparative Manifestos Project." *Electoral Studies* 31:594–404.
Gerhard, Ute. 1990. *Gleichheit ohne Angleichung: Frauen im Recht*. Munich: C. H. Beck.
———. 1999. *Atempause: Feminismus als Demokratisches Projekt*. Frankfurt am Main: Fischer Taschenbuch.
Gerring, John. 1997. "Ideology: A Definitional Analysis." *Political Research Quarterly* 50 (4): 957–994.
Gesley, Jenny. 2016. "60 Year Anniversary of the German Compulsory Military Service Act." Library of Congress Blogs. Available at https://blogs.loc.gov/law/2016/07/60-year-anniversary-of-the-german-compulsory-military-service-act/.
———. 2017. "Germany: The Development of Migration and Citizenship Law in Postwar Germany." Law Library of Congress. LL File No. 2017-014428 LRA-D-PUB-002384.
Gilmore, Glenda Elizabeth. 2019. *Gender and Jim Crow: Women and the Politics of White Supremacy in North Carolina, 1896–1920*. Chapel Hill: University of North Carolina Press.
Goldberg, Gertrude Schaffner. 2010. *Poor Women in Rich Countries: The Feminization of Poverty over the Life Course*. New York: Oxford University Press.
Goldenberg, Rina. 2020. "Germany: Birth Rate Drops, Confirms Dramatic Prediction." *Deutsche Welle*, July 31, 2020. Available at https://www.dw.com/en/demography-german-birthrate-down-in-coronavirus-pandemic/a-54395345.

Golder, Matt. 2003. "Explaining Variation in the Success of Extreme Right Parties in Western Europe." *Comparative Political Studies* 36 (4): 432–466.
Goldstein, Joshua. 2001. *War and Gender*. Cambridge: Cambridge University Press.
Green-Pedersen, Christoffer. 2007. "The Growing Importance of Issue Competition: The Changing Nature of Party Competition in Western Europe." *Political Studies* 55 (3): 607–628.
Green-Pedersen, Christoffer, and Peter B. Mortensen. 2015. "Avoidance and Engagement: Issue Competition in Multiparty Systems." *Political Studies* 63 (4): 747–764.
Grimm, Robert. 2015. "The Rise of the Germany Eurosceptic Party Alternative für Deutschland, between Ordoliberal Critique and Power Anxiety." *International Political Science Review* 36 (3): 264–278.
Gunlicks, Arthur. 2003. *The* Länder *and German Federalism*. Manchester: Manchester University Press.
Gunnarsson, Lena. 2011. "A Defence of the Category 'Women.'" *Feminist Theory* 12 (1): 23–37.
Gutmann, Amy. 1994. *Multiculturalism: Expanded Paperback Edition*. Princeton, NJ: Princeton University Press.
———. 2003. *Identity in Democracy*. Princeton, NJ: Princeton University Press.
Haar, Marleen van der, and Mieke Verloo. 2013. "Unpacking the Russian Doll: Gendered and Intersectionalized Categories in European Gender Equality Policies." *Politics, Groups and Identities* 1 (3): 417–432.
Hagen, Jürgen von. 1992. "Budgeting Procedures and Fiscal Performance in the European Communities." No. 96. Directorate-General for Economic and Financial Affairs, Commission of the European Communities. Brussels.
Hailbronner, Kay. 2006. "Germany." In *Acquisition and Loss of Nationality: Policies and Trends in 15 European Countries*, edited by Rainer Bauböck, Eva Ersbøll, Kees Groenendijk, and Harald Waldrauch, 213–252. Amsterdam: Amsterdam University Press.
Hailbronner, Kay, and Anuscheh Farahat. 2015. "Country Report on Citizenship Law: Germany." EUDO Citizenship Observatory, European University Institute, Florence.
Haklai, Oded, and Rida Abu Rass. 2022. "The Fourth Phase of Palestinian Arab Politics in Israel: The Centripetal Turn." *Israel Studies* 27 (1): 35–60.
Hancock, Ange-Marie. 2007. "Intersectionality as a Normative and Empirical Paradigm." *Politics and Gender* 3 (2): 248–254.
Hanley, Seán. 2004. "Getting the Right Right: Redefining the Centre-Right in Post-Communist Europe." *Journal of Communist Studies and Transition Politics* 20 (3): 9–27.
Hansen, Michael A., and Jonathan Olsen. 2019. "Flesh of the Same Flesh: A Study of Voters for the Alternative for Germany (AfD) in the 2017 Federal Election." *German Politics* 28 (1): 1–19.
Hawkesworth, Mary. 2003. "Congressional Enactments of Race-Gender: Toward a Theory of Raced-Gendered Institutions." *American Political Science Review* 97 (4): 529–550.
Hettling, Manfred. 2022. "Bürger, Bürgertum, Bürgerlichkeit." *Docupedia-Zeitgeschichte*, June 8, 2022. Available at http://docupedia.de/zg/hettling_buerger_v1_en_2016.
Higham, John. [1955] 2002. *Strangers in the Land: Patterns of American Nativism, 1860–1925*. Reprint, New Brunswick, NJ: Rutgers University Press.
Hinojosa, Magda. 2012. *Selecting Women, Electing Women: Political Representation and Candidate Selection in Latin America*. Philadelphia: Temple University Press.
Hix, Simon, Abdul Noury, and Gérard Roland. 2005. "Dimensions of Politics in the European Parliament." *American Journal of Political Science* 50 (2): 494–511.

Holly, Werner. 2009. "Gemeinschaft ohne Solidarität: Zur paradoxen Grundstruktur der 'Du bist Deutschland'—Kampagne." In *Einigkeitsdiskurse: Zur Inszenierung von Konsens in organisationaler und öffentlicher Kommunikation*, edited by Stephan Habscheid and Clemens Knobloch, 154–175. Wiesbaden: VS Verlag für Sozialwissenschaften.

Hooghe, Liesbet, Gary Marks, and Carole J. Wilson. 2002. "Does Left/Right Structure Party Positions on European Integration?" *Comparative Political Studies* 35 (8): 965–989.

Hough, Dan, Michael Koß, and Jonathan Olsen. 2007. *The Left Party in Contemporary German Politics*. New York: Springer.

Htun, Mala, and Juan Pablo Ossa. 2013. "Political Inclusion of Marginalized Groups: Indigenous Reservations and Gender Parity in Bolivia." *Politics, Groups, and Identities* 1 (1): 4–25.

Htun, Mala, and Laurel Weldon. 2018. *The Logics of Gender Justice: State Action on Women's Rights around the World*. Cambridge: Cambridge University Press.

Huber, John, and Ronald Inglehart. 1995. "Expert Interpretations of Party Space and Party Locations in 42 Societies." *Party Politics* 1:73–111.

Hughes, Melanie M. 2011. "Intersectionality, Quotas, and Minority Women's Political Representation Worldwide." *American Political Science Review* 105 (3): 604–620.

Hunt, David Marshall, and Carol Michael. 1983. "Mentorship: A Career Training and Development Tool." *Academy of Management Review* 8 (3): 475–485.

Imbeau, Louise M., Francois Petry, and Moktar Lamari. 2001. "Left Right Ideology and Government Policies: A Meta-Analysis." *European Journal of Political Research* 40 (1): 1–29.

Inglehart, Ronald. 1971. "The Silent Revolution in Europe: Intergenerational Change in Post-Industrial Societies." *American Political Science Review* 65 (4): 991–1017.

———. 1977. "Values, Objective Needs, and Subjective Satisfaction among Western Publics." *Comparative Political Studies* 9 (4): 429–458.

———. 2008. "Changing Values Among Western Publics from 1970 to 2006." *West European Politics* 31 (1): 130–146.

Inglehart, Ronald, and Marita Carballo. 1997. "Does Latin America Exist? (And Is There a Confucian Culture?): A Global Analysis of Cross-Cultural Differences." *PS: Political Science and Politics* 30 (1): 34–47.

Inglehart, Ronald, and Pippa Norris. 2000. "The Developmental Theory of the Gender Gap: Women's and Men's Voting Behavior in Global Perspective." *International Political Science Review* 21 (4): 441–463.

———. 2003. *Rising Tide: Gender Equality and Cultural Change around the World*. Cambridge: Cambridge University Press.

Inglehart, Ronald, and Christian Welzel. 2005. *Modernization, Cultural Change and Democracy*. New York: Cambridge University Press.

Ingram, James D., and Triadafilos Triadafilopoulos. 2010. "Rights, Norms, and Politics: The Case of German Citizenship Reform." *Social Research* 77 (1): 353–382.

"International: Berlin to Bonn." *Time*, September 13, 1948. Available at https://content.time.com/time/subscriber/article/0,33009,888465,00.html.

Inter-parliamentary Union Archive of Statistical Data for August 2009. Available at http://www.ipu.org/wmn-e/arc/classif310809.htm.

Inter-parliamentary Union Women in National Parliaments, data reported for March 2, 2018. Available at http://archive.ipu.org/wmn-e/world.htm.

Ireland, Patrick. 2004. *Becoming Europe: Immigration, Integration, and the Welfare State*. Pittsburgh: University of Pittsburgh Press.

Irving, Helen. 2008. *Gender and the Constitution: Equity and Agency in Comparative Constitutional Design*. Cambridge: Cambridge University Press.
Israel Democracy Institute. Available at https://en.idi.org.il/.
Itzkovich-Malka, Reut, and Chen Friedberg. 2018. "Gendering Security: The Substantive Representation of Women in the Israeli Parliament." *European Journal of Women's Studies* 25 (4): 419–439.
Iversen, Torben, and Frances Rosenbluth. 2008. "Work and Power: The Connection between Female Labor Force Participation and Female Political Representation." *Annual Review of Political Science* 11 (1): 479–495.
Jacobs, Lawrence R., and Theda Skocpol, eds. 2005. *Inequality and American Democracy: What We Know and What We Need to Learn*. New York: Russell Sage Foundation.
Jalalzai, Farida, and Pedro dos Santos. 2021. *Women's Empowerment and Disempowerment in Brazil: The Rise and Fall of President Dilma Rousseff*. Philadelphia: Temple University Press.
Jaquette, Jane S., and Sharon L. Wolchik, eds. 1998. *Women and Democracy: Latin America and Central and Eastern Europe*. Baltimore: Johns Hopkins University Press.
Jónasdóttir, Anna G. 1988. "On the Concept of Interest, Women's Interests, and the Limitations of Interest Theory." In *The Political Interests of Gender*, edited by Katherine B. Jones and Anna Jónasdóttir, 33–65. London: Sage.
Jones, Katherine B., and Anna Jónasdóttir. 1988. *The Political Interests of Gender*. London: Sage.
Jones, Mark P. 1994. "Quota Legislation and the Election of Women: Learning from the Costa Rican Experience." *Journal of Politics* 66 (4): 1203–1223.
Joppke, Christian. 1999. *Immigration and the Nation-State: The United States, Germany, and Great Britain*. Cambridge: Cambridge University Press.
Jordan-Zachery, Julia S. 2017. *Shadow Bodies: Black Women, Ideology, Representation, and Politics*. New Brunswick, NJ: Rutgers University Press.
Kalyvas, Stathis N. 1996. *The Rise of Christian Democracy in Europe*. Ithaca, NY: Cornell University Press.
Kam, Christopher. 2009. *Party Discipline and Parliamentary Politics*. Cambridge: Cambridge University Press.
Kanter, Rosabeth. 1977. *Men and Women of the Corporation*. New York: Basic.
Kaplan, Gisela. 1992. *Contemporary Western European Feminism*. New York: New York University Press.
Karnitschnig, Matthew, and Hans von der Burchard. 2021. "Social Democrat Scholz Channels Merkel to Lead German Election Race." *POLITICO*, September 1, 2021. Available at https://www.politico.eu/article/germany-chancellor-hopeful-social-democrats-angela-merkel-olaf-scholz/.
Katzenstein, Peter. 1987. *The Semisovereign State*. Philadelphia: Temple University Press.
Kaufmann, Karen. 2002. "Culture Wars, Secular Realignment, and the Gender Gap in Party Identification." *Political Behavior* 24 (2): 283–307.
Keman, Hans. 2007. "Experts and Manifestos: Different Sources—Same Results for Comparative Research?" *Electoral Studies* 26 (1): 76–89.
Kennedy-Pipe, Caroline. 2000. "Women and the Military." *Journal of Strategic Studies* 23 (4): 32–50.
Kenny, Meryl. 2013. *Gender and Political Recruitment: Theorizing Institutional Change*. London: Palgrave Macmillan.
Kenworthy, Lane, and Melissa Malami. 1999. "Gender Inequality in Political Representation." *Social Forces* 78 (1): 235–269.

Kimmel, Michael. 2019. *Healing from Hate*. Berkeley: University of California Press.
Kintz, Melanie. 2011. "Intersectionality and Bundestag Leadership Selection." *German Politics* 20 (3): 410–427.
———. 2014. "Many New Faces, but Nothing New? The Sociodemographic and Career Profiles of German Bundestag Members in the Eighteenth Legislative Period." *German Politics and Society* 32 (3): 16–25.
Kittilson, Miki Caul. 2005. "In Support of Gender Quotas: Setting New Standards, Bringing Visible Gains." *Politics and Gender* 1 (4): 638–645.
———. 2006. *Challenging Parties, Changing Parliaments: Women and Elected Office in Contemporary Western Europe*. Columbus: Ohio State University Press.
Kleinnijenhuis, Jan, and Jan A. de Ridder. 1998. "Issue News and Electoral Volatility." *European Journal of Political Research* 33:413–437.
Kloepfer, Inge. 2017. "WERBUNG DER BUNDESWEHR: We Want You!" *Frankfurter Allgemeine*, November 1, 2017. Available at https://www.faz.net/aktuell/karriere-hochschule/buero-co/werbung-der-bundeswehr-youtube-serie-ueber-den-mali-einsatz-15267882.html.
Knight, Ben. 2017. "The Bundeswehr's Troubled Traditions." *Deutsche Welle*, May 16, 2017. Available at https://www.dw.com/en/the-german-military-and-its-troubled-traditions/a-38863290.
———. 2019. "German Military Hit by Damning Report." *Deutsche Welle*, January 29, 2019. Available at https://www.dw.com/en/german-military-lacks-equipment-and-recruits-says-damning-report/a-47281996.
Koenker, Diane P. 1995. "Men against Women on the Shop Floor in Early Soviet Russia: Gender and Class in the Socialist Workplace." *American Historical Review* 100 (5): 1438–1464.
Kolinsky, Eva. 1993. *Women in Contemporary Germany*. Providence, RI: Berg.
Koltermann, Jens Olaf. 2012. "'Citizen in Uniform': Democratic Germany and the Changing Bundeswehr." Carlisle, PA: United States Army War College.
Konrad-Adenauer-Stiftung. 1982. "Die Vorneverteidigung wird schwieriger werden." *CDU-Dokumentation 42*. August 19, 1982. Bonn: Union Betriebs GmbH.
Krehbiel, Keith. 1992. *Information and Legislative Organization*. Ann Arbor: University of Michigan Press.
Kronsell, Annica. 2005. "Gendered Practices in Institutions of Hegemonic Masculinity: Reflections from Feminist Standpoint Theory." *International Feminist Journal of Politics* 7 (2): 280–298.
Krook, Mona Lena. 2009. *Quotas for Women in Politics: Gender and Candidate Selection Reform Worldwide*. New York: Oxford University Press.
Krook, Mona Lena, Joni Lovenduski, and Judith Squires. 2009. "Gender Quotas and Models of Political Citizenship." *British Journal of Political Science* 39 (4): 781–803.
Krook, Mona Lena, and Pippa Norris. 2014. "Beyond Quotas: Strategies to Promote Gender Equality in Elected Office." *Political Studies* 62:2–20.
Kucera, Tomás. 2017. *The Military and Liberal Society: Societal-Military Relations in Western Europe*. London: Taylor and Francis.
Kuhlmann, Jürgen, and Ekkehard Lippert. 1993. "The Federal Republic of Germany: Conscientious Objection as Social Welfare." In *The New Conscientious Objection*, edited by C. C. Moskos and J. W. Chambers, 98–105. Oxford: Oxford University Press.
Kümmel, Gerhard. 2002. "Complete Access: Women in the Bundeswehr and Male Ambivalence." *Armed Forces and Society* 28:555–573.

Kunovich, Sherri, and Pamela Paxton. 2005. "Pathways to Power: The Role of Political Parties in Women's National Political Representation." *American Journal of Sociology* 111 (2): 505–552.

Kutz, Martin. 2003. "*Innere Führung*: Leadership and Civic Education in the German Armed Forces." *Connections* 2 (3): 109–124.

Kymlicka, Will. 1995. *Multicultural Citizenship: A Liberal Theory of Minority Rights*. New York: Oxford University Press.

Lane, Guy. 2021. "Angela Merkel's Long Reign as Chancellor of Germany—In Pictures." *The Guardian*, September 24, 2021. Available at https://www.theguardian.com/world/gallery/2021/sep/24/angela-merkels-long-reign-as-chancellor-of-germany-in-pictures.

Lane, Jan-Erik, David McKay, and Kenneth Newton. 1997. *Political Data Handbook: OECD Countries*. Oxford: Oxford University Press.

Lapidus, Gail. 1975. "Political Mobilization, Participation, and Leadership: Women in Soviet Politics." *Comparative Politics* 8 (1): 90–118.

Larntz, Kinley. 1978. "Small-Sample Comparisons of Exact Levels for Chi-Squared Goodness-of-Fit Statistics." *Journal of the American Statistical Association* 73 (362): 253–263.

Laurence, Jonathan, and Rahsaan Maxwell. 2012. "Political Parties and Diversity in Western Europe." In *Immigrant Politics: Race and Representation in Western Europe*, edited by Terri Givens and Rahsaan Maxwell, 13–31. Boulder, CO: Lynne Rienner.

Laver, Michael. 2001. "On Mapping Policy Preferences Using Manifesto Data." Unpublished paper, Trinity College Dublin.

Leuschner, Udo. 2005. *Die Geschichte der FDP: Metamorphosen einer Partei zwischen rechts, sozialliberal und neokonservativ*. Münster: Verl.-Haus Monsenstein und Vannerdat.

Levy, Yagil, Edna Lomsky-Feder, and Noa Harel. 2007. "From 'Obligatory Militarism' to 'Contractual Militarism'—Competing Models of Citizenship." *Israel Studies* 12 (1): 127–148.

Liebert, Ulrike. 2004. "Europeanizing the Military: The ECJ and the Transformation of the Bundeswehr." In *Equity in the Workplace: Gendering Workplace Policy Analysis*, edited by Heidi Gottfried and Laura A. Reese, 325–340. New York: Lexington Books.

Lijphart, Arend. 1999. *Patterns of Democracy: Government Forms and Performance in Thirty-Six Countries*. New Haven, CT: Yale University Press.

Lindblom, Charles Edward. 1968. *The Policy-Making Process*. Englewood Cliffs, NJ: Prentice-Hall.

Lipset, Seymour, and Stein Rokkan. 1967. *Cleavage Structures, Party Systems, and Voter Alignments: An Introduction*. New York: Free Press.

Livingstone, Helen, and John Henley. 2021. "German Election: Social Democrats Secure Narrow Win as CDU Plunges to Historic Low." *The Guardian*, September 27, 2021. Available at https://www.theguardian.com/world/live/2021/sep/26/germany-election-2021-results-reaction-angela-merkel-era-ends-baerbock-scholz-laschet-spd-greens-cdu-live-latest-updates.

Lloren, Anouk. 2015. "Women's Substantive Representative: Defending Feminist Interests or Women's Electoral Preferences?" *Journal of Legislative Studies* 21 (2): 144–167.

Lombardo, Emanuela, and Petra Meier. 2014. *The Symbolic Representation of Gender: A Discursive Approach*. New York: Routledge.

Louis, Chantal. 2000. "Kreil Gegen Deutschland," *EMMA*, January 1, 2000. Available at https://www.emma.de/artikel/frauen-militaer-kreil-gegen-deutschland-263590.

Lovenduski, Joni, and Marila Guadagnini. 2010. "Political Representation." In *The Politics of State Feminism*, edited by Dorothy E. McBride and Amy Mazur. Philadelphia: Temple University Press.

Lowndes, Vivien. 2020. "How Are Political Institutions Gendered?" *Political Studies* 68 (3): 543–564.

Lührmann, Anna, Nils Düpont, Masaaki Higashijima, Yaman Berker Kavasoglu, Kyle L. Marquardt, Michael Bernhard, Holger Döring, Allen Hicken, Melis Laebens, Staffan I. Lindberg, Juraj Medzihorsky, Anja Neundorf, Saskia Ruth–Lovell, Keith R. Weghorst, Nina Wiesehomeier, Joseph Wright, Ora John Reuter, Nazifa Alizada, Paul Bederke, Lisa Gastaldi, Sandra Grahn, Garry Hindle, Nina Ilchenko, Johannes von Römer, Daniel Pemstein, and Brigitte Seim. 2020. "Codebook Varieties of Party Identity and Organisation (V-Party) V1." *Varieties of Democracy (V–Dem) Project*. Available at https://www.v-dem.net/data/the-v-dem-dataset/.

MacGregor, Neil. 2016. *Germany: Memories of a Nation*. New York: Knopf.

Mackay, Fiona, Meryl Kenny, and Louise Chappell. 2010. "New Institutionalism through a Gender Lens: Towards a Feminist Institutionalism?" *International Political Science Review* 31 (5): 573–588.

Mair, Peter, and Francis G. Castles. 1997. "Revisiting Expert Judgements." *European Journal of Political Research* 31:150–157.

Mair, Peter, and Cas Mudde. 1998. "The Party Family and Its Study." *Annual Review of Political Science* 1:211–229.

Mair, Peter, Wolfgang C. Müller, and Fritz Plasser. 2004. *Political Parties and Electoral Change: Party Responses to Electoral Markets*. London: Sage.

Mair, Peter, and Ingrid van Biezen. 2001. "Party Membership in Twenty European Democracies, 1980–2000." *Party Politics* 7 (1): 5–21.

Mansbridge, Jane. 1999. "Should Blacks Represent Blacks and Women Represent Women? A Contingent 'Yes.'" *Journal of Politics* 61 (3): 628–657.

Mansbridge, Jane, and Katherine Tate. 1992. "Race Trumps Gender: The Thomas Nomination in the Black Community." *PS: Political Science and Politics* 25 (3): 488–492.

Marks, Gary, Carole J. Wilson, and Leonard Ray. 2002. "National Political Parties and European Integration." *American Journal of Political Science* 46 (3): 585–594.

Marshall, T. H. 1950. "Citizenship and Social Class." London: Pluto.

Martin, Philip L. 1981. "Germany's Guestworkers." *Challenge* 24 (3): 34–42.

Marx, Karl, and Friedrich Engels. 1970. *The German Ideology*. New York: International.

Matland, Richard E. 1993. "Institutional Variables Affecting Female Representation in National Legislatures: The Case of Norway." *Journal of Politics* 55 (3): 737–755.

Matland, Richard E., and Donley T. Studlar. 1996. "The Contagion of Women Candidates in Single-Member District and Proportional Representation Electoral Systems: Canada and Norway." *Journal of Politics* 58 (3): 707–733.

Matland, Richard E., and Michelle M. Taylor. 1997. "Electoral System Effects on Women's Representation: Theoretical Arguments and Evidence from Costa Rica." *Comparative Political Studies* 30 (2): 186–210.

McCall, Leslie. 2005. "The Complexity of Intersectionality." *Signs* 30 (3): 1771–1800.

McConnaughy, Corrine M. 2013. *The Woman Suffrage Movement in America: A Reassessment*. Cambridge: Cambridge University Press.

McDonagh, Eileen. 2009. *The Motherless State: Women's Political Leadership and American Democracy*. Chicago: University of Chicago Press.

McFadden, Susan Willis. 2019. "German Citizenship Law and the Turkish Diaspora." *German Law Journal* 20:72–88.

McKay, Joanna. 2004. "Women in German Politics: Still Jobs for the Boys?" *German Politics* 13 (1): 56–80.
Mediendienst Integration. 2021. "Mehr Abgeordnete mit Migrationshintergrund." September 29, 2021. Available at https://mediendienst-integration.de/artikel/mehr-abgeordnete-mit-migrationshintergrund-1.html.
Meiers, Franz-Josef. 2005. "Germany's Defence Choices." *Survival* 47 (1): 153–165.
Meyer, Birgit. 2003. "Much Ado about Nothing? Political Representation Policies and the Political Influence of Women in Germany." *Review of Policy Research* 20 (3): 401–421.
Mölder, Martin. 2016. "The Validity of the RILE Left–Right Index as a Measure of Party Policy." *Party Politics* 22 (1): 37–48.
Mostafa, Mohamed. 2013. "Wealth, Post-materialism and Consumers' Pro-environmental Intentions: A Multilevel Analysis across 25 Nations." *Sustainable Development* 21 (6): 385–399.
Mudde, Cas. 2007. *Populist Radical Right Parties in Europe*. Cambridge: Cambridge University Press.
Müller, Claus. 2006. "Integrating Turkish Communities: A German Dilemma." *Population Research and Policy Review* 25:419–441.
Murray, Laura M. 1994. "Einwanderungsland Bundesrepublik Deutschland? Explaining the Evolving Positions of German Political Parties on Citizenship Policy." *German Politics and Society* 33 (Fall): 23–56.
Murray, Rainbow. 2007. "How Parties Evaluate Compulsory Quotas: A Study of the Implementation of the 'Parity' Law in France." *Parliamentary Affairs* 60 (4): 568–584.
Mushaben, Joyce. 2009. "Madam Chancellor: Angela Merkel and the Triangulation of German Foreign Policy." *Georgetown Journal of International Affairs* 10 (1): 27–35.
———. 2017. *Becoming Madam Chancellor: Angela Merkel and the Berlin Republic*. Cambridge: Cambridge University Press.
———. 2022. "Against All Odds: Angela Merkel, Ursula von der Leyen, Annegret Kramp-Karrenbauer and the German Paradox of Female CDU Leadership." *German Politics* 31 (1): 20–39.
Nash, Jennifer C. 2008. "Re-thinking Intersectionality." *Feminist Review* 89:1–15.
Nasr, Joseph. 2021. "Greens Candidate for German Chancellor Says Sexist Scrutiny Holding Her Back." *Reuters*, July 8, 2021. Available at https://www.reuters.com/world/europe/greens-candidate-german-chancellor-says-sexist-scrutiny-holding-her-back-2021-07-08/.
Ngai, Mae M. 1999. "The Architecture of Race in American Immigration Law: A Reexamination of the Immigration Act of 1924." *Journal of American History* 86 (1): 67–92.
Nicholson, Esme. 2021. "Germany Debates How to Form Gender-Neutral Words out of its Gendered Language." *NPR*, October 20, 2021. Available at https://www.npr.org/2021/10/30/1049603171/germany-gender-neutral-language-german.
Norris, Pippa. 1996. "Mobilising the 'Women's Vote': The Gender-Generation Gap in Voting Behaviour." *Parliamentary Affairs* 49 (2): 333–343.
———. 2004. *Electoral Engineering: Voting Rules and Political Behavior*. Cambridge: Cambridge University Press.
Norris, Pippa, and Joni Lovenduski. 1995. *Political Recruitment: Gender, Race and Class in the British Parliament*. Cambridge: Cambridge University Press.
O'Brien, Diana Z. 2015. "Rising to the Top: Gender, Political Performance, and Party Leadership in Parliamentary Democracies." *American Journal of Political Science* 59 (4): 1022–1039.

———. 2018. "'Righting' Conventional Wisdom: Women and Right Parties in Established Democracies." *Politics and Gender* 14 (1): 27–55.

O'Brien, Diana Z., and Johanne Rickne. 2016. "Gender Quotas and Women's Political Leadership." *American Political Science Review* 110 (1): 112–126.

Och, Malliga, and Shauna L. Shames, eds. 2018. *The Right Women: Republican Party Activists, Candidates, and Legislators*. Santa Barbara, CA: ABC-CLIO.

Oestreich, Heide. 1999. "Frauen zu den Waffen." *taz, die tageszeitung*, October 30, 1999.

Offen, Karen. 1988. "Defining Feminism: A Comparative Historical Approach." *Signs* 14 (1): 119–157.

Okin, Susan Moller. 1998. "Feminism, Women's Human Rights, and Cultural Differences." *Hypatia* 13 (2): 32–52.

———. 1999. "Is Multiculturalism Bad for Women?" In *Is Multiculturalism Bad for Women?* edited by Martha Nussbaum, Joshua Cohen, and Matthew Howard. Princeton, NJ: Princeton University Press.

Oltermann, Philip. 2021. "Merkel Rejects Deputy's Claim He Is Continuity Candidate for Chancellor." *The Guardian*, September 1, 2021. Available at https://www.theguardian.com/world/2021/sep/01/merkel-rejects-deputy-claim-continuity-candidate-chancellor-scholz.

O'Neill, Brenda, and David K. Stewart. 2009. "Gender and Political Party Leadership in Canada." *Party Politics* 15 (6): 737–757.

O'Regan, Valerie R. 2000. *Gender Matters: Female Policymakers' Influence in Industrialized Nations*. Westport, CT: Greenwood.

The ParlGov Project. Codebook available at https://parlgov.org/data/codebook.pdf.

Partridge, Damani. 2012. *Hypersexuality and Headscarves: Race, Sex, and Citizenship in the New Germany*. Bloomington: Indiana University Press.

Pate, Jennifer, and Richard Fox. 2018. "Getting Past the Gender Gap in Political Ambition." *Journal of Economic Behavior and Organization* 156:166–183.

Paxton, Pamela, Melanie Hughes, and Tiffany Barnes. 2020. *Women, Politics, and Power: A Global Perspective*, 4th ed. Washington, D.C.: Rowman and Littlefield.

Paxton, Pamela, and Sherri Kunovich. 2003. "Women's Political Representation: The Importance of Ideology." *Social Forces* 82 (3): 87–113.

Peleg, Ilan. 2007. *Democratizing the Hegemonic State: Political Transformation in the Age of Identity*. Cambridge: Cambridge University Press.

Pfau-Effinger, Birgit. 2004. "Socio-historical Paths of the Male Breadwinner Model—An Explanation of Cross-national Differences." *British Journal of Sociology* 55 (3): 377–399.

Phillips, Anne. 1998. *The Politics of Presence*. New York: Oxford University Press.

———. 2010. *Gender and Culture*. Malden, MA: Polity.

Piscopo, Jennifer M. 2011. "Rethinking Descriptive Representation: Rendering Women in Legislative Debates." *Parliamentary Affairs* 64 (3): 448–472.

———. 2019. "The Limits of Leaning In: Ambition, Recruitment, and Candidate Training in Comparative Perspective." *Politics, Groups, and Identities* 7 (4): 817–828.

———. 2021. "Women Running in the World: Candidate Training Programs in Comparative Perspective." In *Good Reasons to Run: Women and Political Candidacy*, edited by Shauna Shames, Rachel Bernhard, Mirya Holman, and Dawn Teele, 215–232. Philadelphia: Temple University Press.

Piscopo, Jennifer M., and Shauna Shames. 2020. "The Right to Be Elected." *Boston Review Forum*. Cambridge, MA: MIT Press.

Piscopo, Jennifer M., and Peter Siavelis. 2021. "Chile's Constitutional Moment." *Current History* 120, no. 823 (February): 43–49.

Pitkin, Hanna. (1967) 1972. *The Concept of Representation*. Reprint, Berkeley: University of California Press.

Plumb, Alison. 2016. "The Substantive Representation of Women on 'Morality Politics' Issues in Australia and the UK: How Does the Substantive Representation of Women Occur in Conservative Parties?" *Political Science* 68 (1): 22–35.

Prinz, Tanja. 2003. *Ausgewählte Mentoring-Programme für Frauen in der Politik in Deutschland*. Diplom-Arbeit, Universität Bremen.

Putnam, Robert. 1971. "Studying Elite Political Culture: The Case of 'Ideology.'" *American Political Science Review* 65 (3): 651–681.

Rashkova, Ekaterina R., and Emilia Zankina. 2017. "Are (Populist) Radical Right Parties *Männerparteien*? Evidence from Bulgaria." *West European Politics* 40 (4): 848–868.

Rath, Christian, and Heide Oestreich. 1999. "Bedrohen Frauen das militaerische Klima?" *taz, die tageszeitung*, June 29, 1999.

Reingold, Beth, Kerry L. Haynie, and Kirsten Widner. 2020. *Race, Gender, and Political Representation: Toward a More Intersectional Approach*. New York: Oxford University Press.

Reingold, Beth, and Adrienne R. Smith. 2012. "Welfare Policymaking and Intersections of Race, Ethnicity, and Gender in US State Legislatures." *American Journal of Political Science* 56 (1): 131–147.

Reuters. 2020. "Exasperated Merkel Backs Widening Boardroom Quota for Women." July 1, 2020. Available at https://www.reuters.com/article/uk-germany-companies-women/exasperated-merkel-backs-widening-boardroom-quota-for-women-idUKKBN2426RM?edition-redirect=uk.

Rifkin, Janet. 1980. "Toward a Theory of Law and Patriarchy." *Harvard Women's Law Journal* 3:83–95.

Rimonte, Nilda. 1991. "A Question of Culture: Cultural Approval of Violence against Women in the Pacific-Asian Community and the Cultural Defense." *Stanford Law Review* 43 (6): 1311–1326.

Rimscha, Robert von. 2001. "Meinung Kriminalitätsstatistik: Im besten Kardinalsalter." *Tagesspiegel*. May 22, 2001. Available at https://www.tagesspiegel.de/meinung/kriminalitatsstatistik-im-besten-kardinalsalter-796804.html.

Roberts, Geoffrey. 1988. "The German Federal Republic: The Two-lane Route to Bonn." In *Candidate Selection in Comparative Perspective: The Secret Garden of Politics*, edited by Michael Gallagher and Michael Marsh. London: Sage.

Robinet-Borgomano, Alexandre. 2021. "Chancellor Olaf Scholz? Change without Disruption." *Institut Montaigne*, November 9, 2021. Available at https://www.institutmontaigne.org/en/expressions/chancellor-olaf-scholz-change-without-disruption.

Rogers, JoAnn, and Jacquelyn S. Litt. 2003. "Normalizing Racism: A Case Study of Motherhood in White Supremacy." In *Home Grown Hate: Gender and Organized Racism*, edited by Abby L. Ferber. New York: Routledge.

Romaniec, Rosalia. 2021. "Merkel's Political Style Remains." *Deutsche Welle*, December 7, 2021. Available at https://www.dw.com/en/opinion-cool-calm-and-collected-merkel-has-left-but-her-political-style-remains/a-60050220.

Ross, Fiona. 2000. "Beyond Left and Right: The New Partisan Politics of Welfare." *Governance* 13 (2): 155–183.

Rübsam, Jens. 1999. "Tanjas Einsatz fürs Vaterland." *taz, die tageszeitung*, August 6, 1999.

Ruf, Florian. 2021. "Does Non-Quota Strategy Matter? A Comparative Study on Candidate Selection and Women's Representation at the Local Level in Germany." *Politics and Gender* 17 (1): 74–103.

Rule, Wilma. 1987. "Electoral Systems, Contextual Factors and Women's Opportunity for Election to Parliament in Twenty-Three Democracies." *Western Political Quarterly* 40 (3): 477–498.
Rürup, Miriam. 2016. "Das Geschlecht der Staatenlosen. Staatenlosigkeit in der Bundesrepublik Deutschland nach 1945." *Journal of Modern European History / Zeitschrift für moderne europäische Geschichte* 14 (3): 411–430.
Safran, William. 1997. "Citizenship and Nationality in Democratic Systems: Approaches to Defining and Acquiring Membership in the Political Community." *International Political Science Review* 18 (3): 313–335.
Sanbonmatsu, Kira. 2002. "Political Parties and the Recruitment of Women to State Legislatures." *Journal of Politics* 64 (3): 791–809.
Sapiro, Virginia. 1981. "Research Frontier Essay: When Are Interests Interesting? The Problem of Political Representation of Women." *American Political Science Review* 75 (3): 701–716.
Sartori, Giovanni. 1970. "Concept Misformation in Comparative Politics." *American Political Science Review* 64 (4): 1033–1053.
———. 1976. *Parties and Party Systems: A Framework for Analysis.* Cambridge: Cambridge University Press.
———. 1991. "Comparing and Miscomparing." *Journal of Theoretical Politics* 3 (3): 243–257.
Sasson-Levy, Orna. 2013. "A Different Kind of Whiteness: Marking and Unmarking of Social Boundaries in the Construction of Hegemonic Ethnicity." *Sociological Forum* 28 (1): 27–50.
Schattschneider. E. E. 1960. *The Semi-Sovereign People.* New York: Holt, Rhinehart, and Winston.
Schiller, Kay. 2003. "Political Militancy and Generation Conflict in West Germany during the 'Red Decade.'" *Debatte* 11 (1): 19–38.
Schilt, Kristen. 2006. "Just One of the Guys? How Transmen Make Gender Visible at Work." *Gender and Society* 20 (4): 465–490.
Schlegel, Erik. 2016. *Quo Vadis Piratenpartei?* Nomos E-Library. Available at https://doi.org/10.5771/9783845274591.
Schmitt-Beck, Rüdiger. 2017. "The 'Alternative für Deutschland in the Electorate': Between Single-Issue and Right-Wing Populist Party." *German Politics* 26 (1): 1–25.
Schneider, Monica, Mirya Holman, Amanda B. Diekman, and Thomas McAndrew. 2016. "Power, Conflict, and Community: How Gendered Views of Political Power Influence Women's Political Ambition." *Political Psychology* 37 (4): 515–531.
Schönwälder, Karen. 2012. "Cautious Steps: Minority Representation in Germany." In *Immigrant Politics: Race and Representation in Western Europe,* edited by Terri E. Givens and Rahsaan Maxwell, 67–86. Cambridge: Cambridge University Press.
Schreurs, Miranda A. 2003. *Environmental Politics in Japan, Germany, and the United States.* Cambridge: Cambridge University Press.
Schultheis, Emily. 2021. "Being a Woman in German Politics Still Isn't Easy. Annalena Baerbock's Rise and Fall Shows Why." *POLITICO,* September 25, 2021. Available at https://www.politico.com/news/magazine/2021/09/25/german-election-annalena-baerbock-women-514150.
Schulze, Andreas. 2004. *Kleinparteien in Deutschland.* Deutscher Universitätsverlag.
Schulze, Hagen. 1998. *Germany: A New History.* Cambridge, MA: Harvard University Press.
Schumacher, Elizabeth. 2021. "Bloated Bundestag: Trouble for German Democracy?" *Deutsche Welle,* September 15, 2021. Available at https://www.dw.com/en/bloated-bundestag-trouble-for-german-democracy/a-59188371.

Schwarze, Jürgen. 2002. "Judicial Review in EC Law." *International and Comparative Law Quarterly* 51 (1): 17–33.
Schwindt-Bayer, Leslie. 2009. "Making Quotas Work: The Effect of Gender Quota Laws on the Election of Women." *Legislative Studies Quarterly* 34 (1): 5–28.
Segal, Mady. W. 1995. "Women's Military Roles Cross-Nationally: Past, Present, and Future." *Gender and Society* 9 (6): 757–775.
Seidel, Gill. 1988. *The Nature of the Right: A Feminist Analysis of Order Patterns*. Critical Theory, Volume 6. Amsterdam: John Benjamins Publishing Company.
Seiler, Daniel-Louis. 1980. *Partis et Familles Politiques*. Paris: Presses Universitaires de France.
Severs, Eline. 2010. "Representation as Claims-Making: Quid Responsiveness?" *Representation* 46 (4): 411–423.
Shames, Shauna, Rachel Bernhard, Mirya Holman, and Dawn Teele, eds. 2021. *Good Reasons to Run: Women and Political Candidacy*. Philadelphia: Temple University Press.
Shames, Shauna, Malliga Och, and Rosalyn Cooperman. 2020. "Sell-Outs or Warriors for Change? A Comparative Look at Rightist Political Women in Democracies." *Journal of Women, Politics and Policy* 41 (1): 1–6.
Shepsle, Kenneth A., and Barry R. Weingast. 1984. "When Do Rules of Procedure Matter?" *Journal of Politics* 46 (1): 206–221.
Showalter, Kathryn. 2016. "Women's Employment and Domestic Violence: A Review of the Literature." *Aggression and Violent Behavior* 31:37–47.
Shutes, Isabel, and Carlos Chiatti. 2012. "Migrant Labour and the Marketisation of Care for Older People: The Employment of Migrant Care Workers by Families and Service Providers." *Journal of European Social Policy* 22 (4): 392–405.
Siavelis, Peter. 1997. "Continuity and Change in the Chilean Party System: On the Transformational Effects of Electoral Reform." *Comparative Political Studies* 30 (6): 651–674.
Simonazzi, Annamaria. 2008. "Care Regimes and National Employment Models." Working Paper #113. Dipartimento Di Economia Pubblica. Università Degli Studi di Roma "La Sapienza."
Sjoberg, Laura. 2016. *Women as Wartime Rapists: Beyond Sensation and Stereotyping*. New York: New York University Press.
Slagter, Tracy Hoffmann. 2006. "Legislative Responses to Supranational Courts: The German Bundestag and the European Court of Justice." Ph.D. diss., University of Iowa. UMI# 3229703.
Smooth, Wendy. 2006. "Intersectionality in Electoral Politics: A Mess Worth Making." *Politics and Gender* 2 (3): 400–414.
Squires, Judith. 1999. *Gender and Political Theory*. Cambridge: Polity.
Stegmaier, Mary. 2022. "Forecasting German Elections." *PS: Political Science and Politics* 55 (1): 64–68.
Stiehm, Judith Hicks. 1982. "The Protected, the Protector, the Defender." *Women's Studies International Forum* 5 (3–4): 367–376.
Strolovitch, Dara Z. 2006. "Do Interest Groups Represent the Disadvantaged? Advocacy at the Intersections of Race, Class, and Gender." *Journal of Politics* 68 (4): 894–910.
Summers, Sarah E. 2015. "'Thinking Green!' (And Feminist) Female Activism and the Greens from Wyhl to Bonn." *German Politics and Society* 33 (4): 40–52.
Swers, Michele. 1998. "Are Women More Likely to Vote for Women's Issue Bills Than Their Male Colleagues?" *Legislative Studies Quarterly* 23 (3): 435–448.
———. 2002. *The Difference Women Make*. Chicago: University of Chicago Press.
———. 2013. *Women in the Club*. Chicago: University of Chicago Press.

Taagepera, Rein. 1999. "The Number of Parties as a Function of Heterogeneity and Electoral System." *Comparative Political Studies* 32 (5): 531–548.

Tarrow, Sidney G. 2011. *Power in Movement: Social Movements and Contentious Politics.* Cambridge: Cambridge University Press.

Taylor, Charles. 1994. *Multiculturalism.* Princeton, NJ: Princeton University Press.

Teele, Dawn Langan. 2018. "How the West Was Won: Competition, Mobilization, and Women's Enfranchisement in the United States." *Journal of Politics* 80 (2): 442–461.

Thomas, Sue. 1994. *How Women Legislate.* New York: Oxford University Press.

Thomassen, Jacque, ed. 2005. *The European Voter: A Comparative Study of Modern Democracies.* New York: Oxford University Press.

Thomsen, Danielle. 2015. "Why So Few (Republican) Women? Explaining the Partisan Imbalance of Women in the U.S. Congress." *Legislative Studies Quarterly* 40 (2): 295–323.

———. 2017. *Opting Out of Congress: Partisan Polarization and the Decline of Moderate Candidates.* New York: Cambridge University Press.

Tickner, Ann. 1992. *Gender in International Relations: Feminist Perspectives on Achieving Global Security.* New York: Columbia University Press.

Tobar, Marcéla Rios. 2021. "Chile's Constitutional Convention: A Triumph of Inclusion." *UNDP: Latin America*, June 3, 2021. Available at https://www.undp.org/latin-america/blog/chiles-constitutional-convention-triumph-inclusion.

Tomescheit, Wiebke. 2021. "Die seltsamen Zweifel an Annalena Baerbock: Deutschland braucht ein neues Familienbild—dringend!" *Stern*, April 21, 2021. Available at https://www.stern.de/politik/deutschland/annalena-baerbocks-eignung-wird-infrage-gestellt---weil-sie-mutter-ist-30489584.html.

Triadafilopoulos, Triadafilos. 2012. "Assessing the Consequences of the 1999 German Citizenship Act." *German Politics and Society* 30 (1): 1–16.

UN Refugee Agency, UNCHR. Available at https://www.unhcr.org/en-us/germany.html.

Valdini, Melody E. 2019. *The Inclusion Calculation: Why Men Appropriate Women's Representation.* New York: Oxford University Press.

Valenzuela, Arturo. 1994. "Party Politics and the Crisis of Presidentialism in Chile: A Proposal for a Parliamentary Form of Government." In *The Failure of Presidential Democracy*, edited by Juan J. Linz and Arturo Valenzuela, 91–150. Baltimore: The Johns Hopkins University Press.

Verba, Sidney, Kay Schlozman, and Henry E. Brady. 1995. *Voice and Equality: Civic Voluntarism in American Politics.* Cambridge, MA: Harvard University Press.

Vössing, Konstantin. 2017. *How Leaders Mobilize Workers.* Cambridge: Cambridge University Press.

Walby, Sylvia. 1989. "Theorizing Patriarchy." *Sociology* 23 (2): 213–234.

———. 1994. "Is Citizenship Gendered?" *Sociology* 28 (2): 379–395.

Walsh, Shannon Drysdale, and Christina Xydias. 2014. "Women's Organizing and Intersectional Policy-Making in Comparative Perspective: Evidence from Guatemala and Germany." *Politics, Groups, and Identities* 2 (4): 549–572.

Watson, Bruce. 2005. *Bread and Roses: Mills, Migrants, and the Struggle for the American Dream.* New York: Viking.

Waylen, Georgina. 2017. *Gender and Informal Institutions.* Washington, D.C.: Rowman and Littlefield.

Webb, Paul, and Sarah Childs. 2012. "Gender Politics and Conservatism: The View from the British Conservative Party Grassroots." *Government and Opposition* 47 (1): 21–48.

Weeks, Anna Catalano. 2018. "Why Are Gender Quota Laws Adopted by Men? The Role of Inter- and Intraparty Competition." *Comparative Political Studies* 51 (14): 1935–1973.

---. 2022. *Making Gender Salient*. Cambridge: Cambridge University Press.

Weldon, Laurel. 2008. "Intersectionality." In *Politics, Gender, and Concepts*, edited by Gary Goertz and Amy Mazur, 193–218. Cambridge: Cambridge University Press.

---. 2011. *When Protest Makes Policy: How Social Movements Represent Disadvantaged Groups*. Ann Arbor: University of Michigan Press.

West, Candace, and Don H. Zimmerman. 1987. "Doing Gender." *Gender and Society* 1 (2): 125–151.

WHO. 2017. "Violence against Women—Fact Sheet." Available at http://www.who.int/mediacentre/factsheets/fs239/en/.

Wiliarty, Sarah. 2008. "Angela Merkel's Path to Power: The Role of Internal Party Dynamics and Leadership." *German Politics* 17 (1): 81–96.

---. 2010. *The CDU and the Politics of Gender in Germany: Bringing Women to the Party*. Cambridge: Cambridge University Press.

Williams, Helen. 2011. "Crossing the Divide: Building and Breaking Down Borders through Discourse on Citizenship and Naturalisation Policy in Germany and the UK, 2000–2010." *Eurostudia* 7 (1–2): 87–103.

---. 2014. "Changing the National Narrative: Evolution in Citizenship and Integration in Germany, 2000–10." *Journal of Contemporary History* 49 (1): 54–74.

Williams, Melissa S. 1998. *Voice, Trust, and Memory: Marginalized Groups and the Failings of Liberal Representation*. Princeton, NJ: Princeton University Press.

Wolbrecht, Christina. 2009. *The Politics of Women's Rights: Parties, Positions, and Change*. Princeton, NJ: Princeton University Press.

Wolbrecht, Christina, and J. Kevin Corder. 2020. *A Century of Votes for Women: American Elections since Suffrage*. Cambridge: Cambridge University Press.

"Women's Rights Organizations." Womankind Worldwide. Available at https://www.womankind.org.uk/policy-and-campaigns/women's-rights/women's-rights-organisations.

Woodrum, Eric, and Michelle J. Wolkomir. 1997. "Religious Effects on Environmentalism." *Sociological Spectrum* 17 (2): 223–234.

World Economic Forum. "The Global Gender Gap Report 2017." Available at http://reports.weforum.org/global-gender-gap-report-2017/.

World Values Survey, available at https://www.worldvaluessurvey.org/wvs.jsp.

Wüst, Andreas M. 2016. "Incorporation beyond Cleavages? Parties, Candidates and Germany's Immigrant-Origin Electorate." *German Politics* 25 (3): 414–432.

Wüst, Andreas M., and Thorsten Faas. 2018. *Politische Einstellungen von Menschen mit Migrationshintergrund*. Friedrich-Ebert-Stiftung.

Xydias, Christina. 2013. "Mapping the Language of Women's Interests: Sex and Party Affiliation in the Bundestag." *Political Studies* 61 (2): 319–340.

---. 2014. "Women's Rights in Germany: Generations and Gender Quotas." *Politics and Gender* 10 (1): 4–32.

---. 2017. "The Last Occupational Prohibition: Constructing Women's Entrance into the Bundeswehr." In Davidson-Schmich 2017.

---. 2020. "This Was the One for Me: AfD Women's Origin Stories," *German Politics and Society* 38 (1): 10–125.

---. 2021. "Political Ideologies." In *political science is for everybody*, edited by Amy L. Atchison. Toronto: University of Toronto Press.

---. 2022. "Left, Right, and Center: Women's Political Incorporation in the OECD." In *Sell-Outs or Warriors for Change? A Comparative Look at Conservative Women in Politics in Democracies*, edited by Shauna Shames, Malliga Och, and Rosalyn Cooperman. New York: Routledge.

Yeoh, Brenda S. A., Heng Leng Chee, Rohini Anant, and Theodora Lam. 2021. "Transnational Marriage Migration and the Negotiation of Precarious Pathways beyond Partial Citizenship in Singapore." *Citizenship Studies* 25 (7): 898–917.

Young, Iris Marion. 1997. "Difference as a Resource for Democratic Communication." In *Deliberative Democracy: Essays on Reason and Politics*, edited by James Bohman and William Rehg. Cambridge, MA: MIT Press.

———. 2003. "The Logic of Masculinist Protection: Reflections on the Current Security State." *Signs* 29 (1): 1–25.

Yuval-Davis, Nira. 1997. "Women, Citizenship and Difference." *Feminist Review* 57:4–27.

ZeitOnline. 2019. "Die FDP will mehr Frauen, aber keine Quote." April 28, 2019. Available at https://www.zeit.de/politik/deutschland/2019-04/fdp-parteitag-frauenanteil-zielvereinbarung-gleichstellung.

Index

Page numbers followed by the letter t *refer to tables.*

advocacy for women and multiply marginalized women: formal mechanisms, 81–92; informal mechanisms, 81–85, 92–111. *See also* names of specific political parties

Alliance 90/Greens (B90/Gr): acknowledgement of women's underrepresentation and, 70t, 71–72; actions to promote women's political representation, 92–93, 95t, 105–106, 110–111; Annalena Baerbock and, 19, 114–115, 128–129; distinctiveness from TIER, 112; expanding citizenship, 155–157; gender quotas and, 87t, 87–88; ideological orientations and, 55t, 59, 87–88, 149t; Migrationshintergrund, 118t, 188; origins of, 50–51, 61; September 2021 elections and, 19, 60–61, 129, 186–189; Vera Lengsfeld and, 97; women's inclusion in party leadership and, 74, 117, 127, 128t; women's inclusion in the military and, 141, 145–150, 149t; women's rates of candidacy and, 119t, 120, 122; women's rates of election and, 43, 73, 122, 124t

Alternative for Germany (AfD): acknowledgement of women's underrepresentation and, 70t, 71; actions to promote women's political representation, 93–94, 95t, 96–97; gender quotas and, 87t, 90–92; ideological orientations and, 52, 55t, 61, 92, 188; Martin Hohmann and, 147; Migrationshintergrund and, 118; origins of, 50, 52; September 2021 elections and, 188–189; women's inclusion in party leadership and, 128t; women's inclusion in the military and, 141t, 148; women's rates of candidacy and, 119t, 120; women's rates of election and, 43t, 122, 124t

Alternative für Deutschland. *See* Alternative for Germany (AfD)

anti-Islamic movement, 10, 46–47, 52

Argentina, 28

article 12a, 130–131, 141t, 142, 145–147

authoritarianism, 15, 17, 27, 58, 183, 215n6

Baerbock, Annalena, 19, 114–115, 128–129, 186

Basic Law: armed forces and, 130–131, 138–139, 141t, 142–148; article 116, 46, 153; gender equality and, 215n1; gender quotas and, 71; marriage and family

246 / Index

Basic Law (*continued*)
and, 4; political parties and, 47. *See also* article 12a
Baudissin, Wolf Graf von, 158
Bavaria, 49, 51, 72–73, 100–101, 105
Beggerow, Bettina, 138, 144
Blank, Theodor, 158
Bundestag (lower legislative house): 2017 elections and, 70; debates over citizenship laws and, 151–157; debates over compulsory military service and exclusion of women, 136–151; electoral system of, 48–49, 117; Law on the Equality of Men and Women's Civil Rights, 154; Migrationshintergrund and, 117–118, 118t; political parties and, 50–54, 55t; women in leadership and, 45, 127–128, 128t, 187; women's rates of candidacy, 117–122, 119t, 121t; women's rates of election and, 42, 43t, 122–126, 124t, 125t, 126t; working groups and, 93–94, 97, 99, 104, 108, 110
Bundeswehr: compulsory military service (Wehrpflicht) and gender inclusion, 131–132, 136–151, 141t; expansion of, 137, 158; expansion of women's roles, 138, 143; leadership principle (Innere Führung), 157–159; origins of, 137–140
Bündnis 90/Die Grünen. *See* Alliance 90/Greens (B90/Gr)

center, The (ideology): actions to promote women's political representation and, 170t, 173, 176t; cross-national analyses and, 161, 170t, 173t; political parties and, 17, 49–51, 89, 140, 143, 155; postwar period, 49–50; support for promoting marginalized groups' rights and, 155; WLFP policies and, 177–180; women in the military and, 140
childcare, 7, 45–46, 75, 79, 100, 166, 177
Chile, 162, 163t, 167, 183–185
Christian Democratic Union (CDU): acknowledgement of women's underrepresentation and, 70t, 72; actions to promote women's political representation, 93–94, 95t, 97–99, 111, 117; alliance with CSU, 49, 51, 99; Angela Merkel and, 59–61, 160; expanding citizenship and, 155–156; gender quotas and, 87t, 88–89, 91t; ideological orientations and, 50–51, 55t, 57, 60–61, 149t, 150; Junge Union and, 88; Karl Arnold and, 48; Konrad-Adenauer-Stiftung (KAS) and, 93, 98; Migrationshintergrund, 118t; Rita Süssmuth and, 45; role in coalition governments, 48–50; September 2021 elections and, 186–189; state legislatures and, 49; Thomas de Maizière and, 149; Ursula von der Leyen and, 136; Vera Lengsfeld and, 97; Volker Rühe and, 136; women's inclusion in party leadership, 127, 128t; women's inclusion in the military and, 136, 141t, 143, 145–151, 149t; women's organizations and, 93, 99; women's rates of candidacy and, 119t, 123t; women's rates of election and, 43t, 124t, 126t
Christian Social Union (CSU): acknowledgement of women's underrepresentation and, 70t, 72–73; actions to promote women's political representation, 93–94, 95t, 100–101; alliance with CDU, 49, 51, 99; expanding citizenship and, 155–156; gender quotas and, 87, 89; Hanns-Seidel-Stiftung and, 93; ideological orienations and, 51–52, 55t, 57; Migrationshintergrund, 118t; role in coalition governments, 48–50; women's groups and organizations and, 93, 99; women's inclusion in party leadership and, 128t; women's inclusion in the military and, 141t, 143, 145–151, 149t; women's rates of candidacy and, 119t; women's rates of election and, 43t, 124t
Christlich Demokratische Union Deutschlands. *See* Christian Democratic Union (CDU)
Christlich-Soziale Union in Bayern. *See* Christian Social Union (CSU)
citizenship: "Germanness" and, 19, 131, 152, 154, 156; ideology and, 140, 156–157, 193t; Innere Führung and, 132, 157–159; marginalized groups and, 6–10, 23, 42, 46, 64–65, 70, 117, 118t, 127, 135–136, 152–153, 154, 156–157, 188–189; role of warrior and, 133–134, 137, 151; women and, 19, 21–22, 38–39, 43, 45–47, 64, 130–138, 148, 151–154
citizenship laws: 1913 Nationality Act, 152–153; 1980s and 1990s, 154–156; 2000

Nationality Act, 9, 47, 154; German Empire and, 151–152; immigration and, 46, 153–155, 193t; jus sanguinis (citizenship by blood or inheritance) and, 46, 135, 153–154; jus soli (citizenship is associated with being born in-country) and, 46, 135–136, 155, 157; Law on the Revocation of Naturalizations and the Deprivation of German Citizenship (July 1933), 152–153; post-World War II, 153–154; United States and, 135

civil society organizations, 1, 3, 8–9, 39, 85; German Armed Force Association (Deutscher Bundeswehrverband [DBwV]), 139, 142; Turkish-Islamic Union for Religious Affairs, 46–47

COVID-19, 100, 102, 107–108, 188

cross-national analyses: contextual and dependent variables and, 168–171; data and, 13, 164–167; electing women to national legislative office and, 171–174; inclusion of small parties and, 53; legislative rules and, 37–38; limitations of left-right axes and, 3–4, 15–16, 20, 161–164; marginalized groups and political leadership, 115–116; mutipartism and, 35–36; party families and, 16–17; political marginalization of women and marginalized groups, 136; rationale for, 4, 8; social traditionalism and, 29; support for protecting marganizalized groups' rights and, 180–183; support for WLFP and, 175–180; TIER and, 111; wider political context and, 39; women in party leadership and, 174–175

data, 3–4, 9, 13, 164–167; Chapel Hill Expert Survey (CHES) and, 57, 165–166, 220n3; Comparative Manifesto Project (CMP) and, 16, 56–57; Comparative Political Dataset (CPDS) and, 164, 185; ParlGov and, 57, 77, 120, 122, 164–167; Varieties of Democracy (V-Dem) and, 165–166, 169, 176, 180; V-Party, 57–59, 167

Deutsche Volksunion (DVU), 53

Die Republikaner. *See* Republicans (REP)

Eastern Europe, 15, 46

East Germany. *See* German Democratic Republic (GDR)

Ecological Democratic Party (ÖDP), 54; gender quotas and, 87t, 90–91; ideological orientations and, 55t; women's inclusion in party leadership and, 127, 128t; women's political underrepresentation and, 70t, 75; women's rates of candidacy and, 118, 119t

economic liberalism: cross-national analyses and, 167t; definitions of, 27–29, 32, 44t, 57; gender quotas and, 90, 91; intersection with social progressivism, 148; ParlGov and, 165; political parties and, 52, 55t, 60, 78, 89; women's and minorities' rights and, 5, 40t, 76–77, 95, 95t, 120–123, 125t, 126t, 131, 136, 140, 141t, 149t, 172t, 173t, 175t, 176t, 177–180, 181t, 182t, 183

economic redistributionism: cross-national analyses and, 167t; definitions of, 27–29, 44t, 57; gender quotas and, 90–91; ParlGov and, 165; political parties and, 54, 55t; women's and minorities' rights and, 5, 40t, 76–77, 95t, 120–123, 125t, 126t, 136, 141t, 149t

elections, federal: 2021 elections, 19, 42–43, 51, 60–61, 114–115, 117, 128–129, 186–189; issue competition and, 16; marginalized groups' rates of candidacy and, 118t; marginalized groups' rates of election and, 116–117; mixed-member proportional system and, 47–50; women's rates of election and candidacy, 43t, 117–126, 119t, 121t, 123t, 124t, 125t, 126t

elections, local, 49, 84, 89, 99–100, 117

elections, state, 49, 89, 117

ethnicity: gender and, 5–10, 12–13, 19, 24, 153; "Germanness" and, 131, 152–153; religion and, 46–47

ethnic minorities. *See* marginalized groups

European Union: Council Directive 76/207/EEC, 139; elections and, 52, 89, 112, 128; European Court of Justice (ECJ), 131, 137, 139. *See also Kreil v. Federal Republic of Germany*

far right, 17–18, 31–32, 52–53, 174

Federal Defense Ministry, 139, 142–143, 149

Federal Republic of Germany (FRG), 45, 131, 137, 158

feminism: B90/Gr and, 105–106, 111; Germany and, 42–44, 130–131, 142–143;

feminism (*continued*)
ideology and, 11, 28; multiculturalism and, 33; opposition to, 11, 52; PDS/LINKE and, 107–108; political parties and, 26; SPD and, 109; United States and, 111

feminist institutionalism, 83

Free Democratic Party (FDP): acknowledgement of women's underrepresentation and, 70t, 73; actions to promote women's political representation, 89, 94, 95t, 101–105, 110; expanding citizenship and, 155–157, 183; Friedrich-Naumann-Stiftung (FNF) and, 93, 102–104; gender quotas and, 87t, 101; ideological orientations and, 28, 55t, 57–58, 89, 148, 183, 189; Ina Lenke and, 19, 63–64, 78–80, 145; Migrationshintergrund, 118t; origins of, 51; role in coalition governments, 49–50; September 2021 elections and, 60, 129, 186–188; women's inclusion in party leadership and, 103, 128t; women's inclusion in the military and, 140, 141t, 143–146, 148–150, 149t; women's organizations and, 93, 104; women's rates of candidacy and, 119t; women's rates of election and, 43t, 124t

Free Voters (FW/FWD), 54; acknowledgement of women's underrepresentation, 70t, 75; gender quotas and, 87t; ideological orientations and, 55t, 121; women's inclusion in party leadership and, 128t; women's rates of candidacy and, 119t; women's rates of election and, 124t

Freie Demokratische Partei. *See* Free Democratic Party (FDP)

gender: citizenship and, 19, 21–22, 38–39, 43, 45–47, 64, 130–138, 148, 151–154; definitions of, 10–11; ethnicity and, 5–10, 12–13, 19, 24, 153; ideological dimensions and, 27–33, 50, 131, 140, 161–162; institutions and, 34–38; intersectionality and, 6–10, 12–13, 24, 64–65, 70–71

gender egalitarianism, 5, 33, 90

gender norms and roles: military and, 5, 19, 130–131, 133–134; social attitudes and, 26, 38–39, 162, 163t

gender quotas: cross-national analysis and, 163, 163t, 168–169, 173–174, 177, 185; effectiveness of, 82–86, 115–116, 122, 123t, 124t, 125, 126t, 173–174; as formal mechanism, 81; ideological orientations and, 18, 91t, 125, 125t, 171–172, 172t; Ina Lenke and, 78–80; multiply marginalized women and, 85, 188; political parties and, 5, 61, 71–76, 86–92, 87t, 97–98, 101–102, 105–106, 108–109, 119t; United States and, 86

German Democratic Republic (GDR): feminist organizations and, 44, 142; reunification and, 51–52, 140, 143

Germany: anti-militarism and, 141t, 142–143, 145, 149–150; immigration and, 46–47, 153–155, 193t; as a party state (Parteienstaat), 48; reunification of (1990), 51–52, 59, 61, 77, 140, 143; unification of (1871), 152, 214n14. *See also* Basic Law

green (ideology), 17, 55t, 106, 166

Green Party, 16, 50–51, 61, 143, 155. *See also* Alliance 90/Greens (B90/Gr)

Guatemala, 8, 22

hegemonic-ethnic supremacy: anticonstitutional activities and, 158–159; cross-national analyses and, 161, 167t, 172t, 173, 173t, 174, 177, 180, 183, 185; definitions of, 31–32, 44t; gender quotas and, 90–92, 91t; political parties and, 32, 52, 55t, 157, 188; women's and minorities' rights and, 5, 33, 39, 40t, 76t, 77, 95, 120–122, 121t, 123t, 124, 131, 136, 141t, 148, 149t; xenophobia and, 27, 58–59, 213n7

ideology: aspects of women's political representation and, 25–27; cultural systems and, 25; definitions of, 14–18; left-right axes and, 2–6, 14–16, 19, 22, 26, 44, 54–57, 55t; "new politics," 14–15, 50; party families and, 16–17, 54–56

intersectionality, 6–9, 24, 64. *See also* ethnicity; gender

intersectionality-plus, 6–9, 12, 24

Kreil, Tanja, 131, 139, 145

Kreil v. Federal Republic of Germany, 131–132, 139–140, 141t; broader context, 151–159; end of compulsory military service and, 148–151, 149t; post-ECJ ruling responses, 144–148; pre-2000 positions, 140–144

labor parties, 17
labor policy, 153
left, The (ideology): actions to promote women's political representation and, 18, 77, 87–88, 117, 120, 122, 169, 171–174, 176t, 185, 188; economic redistributionism and, 27–28; environmentalism and, 51, 91–92; multiculturalism and, 31–33; parental leave and, 45–46; political parties and, 15–17, 51, 75, 87–88, 91–92, 110; postmaterialism and, 14–15, 30–31; social progressivism and, 29–30; state intervention in the economy and, 14, 91; support for promoting marginalized groups' rights and, 6, 23, 90, 131; support for promoting women's rights and, 1–3, 5, 21, 23, 36, 114, 171; WLFP policies and, 177–180; women in the military and, 131, 141t
Left, The (party). *See* Party of Democratic Socialism/The Left (PDS/LINKE)
legislation: Civil Code (1900), 45, 153; Conscription Act (Wehrpflichtgesetz) (1956), 138, 149t; Law on the Revocation of Naturalizations and the Deprivation of German Citizenship (1933), 152–153; Marriage and Family Law Reform Act (1976-1977), 45, 78; Nationality Act (1913), 152–153; Nationality Act (2000), 9, 47, 154; Party Act of 1967 (Parteiengesetz), 47; Wehrrechtsänderungsgesetz (WehrRÄndG) (2011), 149, 151. *See also* Basic Law
legislative rules, 34, 37–38
Lenke, Ina, 19, 63–64, 78–80, 144–145
libertarianism, 58, 80, 165–166
Linke, Die. *See* Party of Democratic Socialism/The Left (PDS/LINKE)

marginalized groups: advocacy for, 2, 22–23, 34, 38–39, 47, 63–65, 154, 180–183; citizenship and, 6–10, 23, 42, 46, 64–65, 70, 117, 118t, 127, 135–136, 152–153, 154, 156–157, 188–189; Germany and, 46–47; military and, 131–132, 134; Nazi regime and, 152–153; party leadership and, 127, 128t; political marginalization of, 2, 6–10, 19, 23, 31, 42, 64–65, 70, 77, 125, 135–136, 152–153, 156–157; quotas and, 163, 188; rates of candidacy and election of, 115–118, 118t, 127, 188; United States and, 23, 64, 135; women, 2, 7–10, 31, 34, 40t, 63–67, 69, 81–111, 176

Marxistisch-Leninistische Partei Deutschlands. *See* Marxist-Leninist Party of Germany (MLPD)
Marxist-Leninist Party (MLPD), 54; acknowledgement of women's underrepresentation, 70t; actions to promote women's political representation, 75; ideological orientations and, 55t; women's inclusion in party leadership and, 128t; women's rates of candidacy and, 119t
materialism: cross-national analyses and, 161, 167t, 172t, 173t, 175t, 176t, 177–180, 185; definitions of, 27, 30–32, 44t; distinctiveness from social traditionalism, 165–166; gender quotas and, 90, 91t, 124; political parties and, 54, 55t, 147–148, 150; women's and minorities' rights and, 5, 39, 40t, 76t, 77, 95, 120, 121t, 123t, 134
mentoring and training programs: AfD and, 96–97; B90/Gr and, 105–106, 110–111, 117; CDU and, 97–99, 117; corporate and business roots of, 111; CSU and, 100–101; FDP and, 101–105; historical context and, 92–96, 110; as informal mechanisms, 63, 81, 84, 86; LINKE and, 106–108, 110–111; SPD and, 108–110, 117
Merkel, Angela, 42–43, 47, 59–61
methods, 26–27, 44, 50, 56–57, 164–167
Migrationshintergrund, 46, 70, 117, 118t, 127, 154, 188
Militärischer Abschirmdienst. *See* Military Counter Intelligence Service (MAD)
Military Counterintelligence Service (MAD), 158–159
multiculturalism: cross-national analyses and, 164, 167, 167t, 173; definitions of, 27, 31–33, 44t; gender quotas and, 90, 91t; political parties and, 54, 55t, 58–60, 78–79; women's and minorities' rights and, 5, 40t, 76t, 77, 95t, 120–122, 121t, 125t, 141t, 149t
multipartism, 34–37, 40t, 113, 116, 180

National Democratic Party (NPD), 53–54; acknowledgement of women's underrepresentation and, 70t, 75; gender quotas and, 87, 90–91; ideological

National Democratic Party (*continued*)
orientations and, 55–56, 92, 121; women's inclusion in party leadership and, 128; women's rates of candidacy and, 118, 119t
Nationaldemokratische Partei Deutschlands. *See* National Democratic Party (NPD)
nationalism, 15, 27, 52, 58–59
"1968 Generation," 78

Ökologisch-Demokratische Partei. *See* Ecological Party of Germany (ÖDP)
Organization for Economic Cooperation and Development (OECD), 19–20, 160, 162, 163t. *See also* cross-national analyses

Parliamentary Council (Parliamentarischer Rat), 47–48
Partei des Demokratischen Sozialismus/Die Linke. *See* Left, The (political party)
Partei Mensch Umwelt Tierschutz. *See* Party for the Wellbeing of Humankind, the Environment, and Animals (TIER)
Party of Democratic Socialism/The Left (PDS/LINKE), 48–49; acknowledgement of women's underrepresentation and, 73; actions to promote women's political representation, 106–108, 110; expanding citizenship and, 156; gender quotas and, 87t; ideological orientations and, 52, 141f; Migrationshintergrund and, 118t, 188; origins in GDR, 51–52, 61, 107, 111; origins of, 50–52, 61, 111; Rosa-Luxemburg-Siftung and, 93; September 2021 elections and, 188–189; women's inclusion in party leadership and, 128t; women's inclusion in the military and, 141t, 144–145, 147, 149, 149t; women's organizations and, 108; women's rates of candidacy and, 119t; women's rates of election and, 43t, 124t. *See also* Left, The (party)
party foundations, 92–94; Desiderius-Erasmus-Stiftung (DES), 93, 96; Friedrich-Ebert-Stiftung (FES), 93, 109; Friedrich-Naumann-Stiftung für die Freiheit (FNF), 93, 102–104, 143; Hanns-Seidel-Stiftung (HSS), 93, 100–101; Heinrich-Böll-Stiftung (HBS), 93, 105–106; Konrad-Adenauer-Stiftung (KAS), 93, 98–99; Rosa-Luxemburg-Stiftung (RLS), 93, 107
party manifestos, 16, 52, 69

Party for the Wellbeing of Humankind, the Environment, and Animals (TIER), 19, 54; acknowledgement of women's underrepresentation and, 70t; actions to promote women's political representation, 82; gender quotas and, 86, 87t, 91t; ideological orientations and, 55t, 76, 82, 91t, 111–113, 121–122; origins of, 111–112; women's inclusion in party leadership and, 112, 127, 128t; women's rates of candidacy and, 112–113, 119t, 120, 123t; women's rates of election and, 118, 126t
patriarchy: pervasiveness of, 2, 5, 10, 23–25, 31, 36, 40t, 131, 134, 145; Volksgeist and, 156
Piratenpartei Deutschland. *See* Pirate Party (PIR)
Pirate Party (PIR), 54; acknowledgement of women's underrepresentation and, 70t, 76; gender quotas and, 87t; ideological orientations and, 55t; origins of, 52–53; women's inclusion in party leadership and, 127, 128t; women's rates of candidacy and, 118, 119t
political environment: citizenship laws and, 132–133, 151–154; cross-national analyses and, 168, 172, 174–175; gender quotas and, 83; ideological context, 4, 21–22, 24–27, 34, 161, 171, 183–185; Ina Lenke and, 78; institutional context, 4, 21–22, 27, 37, 116, 161, 171, 183–185; intersectionality-plus and, 12; pro-gender-equality attitudes, 161, 168, 172–182; sociocultural and historical context, 38–39, 40t, 93, 107, 110, 183–185
political parties: as key actors, 3; leadership boards and, 89; policy change and, 156–157; voters' weakening attachment to, 92
political representation: descriptive, 32, 65–66, 189; men's overrepresentation and, 63, 67–69; role of ideologies in shaping, 2–3, 18, 34; significance for women's rights and interests, 13, 21–22, 64–67; substantive, 1, 11–12, 15, 65–66, 211n1; women's underrepresentation and, 18–19, 62–78
postmaterialism: cross-national analyses and, 167t; definitions of, 27, 30–31, 44t; gender quotas and, 90, 91t, 124; new politics and, 14–15; political parties and, 54, 55t, 78–79, 89; social traditionalism

and, 166; women's and minorities' rights and, 5, 40t, 76t, 77, 95, 120, 121t, 123t, 188
proequality activities, 39, 40t, 161, 170t, 185; data and methods, 164–171; electing women to national legislative office, 171–174; FDP and, 189; protecting minority groups' rights, 180–183; support for WLFP, 175–180; women in party leadership, 174–175

race-ethnicity. *See* ethnicity
Republicans (REP), 54; acknowledgement of women's underrepresentation and, 70, 75; gender quotas and, 87t; ideological orientations and, 53, 55; women's inclusion in party leadership and, 128t; women's rates of candidacy and, 119t, 121
Republikaner. *See* Republicans
right, The (ideology): actions to promote women's political representation and, 61, 95, 114, 116, 120, 122, 160, 169, 173–174, 176t; economic liberalism and, 27–28; hegemonic ethnic supremacy and, 31–33, 185; materialism and, 30–31, 185; patriarchy and, 5; political parties and, 15–17, 56, 60, 75, 88–89, 91; social traditionalism and, 29–30; state intervention in the economy and, 14; support for promoting marginalized groups' rights and, 61, 131, 136, 171, 183; support for promoting women's rights and, 1; WLFP policies and, 177–180. *See also* far right
Russia, 136, 139–140, 158, 219n10

Scholz, Olaf, 186–189
sex-gender. *See* gender
Social Democratic Party (SPD): acknowledgement of women's underrepresentation and, 70, 74; actions to promote women's political representation, 93, 95t, 108–111, 117; Aydan Özoğuz and, 117; expanding citizenship and, 155–157; Friedrich-Ebert-Stiftung and, 93; gender quotas and, 81, 87t, 89; ideological orientations and, 50, 55t, 59, 110; Migrationshintergrund and, 118t; origins of, 51; Party School (Parteischule) and, 109–110; Political Academy (Politische Akademie) and, 109–110; role in coalition governments, 48–50; September 2021 elections and, 60, 186–189; women's inclusion in party leadership and, 127, 128t; women's inclusion in the military and, 141t, 143–144, 146, 148–150, 149t, 149t; women's rates of candidacy and, 119t; women's rates of election and, 43t, 124t
social movements, 3, 39, 43. *See also* feminist movements
social progressivism: cross-national analyses and, 166, 167t; definitions of, 27, 29–31, 44t, 57–58; gender quotas and, 90, 91t; intersection with economic liberalism, 148; political parties and, 54, 55t; women's and minorities' rights and, 5, 40t, 76t, 95t, 120, 121t, 125t
social traditionalism: cross-national analyses and, 165–166, 167t, 172t, 173, 173t, 175t, 176t, 178t, 179t, 181t, 182t; definitions of, 15, 27, 29–32, 44t, 57–58; distinctiveness from materialism, 165–166; gender quotas and, 90, 91t; political parties and, 54, 55t, 58, 60, 78, 140, 147–148, 151; women's and minorities' rights and, 40t, 76t, 77, 95t, 120–121, 121t, 123t, 125t, 126t, 134, 140
Soviet Union, 28, 214n9
Sozialdemokratische Partei Deutschlands. *See* Social Democratic Party (SPD)

United States: citizenship laws and, 135; feminism and, 111; gender quotas and, 86; marginalized groups and, 23, 64, 135; nativism and, 135

Western Europe, 16, 38, 56
Westerwelle, Guido, 79, 144
West Germany. *See* Federal Republic of Germany
women: definitions of, 10–12; as mothers, 32, 45, 68, 72, 79, 129, 166; as non-homogeneous group, 2; pay equity and, 76, 112, 176, 212n17
women, multiply marginalized: advocacy for, 22–23, 27, 31, 34, 39, 40t, 63, 66–67, 69, 82, 84, 114, 125, 180; intersectionality and, 8, 10, 24–25; lack of political representation and inclusion, 2, 19, 38, 64–66, 69, 77, 115, 176

xenophobia, 15, 27, 31–32, 52, 58, 61, 135

Christina Xydias is Associate Professor of Political Science at Bucknell University.